OXFORD STUDIES IN ANCIENT PHILOSOPHY

OXFORD STUDIES IN ANCIENT PHILOSOPHY

EDITOR: JULIA ANNAS

VOLUME V

1987

CLARENDON PRESS · OXFORD
1987

B
1
.09
—
1987

Oxford University Press, Walton Street, Oxford OX2 6DP

Oxford New York Toronto
Delhi Bombay Calcutta Madras Karachi
Petaling Jaya Singapore Hong Kong Tokyo
Nairobi Dar es Salaam Cape Town
Melbourne Auckland
and associated companies in
Beirut Berlin Ibadan Nicosia

Oxford is a trade mark of Oxford University Press

Published in the United States
by Oxford University Press, New York

British Library Cataloguing in Publication Data
Oxford studies in ancient philosophy.—
Vol. 5 (1987)-
1. Philosophy, Ancient
180'.938   B505
ISBN 0–19–824458–4
ISBN 0–19–824457–6 Pbk

Library of Congress Cataloging in Publication Data
Oxford studies in ancient philosophy.—
Vol. 5 (1987)- —Oxford: Clarendon Press;
New York: Oxford University Press, 1983–
v.; 22 cm. Annual.
1. Philosophy, Ancient—Periodicals.
B1.O9   180.'5—dc.19   84–645022
AACR 2   MARC-S
ISBN 0–19–824458–4
ISBN 0–19–824457–6 (Pbk)

Set by Hope Services, Abingdon
Printed in Great Britain
at the University Printing House, Oxford
by David Stanford
Printer to the University

ADVISORY BOARD

CONTENTS

SOCRATES ON GOODS, VIRTUE, AND HAPPINESS*

THOMAS C. BRICKHOUSE and NICHOLAS D. SMITH

IN recent years there has been vigorous and instructive debate over how Socrates conceives the relationship between virtue and happiness.[1] One feature common to the various positions taken, however, is the attribution to Socrates of the doctrine that virtue is sufficient for happiness.[2] in *Plato's Moral Theory*, T. H. Irwin sums up the doctrine as follows: 'being virtuous is not simply our best prospect for happiness.[2] In *Plato's Moral Theory*, T. H. Irwin sums up the doctrine fail to achieve happiness for reasons beyond his control.'[3] On this view, Socrates believes that virtue alone will absolutely secure every benefit necessary for happiness. Thus, although the vicissitudes of fortune and the injustices of others may strip the morally good person of everything

---

* © Thomas C. Brickhouse and Nicholas D. Smith

[1] We see no reason, for the purposes of this paper, to concern ourselves with what is called 'The Socratic Problem', the problem of determining the extent to which Plato accurately represents the views of the historical Socrates. In this paper we wish to investigate only what is said about the relationships among goods, virtue, and happiness in Plato's early dialogues. Thus, for those especially concerned by the problem of the historical accuracy of those views, let us stipulate now that all we mean by 'Socrates' in this paper is the speaker by that name in Plato's early dialogues.

[2] For examples, cf. Terence H. Irwin, *Plato's Moral Theory* (Oxford, 1977) (hereinafter referred to as *PMT*), 100 (cf. also his paper, 'Socrates the Epicurean?' (hereinafter referred to as SE), presented at the Society for Ancient Greek Philosophy meetings in New York, 28 December 1984, esp. 2–6), forthcoming in a revised version in *Illinois Classical Studies* 1986; Gregory Vlastos, 'Happiness and Virtue in Socrates' Moral Theory', *Proceedings of the Cambridge Philological Society*, XXX (1984) (hereinafter referred to as 1984), 181–213, esp. 191–213 (cf. also his review of *PMT*, 'The Virtuous and the Happy', *Times Literary Supplement*, 24 Feb. 1978 (hereinafter referred to as 1978), 230–1, and his paper 'Socrates' Contribution to the Greek Sense of Justice', *Arkaiognosia*, I (1980) (hereinafter referred to as 1980), 301–24, esp. 318–23; Donald Zeyl, 'Socratic Virtue and Happiness', *Archiv fur Geschichte der Philosophie*, LXIV (1982), 225–38; Myles Burnyeat, 'Virtues in Action', in *The Philosophy of Socrates*, ed. Gregory Vlastos (Garden City, 1971), 210–11; Norman Gulley, *The Philosophy of Socrates* (New York, 1968), 200. Gerasimos Santas (*Socrates* (London, Boston, and Henley, 1979)) and Vlastos (1984) provide a hierarchy of the levels of happiness one might obtain, but believe that virtue is sufficient for at least the minimal level (251–2).

[3] Irwin, *PMT*, 100.

but virtue, its possession provides its possessor with an absolute immunity against such losses ever destroying his or her happiness.

The attribution to Socrates of the sufficiency of virtue doctrine has at least an initial air of plausibility. The testimony of Plato is uniformly supported by other ancient writers in revealing Socrates' low regard for what his fellow Athenians regard as life's most important treasures.[4] Wealth and its trappings, the esteem of others, and political power, obviously do not impress him. Unlike other Athenians, who scramble after what they mistakenly think will make them happy, Socrates is concerned with but one thing: living a virtuous life that can come only through the perfection of the soul. Thus, whether on the battlefield or on trial for his life, Socrates considers only what is just, oblivious to the dangers that swirl around him.

But the attribution of the sufficiency of virtue doctrine to Socrates has a high cost as well. Though he none the less argues that Socrates is committed to this doctrine, Irwin has pointed out that it saddles Socratic philosophy with two patently undesirable features. First, the doctrine cannot be made consistent with Socrates' various remarks about the ways in which a good person could be harmed in spite of his or her virtue.[5] Secondly, Socrates could defend such a doctrine only by advancing arguments that run directly counter to his often repeated view that vice is always to be avoided.[6] In this essay we shall defend Socrates' view of the value of virtue by offering an interpretation that not only shows the various texts to be consistent with one another, but also forms a defensible position regarding the choiceworthiness of virtue over vice. We begin in Part I by identifying the issues in question, and then in Part II offer an interpretation of what Socrates says about the various goods. In Part III, we draw what we argue is a Socratic distinction between virtue, considered as a condition of the soul, and virtuous activity. Accordingly we undertake to show how Socrates takes the former to be necessary, but only the latter to be sufficient for happiness. In Part IV we draw a distinction from Socratic philosophy between relative and absolute goods and evils in order to explain Socrates' claims in the *Apology* that a worse person cannot harm a better one, and that no evil comes to a good person. Our

---

[4] Perhaps the most descriptive testimony in this regard is to be found in Alkibiades' speech in the *Symposium*, esp. at 216a8–e5, 219b3–220b8. Although the *Symposium* is generally regarded to be a middle-period work, the speech of Alkibiades is regarded by most contemporary Socratic scholars as compatible with the Socrates portrayed in the early dialogues.

[5] Irwin, SE, 6–7.   [6] Ibid, 6.

general thesis is that a coherent account of Socrates' view of the relationship between virtue and happiness requires that he conceives of happiness as ensured by virtuous activity. But, we argue, because virtuous activity can be thwarted by events which the virtuous person may be powerless to prevent, Socates believes that even the good person, under certain conditions, may judge his or her life to be wretched and not worth living.

I Principles and definitions

At the heart of this issue is Socrates' renowned 'eudaimonism', his commitment to the view that the value of something is always to be construed in terms of its connection to happiness. Specifically, to be an eudaimonist is to be committed to what we shall call the 'Principle of Eudaimonism' or just (PE), for short:

(PE) A thing is good only in so far as it is conducive to happiness.

There is no trace of pure duties in the Kantian sense in Socratic thought. What is good is good simply in virtue of its contribution to one's happiness. But there may be many varieties of eudaimonism. One may count many things or only a few as good or goods. Things may be called good only if they are both necessary and sufficient for happiness, or if they are just sufficient, or if they are at least necessary, or even if they are neither necessary nor sufficient but at least contributory. There may be only independent or both independent and dependent goods. Hence, each of these needs to be defined.

A thing is good in itself (or an independent good—IG) if and only if it is a good, and its being a good is in virtue of nothing other than itself.

Given this, the definition of dependent goods is predictable:

A thing is a dependent good (DG) if and only if it is a good, but its being a good is in virtue of its contribution to or employment by some good other than itself.[7]

---

[7] It follows that an IG can never be an evil, for its goodness does not depend upon anything else; but a DG can be an evil, if it contributes to or is employed by an evil. Examples follow.

Santas and Vlastos (1984) argue that Socrates thinks of complete happiness as consisting in a variety of components, of which moral virtue is the most important. Because they see virtue as a part of happiness, Santas and Vlastos (1984) commit Socrates to the view that virtue is of intrinsic value. Irwin (*PMT*, Ch IV) maintains that

The next two definitions are also obvious:

A thing is a necessary good (NG) if and only if there can be no happiness without it.

A thing is a sufficient good (SG) if and only if the having of that thing alone ensures happiness.

How many sorts of goods are there for Socrates?

II Dependence and independence

Irwin believes that an argument in the *Euthydemus* (*Euthyd.*) commits Socrates to the sufficiency of virtue by eliminating all of the other alternatives. Irwin writes: 'In the *Euthyd.* Socrates' attitude to the popular candidates for happiness is highly critical. He agrees with the popular view that it must include all the goods there are; but he claims that wisdom is the only good, and that it is therefore necessary and sufficient for happiness.'[8] Since the 'unity of the virtues' doctrine identifies wisdom with virtue, Socrates must think, according to Irwin, that virtue is necessary and sufficient for happiness. Hence, if Irwin is right, there is only one good—virtue, and it is an IG that is both an NG

Socrates endorses hedonism and, hence, that virtue is of instrumental value only. Gregory Vlastos (1978; cf. Vlastos, 1980), arguing against Irwin, maintains that virtue is of intrinsic value to Socrates because it is the sole component of happiness. Most recently, Zeyl argues a view like that proposed by Vlastos, but adds to it that Socrates also believes that virtue is good for its consequences. We do not wish to argue for one side or another in this particular debate, and thus have avoided the terms 'instrinsic' and 'extrinsic' (or 'instrumental') in our discussion. Rather, we wish only to discuss goods in terms of whether or not they are conducive to happiness through their own agency (such things are IGs), or only through the agency of something else (such things are DGs). It is worth pointing out, however, that given acceptance of PE only happiness is intrinsically good, and virtue can thus be an *intrinsic* good, properly speaking, only if happiness is to be defined in terms of virtue or virtuous activity, and the latter are not simply conditions of its achievement. Otherwise, virtue will be an instrumental good, and only because it contributes to what is intrinsically good, happiness.

[8] SE, 2. Irwin's inference here is actually invalid, unless he is presupposing a strengthened version of PE. One might consistently believe that PE is true, and that wisdom is the only good, but also that wisdom is still insufficient for happiness. 'The only thing conducive to happiness' does not entail 'the only thing sufficient for obtaining happiness'. The latter locution is plainly stronger. Hence Irwin's inference in this case must rely upon the assumption of some version of PE that strengthens 'conducive to' to something like 'necessary and sufficient for'. We believe, however, that the way we have worded PE is the best way to express the commitment to eudaimonism, since a stronger version begs a number of important questions.

and an SG. There are no DGs, on this view, nor are there goods that are NGs but not SGs or SGs but not NGs.

It is beyond dispute that Socrates thinks that virtue is always good (cf. e.g. *Charmides* (*Charm.*) 161a2–10), and that it is always the most important good (*Protagoras* 313a6–b1; *Crito* (*Cri.*) 47e6–48a4; *Gorgias* (*Grg.*) 512a5–6). But the latter claim at least suggests, though it does not entail, that Socrates thinks there are goods other than virtue.

Now Irwin is certainly right in claiming that in the *Euthydemus* Socrates is highly critical of what most of his fellow Athenians would take happiness to be. And it is clear that there Socrates thinks wisdom is the only thing that is *always* good. But is Irwin right in claiming that in the *Euthydemus* Socrates endorses the view that wisdom is the only thing that is good?

The passage in question begins with Socrates and young Cleinias agreeing that all people wish to be happy (278e3–279a1), and that happiness requires the possession of 'many good things' (279a2–3). They then proceed to list a number of things commonly held to be good: wealth, health, good looks, good birth, public honours, the moral virtues, and good fortune. But good fortune, Socrates argues, at least construed as a good to be pursued,[9] is best understood as wisdom, since with the latter one 'could never make a mistake, but must always act correctly and get along correctly' (280a6–8). So far, then, Socrates has collapsed one of the list of goods into wisdom. He cannot, and does not (yet, at least) conclude from this achievement that wisdom is the *only* good.

If wisdom is to be shown the only good in this passage, then, Socrates must go on to show either that all of the other goods in the list (wealth, health, good looks, good birth, public honours, and the other virtues) can be collapsed into wisdom in a similar way as was good fortune, or else that though these others are distinct from wisdom, none are goods. In fact, Socrates does neither of these things; instead he goes on to show that everything in the list except wisdom[10] is a DG,

---

[9] As we shall subsequently argue (cf. n 29, below), we do not take this passage to establish that wisdom *always assures* good luck, but rather only that good luck, in so far as it can be assured, would best be assured by becoming wise.

[10] The other virtues are dropped from this discussion in the *Euthyd.* though this would have given Socrates an excellent opportunity to argue for the unity of the virtues, as Irwin takes the passage to 'suggest' (*PMT*, 87–8 and 301 n 57). In our view, a more plausible interpretation of this is given by Michael Ferejohn in 'Socratic Thought-Experiments and the Unity of Virtue Paradox', *Phronesis*, XXIX (1984), 105–22, esp. 114–20. Ferejohn argues that just as Socrates says in the passage, wisdom is the only IG. The other virtues are DGs, for their value to their possessors depends upon their

dependent upon the uses to which wisdom would put them. Socrates' first summation of the argument is instructive and worth quoting in full:

> ... it seems that as regards the whole group of things we first called goods, the argument is not about how they are in themselves and by nature goods, but rather, I believe, as follows: if they are led by ignorance they are greater evils than their opposites, in so far as they are more able to serve an evil leader. But if understanding and wisdom lead them, they are greater goods, but in themselves neither sort is of any worth.   (281d2–e1)

It would appear from this argument, then, that Socrates believes that only wisdom is an IG. All other goods are DGs, dependent upon the one IG, wisdom.

This way of understanding Socrates' point in the *Euthydemus* gains strong support from the *Apology* where Socrates emphatically states that some things other than virtue, including even money, can be good. As part of his explanation of the nature of his philosophical mission, he tells the jury:

> For I go about doing nothing other than attempting to persuade you young and old not to care first for your bodies and money (*chrēmata*), nor so vehemently, than for your soul, saying that virtue does not come from money, but from virtue comes money *and every other good thing for men both in public and private*.[11]
> (30a7–b4)

possessors' additionally having wisdom. Ferejohn concludes (117) that the other virtues may be said to be 'invariably beneficent' (i.e., always good for their possessors), and that no goods other than the virtues are invariably beneficent, but only wisdom is 'value-independent' (our IG). The 'trick' to this, on Ferejohn's view (cf. 119), is that wisdom is a necessary condition of the rest of the virtues, so one would never realize any of them without in addition realizing wisdom. Since for the purposes of the rest of this paper, we shall be discussing *realized* virtue, that is, with the achieved necessary condition of wisdom (we believe that this is also presumed in most Socratic discussions of virtue—cf. e.g. *Grg.* 507b5–c5), we shall construe (all of) virtue as an IG.

[11] Burnyeat translates the word '*chrēmata*' as 'valuables' rather than as 'money', in part to save Socrates from the claim that a material possession could be a good. But there are a number of reasons for rejecting Burnyeat's rendering. First, although '*chrēmata*' can mean 'valuables', it still strongly connotes material things. It would be odd Greek, then, for Socrates to use the word to refer to strictly psychic benefits rather than tangible assets of some sort. Secondly, Socrates is chastising his fellow citizens for their utterly misplaced values, and he clearly thinks that they have foolishly placed the wrong emphasis on the well-being of their bodies and their material possessions (cf. *Apology* (*Ap.*) 29d7–e3, 41e2–7). To translate '*chrēmata*' simply as 'valuables' is to miss the directness of Socrates' challenge to what his fellow citizens mistakenly believe are the most important goods. Finally, Burnyeat's translation makes Socrates' claim, 'from virtue comes *chrēmata* and all other good things for men ...' hopelessly redundant: what other 'good things' could there be but 'valuable things'?

Socrates is obviously not claiming that virtue always produces financial rewards, as if it were good business sense. His own lack of wealth is testimony to that (cf. 31c2–3). But if we place the passage in context, Socrates' view of the relationship between virtue and money comes into focus. First, he explains that part of his mission is to rebuke his fellow citizens for caring more about such things as 'money, reputation, and honour' and caring nothing for 'wisdom, truth, and the perfection of the soul' (29d7–e2). By so doing, he says, they mistake what is of lesser value for what is of greater value (30a1–2). It is important to notice, then, that Socrates' rebuke has to do initially with the relative value of various goods, and that he is not claiming that what most people take to be the greatest goods can never be of any value. The passage quoted provides Socrates' *explanation* of why his fellow Athenians are mistaken. Their error, he thinks, is not simply that they have mistaken what is of lesser for what is of greater value; they also have the wrong conception of what *aretē* requires. They think that money and other worldly goods will give them *aretē*, whereas, for Socrates, true *aretē* consists in 'wisdom, truth, and the perfection of the soul'. Money, or any other worldly goods, cannot bring about *aretē*, but in adding that 'money and every other good thing' come from virtue, he is telling them that possessions become real goods only after their possessors have attained *aretē*.[12]

In both passages, from the *Euthydemus* and from the *Apology*, we find Socrates committed to the existence of goods other than virtue, but goods whose goodness depends upon virtue.[13] And though Socrates nowhere specifies how virtue transforms other possessions into goods, or in what way something such as money could benefit the virtuous man, little speculation is required to see how this would go. As an example, let us turn again to the *Apology*. At the beginning of his second speech, immediately after his conviction, Socrates considers

---

[12] The language of *Ap.* 36c4–d1 should be seen as making a compatible point: Socrates tells the jury that he has spent his life trying to persuade everyone not to care for their possessions before they have taken care to make sure that they themselves are the best and most prudent they can be. Socrates' use of the superlatives (*beltistos*, *phronimotatos*) in this passage should not be over-interpreted to the degree that no care for possessions would ever be warranted, on the ground that no one would ever be the best they could be. Socrates' point is only, once again, that he believes the highest priority should be put on being moral.

[13] Thus far we see no reason to disagree with Vlastos' (1984, 186–213) attribution to Socrates of what he terms 'the principle of the Sovereignty of Virtue' to characterize the relationship between virtue as an IG and various things that are transformed into DGs by the possession of virtue.

what 'penalty' would be most appropriate for his 'crimes'. He says the most apt 'punishment' would be free meals at the Prutaneion (36d5–7), an honour ordinarily bestowed on Athens' most celebrated heroes. The reason he gives for why this would be fitting is revealing: he says that he is poor but needs leisure to exhort his fellow citizens (36e4–5). He repeats the point about his neediness at 36e1. His argument is simple: poverty might interfere with his good work in Athens; since he is such a great civic benefactor, the Athenians would only be giving Socrates his due if they provided him what he needed to continue his mission without impediment.

From the *Euthydemus* passage, we can recognize that Socrates would not call free meals at the Prutaneion an IG. Bestowed upon one with evil designs, such a reward would be an evil, for it would expedite one's evil-doing. But bestowed upon Socrates, free meals would be a good, for it would contribute to his (and Athens') well-being (36d9–e1). Hence, free meals are a DG, good on the basis of the contribution they would make to beneficent activity. Generalizing this, we derive the following: though one may talk about any variety of goods other than virtue, including many or even most of those things commonly called goods, they are all DGs, dependent upon their employment in the service of virtue. If one employs one's good looks in such a way as to promote and maintain justice, for example, one's good looks are a thing of value. If instead one uses them to seduce others into evil and injustice, they are a grave evil. If a good reputation is enjoyed by a person of moderation and prudence and assists that person in convincing others to live as he or she does, that reputation is a good thing. But if a scoundrel enjoys the esteem of others, that esteem is a dangerous and wicked thing. In so far as a thing serves the ends of virtue, then, it is a good indeed. But only virtue is *always* good, because only virtue is an IG. All other goods are DGs, and thus their value is not secure: for these same things become evils when they serve vice instead of virtue.

So at least sometimes Socrates recognizes the existence of goods other than virtue, but these others goods, he believes, are only DGs whose value can be transformed into evils through the improper or vicious use of them. But does Socrates always allow DGs to be called 'good'? To see that he does not we need only return to the *Euthydemus* passage cited above. There, only a few lines after having drawn the conclusion that virtue is the only IG, as opposed to various DGs, Socrates draws what appears to be a quite different version of the conclusion drawn from the argument he had just given. This time he says: '. . . of all the other things, none is either good or bad, but of these two, wisdom is good and ignorance bad' (281e3–5).[14] He does not say that the goods other than wisdom are goods, but only dependent ones, or (what is compatible with this) stipulate that they are not goods in themselves, as he did in his first concluding statement (281d8–e1); in the second concluding statement he says they are neither good nor bad, without qualification. Drawing this second, quite different conclusion should strike us, initially, as odd indeed, since Socrates has just finished talking about such things as health and wealth as things that are good when used under the guidance of wisdom. Unless we are to convict Socrates of inconsistency within the space of just a few lines, we must suppose that, in drawing the second conclusion, he is relying on the (suppressed) premiss that if a thing is not an IG, it is not *really* a good at all. But the appearance of inconsistency vanishes if we make the quite reasonable assumption that with the second conclusion Socrates is simply emphasizing the difference between an IG and a DG, by claiming that only an IG is really a good.

Keeping in mind the *Euthydemus'* view that only an IG is really a good, let us turn to a well-known passage in the *Gorgias* that might, at first, appear to represent a different way of classifying valuable things for Socrates.

Socrates: Now among existing things, is there anything that is not good or evil or between the two, neither good nor evil?
Polus: Necessarily nothing, Socrates.
Socrates: Well, do you call wisdom and health and wealth and all other things of that sort good, and their opposites evils?
Polus: I do.
Socrates: And by things neither good nor evil, do you refer to such things as sometimes partake (*metechei*) of the good, and sometimes of the evil, and sometimes of neither, for example, to sit and to walk and to run and to sail, or for example, stones and sticks all other things of that sort? Are these not what you refer to? Or are there other things that you call neither goods nor evils?
Polus: No, just these. (467e1–468a4)

Here it is clear that Socrates is not willing to use the terms 'good' and 'evil' to refer to the 'intermediate things' (*ta metaxu*), those things

---

[14] Vlastos (1984, 199–201) takes the second conclusion to stand in need of the unexpressed qualification that wisdom is good (*just by itself*) and ignorance is evil (*just by itself*). Again, we see no reason to disagree with Vlastos on this point, although it must be emphasized that sense can be made of Socrates' stating the second conclusion in such different terms only if he wishes to emphasize the very different status of wisdom as an IG and various DGs and, hence, that, strictly speaking, wisdom is the only good.

that 'sometimes partake of the good and sometimes of the evil'. So unless something is *always* good—which is not true of DGs—it is not *really* good, but instead, neither good nor evil. It is important to notice, however, that this is no different from the way Socrates classifies valuable things in the *Euthydemus*. There we saw that although Socrates is willing to refer to DGs as 'goods', he makes a point of emphasizing that he regards only an IG, something that is of itself beneficial, as good in the proper sense. Now it is clear that in the *Gorgias* passage, Socrates is pointing out to Polus under what conditions it is rational to want 'intermediate things', things that are in themselves neither beneficial nor harmful. In both dialogues the point regarding the desirability of such things is the same: it is rational to want the things that are, in themselves, neither good nor evil when and only when they happen to be truly beneficial. Thus the difference between the two dialogues regarding what is to be called 'good' is merely terminological, and of no consequence for understanding the Socratic classification of valuable things.

Given the way in which Socrates in the *Gorgias* characterizes what will count as a good and what will count as not a good, but merely a neutral thing, we can conclude—thus far with Irwin—that though Socrates is frequently willing to talk as if he recognizes goods other than virtue, when speaking strictly he does not recognize any goods that are not IGs. And if we can accept what is said in the *Euthydemus* and what is said about the unique position enjoyed by virtue in Socratic philosophy as a whole, we may infer that, for Socrates, only virtue counts as an IG. Hence, it appears that within Socratic philosophy, strictly speaking, only virtue is a good.

But the passage in the *Gorgias* to which we have just referred presents another difficulty for understanding Socrates' classification of valuable things: it appears directly to contradict the view defended in the *Euthydemus* that virtue is the only IG, and hence the only thing that is, for Socrates, good strictly speaking. In the *Gorgias* passage Socrates seems to endorse the view that there are a variety of goods, 'wisdom and health and wealth and all other things of that sort'.[15]

In the context in which he says this in the *Gorgias*, however, there is no need for Socrates to undertake to examine any of these goods, their dependence upon, or independence of one another. His argument at this point turns on Polus' acceptance of the assumption, made explicit

[15] Santas and Vlastos (1984), for example, take Socrates to be saying that such goods are components of happiness. As our following argument shows, however, we deny this.

at 477a8–c2, that of the soul, the body, and one's possessions, each has its own good condition, together with Polus' acceptance of the claim that the 'neutral things' are pursued for the sake of whatever is good. The point of this passage is to gain Polus' assent to the reason that must be given for desiring 'neutral things'. Goods are those for the sake of which we do everything (468b7–8, c5); neutrals are performed for the sake of the good, and not for their own sake (468a5–b4, c6); evils are never pursued, if recognized as evils (468c6–7, d5–6). Socrates is not attempting actually to classify any of the particular things listed, for example health or wealth, as good with any finality.[16]

One passage remains, however, that would appear to lend strong support to the view that there is at least one good other than virtue, if only because it plainly identifies an evil other than vice. At *Gorgias* 512a2–b2, Socrates tells Callicles that one with a chronically diseased body, like one with a chronically diseased soul, is 'wretched' (*athlios*) and better off not living, since such a person is bound to live badly. No conditions are put on this claim regarding the person who is virtuous but chronically diseased; we must assume this person, too, would be wretched, and have a life not worth living. If chronic disease is an evil sufficient to make one's life not worth living, as this passage claims, then the evil of disease would appear to be independent of virtue and vice. The correspondingly opposite truth might thus be supposed to follow for health, namely, that it is an IG.

If this is the only way to understand the *Gorgias* passage, we are left with a direct contradiction with the *Euthydemus*, which as we found above, stipulated clearly that health was a DG and not an IG. But we believe a resolution is possible, if we attend to various features of the passage in the *Gorgias*. First, in the *Gorgias* as a whole, as we said earlier, no definitive count of the number of goods is ever undertaken; the argument relies upon what Socrates' interlocutors are prepared to accept, namely, that health is indeed a good and that disease is an evil. But secondly, Socrates gets Callicles to agree in the end that health is the good of the body and virtue is the good of the soul, and that the

[16] At this stage in the *Grg.* Socrates is relying on the quite common Greek usage of 'good'. In this sense, a thing is good when it is in that condition such that it can function well or can be used well. Thus, a knife is 'good', e.g., when it is in that condition such that it can cut well. Similarly, the soul is 'good', when it is in that condition, namely possessing wisdom, such that it can function well as a soul, and the body is 'good', when it is in that condition, namely health, such that it can function well as a body. But this non-moral use of good leaves open the moral question of how anything should be used in such a way that it will conduce to happiness. To gain Polus' assent, at this point in the dialogue, Socrates need not attempt to answer the moral question, which is left open.

latter is an immeasurably greater good than the former, because the soul is 'so much more precious than the body' (512a5–6; cf. 477b5–e6, *Cri.* 47e6–48a3). If the good of the body should come into conflict with the good of the soul, or should in some way contribute to the evil of the soul (e.g. if one's good health contributed to one's pursuing more actively a life of evil and injustice—cf. *Euthyd.* 281b4–e1) then health would become, all things considered, an evil. Thus it is not merely that health is less important than virtue, though it is; health is not *always* good. Hence, health is just another DG, and like other DGs, worth nothing (or even an evil) when not employed by virtue. Disease is a serious matter for Socrates, however, even though it is no evil in itself, from the perspective of the whole person.

III Virtue and activity; necessity and sufficiency

We have seen how Socrates often acknowledges that many things may be goods, but that all depend upon virtue for their goodness, and how this turns out to mean, on his view, that only virtue is, in the strict sense, a good. But a thing may be an IG without being an SG; that is, a thing may, of itself, be *conducive* to happiness (as per PE), but not always *suffice* of itself to *ensure* it. After all, this is precisely Aristotle's view of this issue: he accepts PE and the view that virtue is an IG, but says that virtue does not always suffice in ensuring happiness. Such terrible misfortunes (as, for example, those suffered by Priam) might befall the virtuous man as to prevent him from achieving the happiness that would otherwise be his (*Nicomachean Ethics*) (*NE*) 1100b33–1101a13). So the question remains as to whether or not Socrates thinks virtue is sufficient for happiness, that is, whether virtue is an SG. It is to this question, then, that we must now turn.

Fundamental to the moral philosophy of the early dialogues is Socrates' conviction that one must always act as virtue requires and avoid the commission of any wrong whatever. In the *Apology*, for example, he explains why he will never abandon his virtuous service to the god by telling the jury: 'You are mistaken . . . if you think that a man ought to take into account the danger of life or death and not consider only this when he acts: whether he does just things or unjust and performs the acts of a good or an evil man' (28b5–9; cf. 28d6–10). The same uncompromising view is repeated in response to Crito's appeal that he escape from prison: 'And if it appears that such an action would be unjust, then the fact that I stay here and die or suffer anything else at all ought not to be considered, when the alternative is to do injustice' (48d3–5). He knows all too well that by electing to stay in prison, he will lose everything but his virtue. For Socrates, then, whatever could be gained through the doing of injustice could never outweigh the value of acting in accordance with virtue.

Socrates justifies his conclusion regarding the supreme value of the virtuous life by means of his agreements with Crito that 'it is not living but living well that one must consider most important' and that 'to live well is the same things (*tauton*) as to live rightly' (48b9). Regardless of how Socrates understands the nature of the identity asserted in the second premiss, he believes at least that the virtuous life is both necessary and sufficient for living well.

The expression, 'living well' (*eu zēn*), like the expression, 'doing well' (*eu prattein*) is used by Socrates as a synonym for, or is at least biconditionally related to 'happiness' (*eudaimonia*) (cf. e.g. *Republic* (*R.*) I. 354a1–2[17]). Thus, Socrates believes that 'living rightly and nobly' is both necessary and sufficient for happiness. What is not clear, however, is what he takes 'doing well' and 'living well' to refer to. On the one hand, he may take the terms to refer to a particular condition of the soul, and whatever activities might be performed under the guidance of that condition (cf. e.g. *Ap.* 28b5–9; *Charm.* 160d5–e1; *R.* I. 335d11–12). In this case, that condition alone would appear to be sufficient for happiness. But it might also mean that some level of achievement in one's activity is required, for which the virtuous condition of the soul is a necessary condition, but for which external factors such as opportunity and the powers to accomplish that level of achievement are necessary conditions as well. Such a level of achievement might at least sometimes require the use of the body, or at least that the body not be an impediment to it. In this case, the possession of virtue may not always be sufficient for living rightly and, hence, for living well, since there may be circumstances that prevent one from attaining the necessary level of achievement in one's activities. Deciding, then, upon whether or not certain standards of achievement must be met for 'living well' is crucial to determining

---

[17] The *Euthyd.* may also be cited here, since the argument shifts from talk of *eu prattein* at 278e3, 6, and 279a2 to both *eu prattein* and *eudaimonia* at 280b6, to only *eudaimonia* from 280b7 through the rest of the argument. Given the role of these terms in the argument, logic requires them to be used as synonyms.

whether or not Socrates subscribes to the sufficiency of virtue doctrine.

Towards the end of *Republic* 1 (353d2–354a2), Socrates argues that the soul has a function and that if it is to perform its function well, it must possess its own virtue. Its function is 'management, rule, deliberation, and life'. The evil soul, of course, will perform its function badly, whereas the 'good soul will do all such things well'. Thus, he concludes that the just soul and the just person live well and 'one who lives well is blessed (*makarios*) and happy'. It is not clear from the passage just what Socrates thinks the soul is to manage and rule over. Nowhere, for example, does he specifically exclude the possibility that the soul's function is to manage and to rule over itself. If that is what he means, Socrates would have to judge one happy if and only if one is the master of one's soul, apart from any other consequences of such mastery. But in a passage in the *Gorgias* that is almost certainly intended to make the same point as this passage in *Republic* 1, Socrates explicitly maintains that one is to be called 'blessed and happy' on the basis of his or her actions, and not merely on the condition of his or her soul.

The temperate one will avoid or pursue the things and people as one should, and will resist and endure where one should. And so, Callicles, since the temperate person is just and brave and pious, as we have described him, he definitely must be a completely good person; *and the good person must do whatever he does well and nobly; and the person who does well is blessed and happy; whereas the villain and evil-doer is wretched.*

(507b5–c5)

According to the *Gorgias*, then, the proper 'management and rule' that constitutes the well functioning of the soul, concerns the correct 'avoidance and pursuit of things and people'. Thus, the good soul is concerned with virtuous activities and not merely the maintenance of its own good condition.[18] Moreover, Socrates is attempting to

---

[18] Burnyeat (above n 2, 211, 232) believes that, for Socrates, the well-being of the soul is prior to the performance of virtuous action. From this he appears to infer that the well-being of the soul must be of intrinsic value to Socrates. Irwin points out (*PMT*, 303 n 71) that this inference is a faulty one. Socrates could think that the well-being of the soul is a logically necessary condition for the performance of virtuous action but of value only in respect of its contribution to such virtuous activity. Hence, its necessity for virtuous activity does not confer *intrinsic* value upon it. Its value might none the less be instrumental. Our own view does not concern itself with whether or not virtue has intrinsic value (see n 7, above), but we are committed to the thesis that virtue is at least always preferable to its opposite, but not sufficient in itself to ensure happiness. Happiness is ensured, we believe, only by securing both the well-being of the soul and the achievement of some minimal level of activity that would *ceteris paribus* flow from it.

convince Callicles that the virtuously temperate person is always better off than the unbridled pleasure-seeker Callicles admires. But, as the passage shows, Socrates drives home his point, not by arguing merely that the soul of the good person is more orderly than that of the intemperate person, but rather by showing that the good person always *does well*. What qualifies the good person as being 'blessed and happy', is the fact that he or she succeeds in his or her actions.[19]

It might be thought that Socrates' view that happiness consists in the performance of virtuous activities need not conflict with the sufficiency of virtue doctrine. When Socrates tells Callicles, 'and the good person must do whatever he does well and nobly', he may mean that the virtuous person will always adapt to whatever circumstances arise. When conditions occur that prevent the performance of the actions he or she might otherwise desire to do, the good person simply adjusts his or her desires accordingly, recognizing that under the circumstances those actions cannot be performed.[20]

Certain passages certainly suggest an adaptive strategy, without which Socrates' morality would itself come into question. For example, when the Thirty ordered him to go out and arrest Leon, Socrates simply went home (32c4–d7). He did not, however, undertake to obstruct the arrest in any more aggressive way (and Leon was indeed brought in and executed). Similarly, Gregory Vlastos has questioned the propriety of Socrates' lack of political activity in the Athens that condemned the inhabitants of Scione and Melos to genocide, and decided to undertake what turned out to be the disastrous invasion of Sicily.[21] But as Vlastos recognizes, Socrates' response to such a charge would surely be '. . . you know well that if I had undertaken to do politics long ago, I would have perished long ago and done no good to you or to myself' (*Ap.* 31d7–e1).[22] So, it might be thought that the virtuous person always undertakes to do the best thing available at the time, all things considered. Had Socrates attempted to prevent the arrest of Leon, the condemnation of Scione or Melos, or the invasion of Sicily, he would have diminished or brought to an end the pious

---

[19] It might be thought that this passage indicates that Socrates thinks the good person will always do well and, hence, will always be happy. But Socrates need not mean this, nor does he say it. It is true that whatever the good person does will always be done well. But it does not follow from this that the good person will always be able to act. One's actions may be thwarted by conditions over which one has no control.

[20] This view is defended by Irwin in SE.

[21] Vlastos, 'Reasons for Dissidence', *Times Literary Supplement*, 24 Aug 1984, 932.

[22] ibid, Vlastos's translation.

mission he daily carried out in Athens, a mission so important that it made him Athens' greatest benefactor (*Ap.* 30a5–7).

But the constraints put upon the virtuous person by others and by circumstances may be great ones, so great as effectively to prevent any but the most minimally good action. Would Socrates view the life of a virtuous person under such extremely inhibiting conditions to be a happy one? We think not. Socrates does believe, of course, that the greatest harm is always harm to the soul. But in arguing for this very point in the *Crito*, he states that 'life is not worth living with a diseased and corrupted body' (47e3–5). What is significant is that avoiding a life that is not worth living is also the reason one should avoid having a diseased and corrupted soul (47e6–49a2). Having a diseased and corrupted body, then, must be a sufficiently great impediment to happiness that regardless of how one might try to adjust to it, one's life would not be worth living. As we said earlier, at the end of Part II, the same point is made with even greater emphasis in the *Gorgias*, at 512a2–b2, where we are told that one with a chronically diseased body, like one with a chronically diseased soul, is 'wretched' and better off not living, since such a person is 'bound to live badly'. Even if Socrates thinks that the virtuous person will attempt to adjust his or her goals and activities to some circumstances, he clearly believes that some things could happen, for example falling chronically ill with a disease of sufficient severity, against which one is powerless to defend oneself despite one's virtue, but which would be sufficient to make one's life worse than death. And however one construes Socrates' views on the afterlife, having a life worse than death can hardly count as living well or as having a happy life.[23]

---

[23] It is worth noticing that on Irwin's view in SE, the virtuous person could never suffer (or at least not suffer for long) from unsatisfied desires. It is thus a consequence of Irwin's view that the maximally virtuous person would not desire to see injustices over which he or she had no control righted or brought to an end. This strikes us as more than philosophically repugnant; it strikes us as un-Socratic. After all, Socrates admits that there occur numerous unjust and illegal things that he would not be able to prevent (cf. *Ap.* 31e2–32a3). But nowhere is there the slightest hint that the just person would not desire such injustices to end. Nor is there any hint that Socrates believes that the just person will always have his or her way in 'fighting for the just' (*Ap.* 32a1). He or she will do the best he or she can, and will succeed as much as success is possible for one in such circumstances. But one may not always get what one wants. One's failure, in such cases, moreover, need not change one's view that what one wanted was what was best, and therefore, to be desired even though presently unobtainable. In short, we see nothing in Socrates that, like the Stoics, suggests that one should desire only the way things actually turn out.

Irwin (SE, 6) at least concedes that his account is inconsistent with Socrates' various

Moreover, Socrates' emphasis in *Republic* I on the proper functioning of the soul indicates that he does not see happiness as something that can always be fostered merely by adjusting to circumstances. On the contrary, the possession of virtue requires that the soul always aim at a specific set of activities, actions that improve, and never harm, people (*R.* 1. 335b2–e6). For Socrates, to improve people is always to create or maintain virtue in them. This is precisely what Socrates tells the jury in the *Apology*, as well: it is a central feature of his divine mission to make people care first about wisdom, truth, and the perfection of the soul (29e1–2). But if 'living justly and nobly' and 'living well' refer to the performance of various virtuous activities and not merely to the possession of a particular condition of the soul, it is clear that no adjusting to circumstances can ever save the happiness of the good person if circumstances prevent even the minimal performance of such virtuous actions. This also helps to explain Socrates' obvious concern for the good of the body, health. Having a diseased and corrupted body makes life not worth living precisely because it prevents even the minimum performance of virtuous action required for the happy life.

It is clear from the *Apology* that the improvement of people, the end of virtuous action, can be achieved only (or at least in the main[24]) through the therapeutic effects of philosophical interchange (38a1–8),[25]

remarks about the ways in which the virtuous person may none the less be harmed and come to judge his or her life as miserable and not worth living. He cites Richard Kraut (*Socrates and the State* (Princeton, 1984), 38–9 n 21) as holding a contrary view. We are in basic agreement with the position Kraut sketches. However, Kraut nevertheless fails to distinguish clearly between virtue, considered as the healthy condition of the soul, and virtuous action, saying, e.g. (what we find unacceptable—for more on this, see n 25, below), 'one can no longer be virtuous if his body is ruined'. On our view, harms to the body can prevent virtuous action, but will not alter the virtuous condition of the soul.

[24] We have added the qualification because we believe that Socrates might reasonably be supposed also to accept that one can also improve others by setting a good example in any of one's affairs, as e.g., in one's demeanour on the battlefield.

[25] Kraut says that virtue 'requires such activities as discussion and self-examination'. It is an interesting question whether or not Socrates believes that one cannot maintain whatever degree of health in the soul one has already achieved unless one continues always to engage in discussion and self-examination. Would the health of the soul decay or vanish, if one was prevented somehow from such activities? If so, it is difficult for us to see any way in which the good person can be assured of freedom from harm (for our sense of this, see s IV, below), for on this assumption even his or her soul might suffer harm if he or she were to be unjustly exiled or imprisoned. Instead, we believe that if one is ever to achieve the virtuous condition of the soul, one must first engage in such activities, and that such activities will be prominent among the natural range of activities to which the already virtuous soul would apply itself (with the proviso noted in n 24, above). Kraut's sense of 'requires' might appear to involve a constant and continuing need, however (cf. n 23, above), though he also recognizes that 'the soul is not corrupted if one is the victim of injustice' (38, with passages cited in his n 18).

in which Socrates views himself to be divinely commanded to engage. It is not surprising, then, that after he has been convicted he rejects a number of counter-penalties on the ground that he knows them to be evils: imprisonment, imprisonment until a fine is paid, exile, and a cessation of his philosophical activities (37b7–38b1). Imprisonment, even until a fine is raised and paid on his behalf, would all but bring to an end his philosophical examination of others (37c1–2). Exile would be no solution because other cities will be far less likely than Athens to allow him to philosophize (37c4–e2). Plainly, voluntary silence in Athens has the same consequence (37e3–38a5). So when Socrates says he must 'talk every day about virtue . . . examining myself and others . . . [for] the unexamined life is not worth living' (38a1–6), he shows that he requires more than the virtuous condition of his soul to make his life worth living; in addition, he needs daily to examine himself and others. The penalties he considers and rejects, in the second speech in the *Apology*, therefore, are evils, for they would hinder the performance of even the minimal level of activity necessary to make Socrates' life worth living. Only this conception makes sense of Socrates' claim that such penalties would be evils. If virtue, considered merely as the relevant condition of one's soul, were all that were at stake, no interference in Socrates' life of the relevant sorts—not imprisonment, not exile, and not disease—would be evil or harmful, for none of these are a threat to the virtuous condition of Socrates' soul. But Socrates says they would be evils (37b7–8), and carefully offers the only counter-penalty that he says will do him no harm (38b2).[26]

We are now in a position to understand two passages that provide the strongest apparent evidence for the sufficiency of virtue doctrine, for each appears to be an explicit endorsement of it. At *Gorgias* 470e6–7, Socrates says that he does not know if Archelaus, the king of Macedonia, is happy, because he does not know how he is in terms of education (*paideia*) and justice (*dikaiosunē*). Polus asks, 'Why, is all of happiness in this [education and justice])?' and Socrates responds, 'Yes, according to what I say, Polus; for the good and noble man and woman is happy, I say, and an evil and villainous one is wretched'

---

[26] Kraut also makes this point, amidst an admirably detailed account of why Socratic principles must not be construed as having the consequence that Socrates would be indifferent to suffering injustice (cf. 35–9).

(470e8–11). If all of happiness consists in being good, it would appear beyond cavil that virtue is sufficient for happiness.[27]

Similarly, in the passage from the *Republic* we have already discussed (353d2–354a2), Socrates begins his concluding argument with Thrasymachus by stipulating, with Thrasymachus' now passive agreement, that the virtue of a thing is what allows that thing to fulfil its function. At 353e10–11, the specific conclusion Socrates sought to derive from this premiss is drawn out: 'The just soul and the just person will live well, and the unjust, poorly'. If this conclusion is to be taken literally, virtue does not need enabling conditions; it is sufficient unto itself for its possessor to live well, and hence, happily (354a1–5).

By now, our analysis of these passages should be predictable. When Socrates says in these passages that all of happiness consists in being good, or that the just soul will live well, there is no reason to suppose that he means that goodness or justice are, of themselves, sufficient for happiness, independent of whatever disasters and impediments the person may suffer. Instead, we may suppose that Socrates is referring to goodness and justice in persons *as they are under ordinary circumstances*, that is, suffering no substantially impaired capacity for the sort of agency one could *ceteris paribus* expect from the good man or woman. If Polus or Thrasymachus had interrupted in either passage with the question, 'Do you mean, Socrates, that one would live well even if one was systematically prevented from doing one's soul's virtuous bidding, due to disease, infirmity, or an injustice done to one?' we should expect a more careful presentation of Socrates' position. In response to such a question, Socrates would have to admit that one cannot judge one's life to be worth living under such conditions, but that the just person would bear such sorrows better than would others. But it is not Socrates' point in either passage to distinguish the good-souled, but imprisoned, enfeebled, broken or moribund person from the good person as we would otherwise expect him or her to be. Hence, we should assume the latter to be a sort of individuals referred to by Socrates' 'the good and noble man and woman' (*ton kalon*

---

[27] In fact, *Grg.* 470e6–7 is entirely ambiguous. On the one hand, we might read 'all happiness is in this (i.e. justice and education)' (*en toutō hē pasa eudaimonia estin*) to mean all happiness consists in justice and education. If this is the proper reading, the lines would provide evidence, at least prima facie, for the sufficiency of virtue doctrine. But as Irwin (*Plato's Gorgias* (Oxford, 1979), n on 470e8) points out, the line may be taken to mean 'all happiness *depends upon* justice and education', in which case, Socrates is only asserting that virtue is necessary for happiness. If the latter is all Socrates has in mind, the passage provides no evidence at all for the sufficiency of virtue doctrine.

kagathon andra kai gunaika) at *Gorgias* 470e8–11. Happiness, then, consists in being a good and noble man or woman without such severe external impediments as for all practical purposes to paralyse one or in some other way to prevent one from translating one's goodness into good action.[28]

Of course, Socrates does not make the specification we have relied upon in our interpretation of these passages. His claims are made in an unqualified way. None the less, they need to be read as we have suggested because of the explicitness of Socrates' remarks about the ruinous effects of disease and incapacity. In each case where he addresses such topics self-consciously, he admits that life is not worth living when one is so bitterly afflicted. If one takes the principles of interpretation to require an unqualified reading of passages in which such afflictions are not at issue, on the ground that Socrates' language is unqualified in them, one will be committed to the presence of an irresolvable contradiction in Socrates' views. But we appeal to more than charity in the reading we have proposed. It is not merely that our reading charitably permits Socrates to remain consistent; it is that the principles by which such consistency may be achieved are to be found explicitly stated and repeated in Socrates' own philosophy. Though we are entirely committed to the text's authority in resolving disputes of interpretation, it is clear throughout Plato's early dialogues that Socrates frequently expresses his views by taking the more obvious disclaimers and qualifications as assumed. An overly literal reading of these particular passages must insist that Socrates contradicts himself in the most obvious ways only by resisting the application of his own explicitly held views. And such a reading can make no significantly greater claim to textual support than our more charitable interpretation. Hence, we see no advantage whatever to resisting our reading on the

---

[28] An alternative, which would make the virtuous condition of the soul sufficient for happiness, might be that happiness consists minimally (though not necessarily in its highest form) merely in being the sort of person always disposed to do whatever is the best course of action given the available options. Such an hierarchical account of happiness might be seen as implied by Socrates' occasional use of relative standards of good and evil, benefit and harm (see s IV, below), from which Santas (cf. 251–2) and Vlastos (1984) appear to derive their views. But this, again, appears to us to preserve the sufficiency of virtue doctrine at the expense of all that Socrates says about the relation of happiness to living well, and the sense we are to make of what it is to live well. On our view, one may be virtuous and yet enjoy no residue of happiness, for one may be such as to have a life worse than death (a life not worth living). But such a person will none the less always be better off than the one without virtue, for the latter inevitably suffers a degree of wretchedness far worse than any wretchedness the former can suffer.

basis of an appeal to literality in interpretation. We prefer to allow *all* of what Socrates says to determine our reading of any individual passage, especially, as in this case, when charity may be achieved only by doing so.[29]

IV Relative and absolute good and evil, benefit and harm

Two passages from the *Apology* still require attention, however, for they provide what some commentators believe is compelling evidence from the sufficiency of virtue doctrine.[30] In the first, Socrates explains why he is utterly undaunted in the face of any penalties that may be inflicted on him for having engaged in the pious pursuit of his mission. 'Neither Meletus nor Anytus could harm me—that is not possible—for I do not think it is permitted for a better person to be harmed by a worse' (30c8–d1). In the second, Socrates explains why, having been condemned to death, he can face his death with equanimity. 'No evil comes to a good person either in life or death' (41d1–2). It is not difficult to see why commentators would take these passages to be decisive. Since Socrates is an eudaimonist, that is, subscribes to PE, he accordingly construes evils in terms of being conducive of unhappiness or wretchedness (*athliotēs*). This, then, is the harm that always results from evil (cf., e.g., Grg. 477e3–4; *Meno* 77d2–9). He obviously recognizes that he can be deprived of all of his possessions and put to death. But since none of these things would harm him, it might appear

---

[29] The same argument and one other would apply in our interpretation of *Euthyd.* 279d4–280b3, where Socrates and Cleinias come to agree that 'when wisdom is present, the one in whom it is present is not still in need of good fortune' (280b2–3). We do not believe that this should be read as committing Socrates and Cleinias to the absurd view that no misfortune can befall the wise person, but only that wisdom gives the best access one can pursue to good fortune. (1) When Socrates and Cleinias agree that the wise person is not still in need of good fortune, they may be assumed to be making the same sorts of assumptions as we have argued are presumed by the discussions at *Grg.* 470e6–11 and at *R.* I. 353d2–354a2, namely, that *other things are equal*. The wise person is not omnipotent; whatever one's wisdom, one cannot control all of the things that might happen to one, and some of these things might be quite unlucky. But the wise person, *ceteris paribus* will always be more fortunate than the unwise person. (2) The entire argument here is conditioned by a search for what is good, and one cannot sensibly set out to obtain good fortune, at least much of which would appear to befall one or not regardless of other factors. Socrates argues, however, and Cleinias agrees, that wisdom maximizes one's chances at being fortunate, and so the pursuit of good fortune would be no other than the pursuit of wisdom. (We owe this second point to Michael Ferejohn.)

[30] Cf., e.g., Irwin, *PMT*, 100; Vlastos, 1978, 230; Burnyeat, above n 2, 210; George Grote, *Plato and the Other Companions of Socrates*, vol. i (repr, New York, 1973), 243.

that he cannot believe that any of his possessions, or even life itself, is required for happiness. His virtue alone would appear to be sufficient.

But despite its widespread acceptance, this interpretation is thoroughly problematical. Immediately after Socrates reveals his confidence, in the second passage, that 'no evil comes to a good man in life or in death', he goes on to say: '. . . but this is clear to me, that it was better for me to die and be released from troubles' (41d2–5). His confidence in this regard derives from the fact that his *daimonion* did not warn him either before or during the trial (41d5–6). Now just how Socrates reaches this conclusion from the mere absence of daimonic interference need not concern us here.[31] What is important is that although Socrates is confident that no harm will come to him at death, he is by no means confident about just what will happen at death. Perhaps, he says earlier, his soul will migrate to Hades where he will spend his time 'examining and questioning the people there' (41b5–6). That, he says, would be 'inconceivable happiness' (41c3–4). But at the same time Socrates is aware that death may also be a 'dreamless sleep', void of all perception (40c9–d1). Anyone who claims to know which of the two possibilities will actually come to be is guilty of the very sort of pretence of wisdom from which Socrates has for so long sought to free men (29a4–b2). His last words to the jury are noteworthy: 'But the time has come to go. I go to die, and you to live; but which of us goes to a better thing is clear to none but god' (42a2–5).

At the conclusion of the *Apology* Socrates believes it is better for him to die; but he is not convinced that his is the best lot—some members of the jury, according to his final words at 42a2–5, may enjoy even better. And since death may be utter extinction, Socrates must believe that utter extinction is better than continuing his life with the troubles from whch he now will be relieved. Thus, at the conclusion of the trial, Socrates can hardly be assured of his own happiness, since although he plainly believes himself to be a good man, utter extinction is preferable to continuing his life in his present circumstances. When Socrates claims that 'no evil can come to a good man', whatever else he means, unless we are to convict him of self-contradiction within the briefest of passages, he cannot mean that moral goodness, by itself, is always sufficient for happiness.

There are two ways in which we might interpret 'harm', both of

---

[31] For Socrates' derivation, cf. T. C. Brickhouse and N. D. Smith, 'The Divine Sign Did Not Oppose Me': A Problem in Plato's *Apology*', *The Canadian Journal of Philosophy*, 16.3 (1986) 511–526.

which are used and we believe, used frequently by Socrates. On the one hand, we might interpret something as harmful to the extent that it impedes or removes some benefit one might otherwise enjoy, or increases some disadvantage one would to some degree suffer anyhow. Let us call this a 'relative harm', for harm in this sense may involve no absolutely evil product—the one harmed relatively only enjoys one fewer advantage than he or she might otherwise enjoy. He or she might still, all things considered, have an extremely desirable life. Similarly, though the one suffering relative harm might end up being wretched, it is possible that he or she would have been wretched anyhow, only somewhat less so. So relative harms merely move one from the position one would otherwise enjoy or suffer to a somewhat inferior position, all things considered. This conception of harm appears to be what motivates Socrates' discussion of the various degrees of wretchedness and evil one finds at various places in the *Gorgias* (e.g. 469b3–c1,[32] 472e4–473e1, 475a2–d4), and, in other places in the same dialogue (e.g. 477a5–479e9), the conception of benefit as the making of someone better, even where the result is only that they are less wretched than they would have been (473b6–e1). If this, then, the relative conception of harm (and correspondingly, evil), is what Socrates means to employ when he says 'no evil comes to a good person', he contradicts himself in the *Apology*, for it is clear in that dialogue that by the end of the trial his life has become no better than death, and it is also clear that any number of penalties might have been incurred that would have caused him, for all his virtue, at least relative harm.

But there is another conception of harm in Socrates' discussions as well, which we might call an 'absolute' conception. This conception would appear to be required when Socrates talks about virtue as the only thing that is good in the strict sense, that is, the only thing that is an IG. When he says that virtue is the only thing that is good in this sense, then its loss (or gaining its opposite—vice) is, in the same restricted sense, the only evil or harm. Certainly Socrates thinks that the only harm that can come to the soul is vice (cf. e.g. *Grg.* 477b6–c5, e4–6; *R.* I. 335c1–4) and the Socratic paradox ensures that the possession of virtue is an absolute guarantee against vice or vicious

---

[32] It is noteworthy that at the end of this passage Socrates admits that he would rather not suffer wrong. Cf. also 470a7–8, where to be punished is identified as a bad thing, and 480e6–7, where we must take care not to suffer wrong. Other passages making similar points are cited in Kraut's discussion, esp. 38–9.

activity. An absolute conception of harm, moreover, would be warranted wherever Socrates identifies one with one's soul. That this identification is something he is at least sometimes tempted to do is plain from what he says about the afterlife. Though he is uncertain as to what the afterlife is like—or even if there is one—he believes that it is at least a possibility that it involves a migration to Hades. But surely he believes that what migrates to Hades is only the soul and nothing else. On this conception, it is plain that no evil or harm can come to a good person, for nothing in one's external circumstances can damage one's soul, and the virtue it enjoys. Hence, nothing can make the good person endure the worst kind of suffering, and to be harmed absolutely would be to have the thing harmed endure in the worst condition it can be in.

It is the absolute conception of evil and harm, then, that we believe Socrates employs when he says that 'no evil comes to a good person' and 'it is impossible for a better person to be harmed by worse'. When he says such things, he means that the good person cannot be made vicious. But it might be thought that on our interpretation when Socrates says such things he must be speaking with sheer bravado. Since we maintain that he is claiming that no absolute harm comes to the virtuous soul, Socrates must concede that although neither Meletus nor anyone else could ever harm his soul, unjust treatment could, nevertheless, harm him relatively, indeed, to such a degree as to make his life no longer worth living.

Whatever the oddness of this claim, Socrates *does* come to the conclusion after he has been convicted that it is better for him to die. And he says this with the realization that, for all he knows, death will bring utter extinction. Moreover, in asserting that no harm can come to his soul even if the suffering of injustice can make his life no longer worth living, Socrates is hardly making an empty gesture. There is, on his view, a far worse fate than having one's potential for happiness taken away from one by the evils committed by others. Nowhere in the *Apology* does Socrates explain why the loss of happiness is not the worst thing that can befall a person. But in the *Gorgias*, having stated that he would never want to suffer a wrong (469b12–c1; cf. 480e6–7), he goes on to argue that it would be a far greater evil to do wrong (469c1–2, 473a4–5, 474b7–8, 474c4–475e6). But the greatest evil of all, he says, would be to escape having to pay the penalty of wrong-doing and to live for the longest time possible with the greatest of all afflictions, an evil soul (480e5–481b1). Now when Socrates warns the jury that they will inflict worse harm on themselves than on him if they follow Meletus and Anytus and convict him (*Ap.* 30c6–8), he is relying on his conviction that it is always worse to do wrong than to suffer it, even if the one who suffers it will, as a result, have a life no longer worth living. Thus, when Socrates immediately goes on to say that a good person can never be harmed by a worse, and later, that no evil comes to a good person in life or in death, he is announcing that no one can make the good person suffer the most wretched of lives, life with a corrupted soul.[33]

V Summary and conclusion

We have argued that despite their appearance, Socrates' various discussions of goods, virtue and happiness may be interpreted as consistent with one another. In order to do so, however, we have had to rely in our readings of a number of passages on a variety of distinctions and interpretations that derive from passages other than the ones in question. The alternative to doing this, we believe, requires the extremely uncharitable conclusion that Socrates contradicts himself in Plato's early dialogues, sometimes even within a very brief passage. None of the understandings upon which the interpretation we have offered rely are 'pure' charity, however, since none involve the manufacture of premises or principles from whole cloth. The principles upon which our interpretation of each passage is founded may be seen at work and repeated in more than one of Plato's early dialogues. Accordingly, we have employed them as they are presented in the text in order to make sense of other Socratic principles are arguments.

---

[33] Although Socrates would count the corruption of the body through disease or accident as only a relative harm, yet in some instances a harm sufficient to make even the virtuous person judge his or her life no longer worth living, there is one passage in the *Grg.* (512a2–b2), noted above in S. II and III, where he says that one suffering 'from great and incurable diseases' might count himself 'wretched' (*athlios*). It would none the less be a mistake to infer from this passage that Socrates believes that even the most dreaded diseases could ever bring harm in the absolute sense. The whole thrust of the arguments against Polus and Callicles is to convince them that the worst harm that can come to a person is to be unjust and escape punishment. Though the wretchedness that comes with incurable disease might make the virtuous person see that he or she is better off dead, for Socrates, one will nevertheless always have reason to judge oneself better off than the person who suffers the absolute harm, that harm done to the soul by unpunished injustice.

A summary of the positions we have attributed to Socrates may be helpful. We shall present this summary in terms of each item under discussion, (i) goods, (ii) virtue, (iii) happiness. Unlike our first expressions of these positions, we shall now provide both the positive (good, virtuous, or happy) and negative (evil, vicious, or unhappy) aspects of the positions we attribute to Socrates.

(i) *Goods*

1. (PE) (The Principle of Eudaimonism)—A thing is good only in so far as it is conducive to happiness. A thing is evil only in so far as it is conducive to wretchedness.

2. A thing is good in itself (or an independent good—IG) iff it is a good, and its being a good is in virtue of nothing other than itself. A thing is evil in itself (or an independent evil—IE) iff it is an evil, and its being an evil is in virtue of nothing other than itself. IGs can never be evils and IEs can never be goods.

3. A thing is a dependent good (DG) iff it is a good, and its being a good is in virtue of its contribution to or employment by some good other than itself. A thing is a dependent evil (DE) iff it is an evil, and its being an evil is in virtue of its contribution to or employment by some evil other than itself. DGs can be evils when they contribute to or are employed by evils; DEs can be goods when they contribute to or are employed by goods.

4. Though it is occasionally useful to talk about DGs as goods, since only IGs are always good, they are the only real goods. Similarly, since only IEs are always evil, they are the only real evils.

5. There are different goods and different evils unique to different things, viz., health is good, disease evil, for the body and virtue is good, vice evil, for the soul. But the greatest good of all—so great as to outweigh any consideration of any other goods, should they come into conflict so that one had to choose between them in one's life—is virtue, the good of the soul. The greatest evil of all—so great as to outweigh any consideration of any other evils, were they to come into conflict so that one had to choose between them in one's life—is vice, the evil of the soul. Hence, though health is an IG (and disease an IE) from the point of view of the body alone, health is only a DG (and disease only a DE) from the point of view of the whole person.

6. A relative good is one that moves one's condition more towards the extreme of happiness from where it would otherwise be. A relative evil is one that moves one's condition more towards the extreme of

wretchedness that it would otherwise be. One can receive a relative good and still be wretched, or a relative evil and still be happy.

7. An absolute good is one that makes its possessor absolutely happy. An absolute evil is one that makes its possessor absolutely wretched.

8. The only absolute good is virtuous activity. The only absolute evils are vice and vicious activity.

(ii) *Virtue*

9. Virtue, considered as the good of the soul, is necessary but not sufficient for happiness. Vice is sufficient but not necessary for wretchedness.

10. Only virtue, when not hindered to the point of effective futility in action, will enable us to live a happy life (or alternatively, at or above a certain minimum level of activity, activity that derives from virtue is sufficient for happiness.)

(iii) *Happiness*

11. To be happy is the same as to live well or to do well. To be wretched is the same as to live ill or to do ill.

12. Though nothing can make the good person suffer the most extreme (absolute) wretchedness, circumstances can make his or her life wretched to the point of being no longer worth living, that is, circumstances can make him or her capable no longer of living or doing well, and thus of being happy.

Item number 12 explains the lack of symmetry one finds in items 8 and 9, for one may not live well despite one's virtuous soul, but one will never fail to live ill with a vicious soul. In this asymmetry, we find Socrates' own version of the Greek proverb, '*chalepa ta kala*' (good things are difficult—*Cratylus* 384b1); for evil is always easy to obtain (cf. *Ap.* 39a6–b1), but moral goodness must have a friendly environment in which to achieve its goals.[34]

Lynchburg College, Virginia
Virginia Polytechnic Institute and State University

---

[34] We are indebted to Richard Kraut and to Charles Young , whose criticisms of an earlier version of this paper helped us to make many necessary revisions. Neither should be assumed to agree with us, however.

PERCEIVING, CONSIDERING, AND ATTAINING BEING (*THEAETETUS* 184–186)*

YAHEI KANAYAMA

IN 184–6 of the *Theaetetus* Plato refutes perception's claim to be knowledge by pointing out its inability to attain being. Two main problems we face in interpreting this refutation are:

(1) What is Plato's idea of perception , or more specifically what did Plato understand by '*aisthanesthai*' or '*aisthēsis*'?
(2) What is meant by 'attain being' (*tuchein* or *hapsasthai ousias*)?

Whatever answers we may offer to these questions, they must satisfy at least one condition: as long as one remains at the level of cognition represented by '*aisthanesthai*' or '*aisthēsis*', one cannot 'attain being'. Therefore, the way we answer question (1) affects the way we answer question (2), and vice versa, and it is necessary to tackle these questions together. Firstly, I shall attempt to elucidate what Plato understood by '*aisthanesthai*'. In this attempt special attention will be paid to 185b9–c2 and 185e7, the passages which have usually been taken to describe perception and which have been used as one of the main clues to interpreting Plato's idea of perception.[1] I shall show that contrary to this view these passages should be understood as describing the act of explicit considering, the mind's act which is clearly different from perceiving, though perception may be used in it. The consideration of 184–6 and other relevant texts will lead to the conclusion that the kind of cognition Plato understood by '*aisthanesthai*' is awareness of something as *F*, where '*F*' stands for a sensible quality.

Secondly, I shall deal with question (2). It has often been contended

---

* © Yahei Kanayama 1987
[1] Cf. J. M. Cooper, 'Plato on Sense-Perception and Knowledge (*Theaetetus* 184–186)', *Phronesis*, XV (1970), 131–2; M. F. Burnyeat, 'Plato on the Grammar of Perceiving', *Classical Quarterly*, XXVI (1976), 42, 43, 46; D. K. Modrak, 'Perception and Judgment in the *Theaetetus*', *Phronesis* XXVI (1981), 42–3.

that perception's inability to attain being should be understood as its inability to have a propositional content or frame a propositional structure,[2] and that accordingly for Plato perception has no propositional content or structure; then, it may not be even awareness of something as *F*. In this paper I would like to suggest that 'attain being' should be understood in the sense of 'attain objectivity' or 'find how things are in the world'. My contention is that what is important in the refutation of perception's claim to be knowledge is whether something has resulted from the act of considering (reasoning etc.) rather than whether something has a propositional content or structure. While much attention has been paid by scholars to the notion of propositional content or structure, I suggest that a greater emphasis should be placed on the act of considering. Perception's claim to be knowledge is rejected on the ground that the act of considering, which is distinct from, and is not involved in, perceiving, is necessary for attaining being (objectivity) and for knowledge. I take it that the reason why interpreters have been prevented from duly emphasizing the act of considering in interpreting the refutation at 184–6 lies partly in the fact that the distinction between considering and perceiving has been obscured by taking 185b9–c2 and 185e7 as descriptions of perception. Therefore, our initial examination of these two passages will serve two purposes: to correct a misunderstanding concerning Plato's idea of perception, and to remove an obstacle to recognizing the importance of the act of considering. Our interpretation of 184–6 will also elucidate the place the refutation occupies in relation to Protagoras' position explicated in Part I and to the definition of knowledge newly offered in Part II of the *Theaetetus*.

I Plato's idea of perception

When I use the word 'perception' and attempt to clarify Plato's idea of perception, my objective is to determine how Plato used the verb '*aisthanesthai*' at 184–6. Perception, as Cooper understands it, is used in two different ways. According to him,

Plato is in effect using the notion of *aisthēsis* in two ways. For the perceptual

[2] This is one of the two lines of interpretation suggested by C. H. Kahn, 'Some Philosophical Uses of "to be" in Plato', *Phronesis*, XXVI (1981), 119–27, and Cooper, above n 1, 138–44. Cf. also J. McDowell, *Plato Theaetetus* (Oxford, 1973), 118, 192–3, and Burnyeat, above n 1, 45.

acts of the mind—the acts of seeing, hearing, smelling, etc.—can be called *aisthēseis* (cf. 186d10–e2), as can the powers of the body which Plato says make these acts possible.[3]

Certainly, as Cooper says, the noun '*aisthēsis*' is used by Plato on the one hand to represent the perceptual acts of the mind (186d10–e2), and on the other to represent the powers of the bodily organs, with the nouns '*akoē*', '*opsis*' (184d2, 185a2, b8, c1–2). However, as far as the verbs, '*aisthanesthai*', '*horan*', and '*akouein*', are concerned (184b9, c6–8, d4, e5, 185a1, 6, c8, d4, 186b3, c1), they are used to represent the perceptual acts of the mind, and not the powers of the individual organs. One of Plato's main concerns at 184–6 is to show that the proper subject of our various perceptions is not the individual organs but one and the same mind.[4] What I shall try to present is Plato's idea of perceptual *acts* of the mind, that is, what Plato understood by the verb '*aisthanesthai*'. Cooper says that because the noun '*aisthēsis*' can be used in two ways, we should bear in mind the possibility that what is shown not to be knowledge might be simply the powers of bodily organs.[5] However, it seems clear from the use of verbs, '*aisthanesthai*', '*horan*', '*akouein*', etc. at the final stage of the refutation (186d10–e2) that we don't have to take this possibility into account.

What did Plato understand by '*aisthanesthai*'? Is it the same as what we usually think of by the word 'perception'? It is useful to suppose the following three stages of apprehension or cognition and ask to what stage does Plato's idea of *aisthanesthai* correspond. All three kinds of cognition deal with sensible qualities, which are perceived only through one sense (184e8–185a7): (1) explicit judgement, (2) awareness of something as F (or implicit judgement), (3) feeling comparable to suffering pains. I would like to show that Plato's own idea corresponds to (2).

1. 'aisthanesthai' *and* 'episkopein', skepsasthai'

In 184–6 Plato uses not only '*aisthanesthai*' but also some other words which represent some aspects of the mind's cognition, such as '*dianoeisthai*', '*episkopein*'. When we try to determine how wide an area '*aisthanesthai*' covers in the mind's cognition, it is necessary to take

---

[3] Cooper, above n 1, 129.
[4] cf. Burnyeat, above n 1.
[5] Cooper, above n 1, 129–31.

into account the use of such words and consider its contrasts and similarities with them.

At 185b9–c1 it is said, 'If it should be possible to consider (*skepsasthai*) whether both [i.e. a sound and a colour] are salty or not, you'll be able to say what you'll consider (*episkepsē* (*i*)) with', and at 185e7, 'there are some [i.e. sensible qualities] which the mind considers (*episkopein*) through the capacities of the body'.[6] In these sentences the terms representing sensible qualities are used either as the object or as the predicate term of the object clause of the verbs. This seems to suggest that the activity of the mind represented by the verbs '*skepsasthai*' etc. is perception. This line of interpretation leads to the following conclusion: Plato included in the function of perception the act of considering whether something is salty, and therefore, he thought that in perceiving something the mind might make some judgements. An example of this line of interpretation is illustrated by Modrak.

In the context of the discussion, investigating the question whether something is salty is a function of perception, so answering the question must also be a function of perception. If the mind decides through perception that something is salty, then the mind makes some judgments through perception.[7]

As to the question of what kind of judgement is involved in perception, the answer differs according to interpreters. For instance, Modrak continues,

The exact character of these judgments is underdetermined by the text. It is fairly certain that only judgments of the form, 'this is S' (where S stands for a sensible quality), are made through perception. It is less certain whether these judgments must be articulated or whether they might include non-linguistic representations.[8]

Cooper admits the use of words in perceptual judgements, and says,

---

[6] Needless to say, '*hē psuchē episkopein*' from the '*ta men . . .*' clause is to be supplied also in the '*ta de . . .*' one (185e6–7).

[7] Modrak, above n 1, 43. Modrak adds a note after this sentence and says, 'That the mind makes simple perceptual judgments through perception is also suggested by 186b2–4 where the mind is said to grasp the hardness of the hard and the softness of the soft through touch.' If 186b2–4 is taken to mean that in perceiving hardness the mind is perceiving hardness as a quality which belongs to the hard thing, and is making an elementary judgement that this is hard, then we may be able to understand the passage as Modrak does. However, there is no need to take 186b2–4 in such a way. We don't have to regard 'of the hard' and 'of the soft' as factors perceived by the mind.

[8] Modrak, above n 1, 43

... Plato says (185b9–c3), we investigate whether a couple of things are bitter by means of a bodily power, namely the sense of taste. This clearly means that in operating through the senses the mind applies the words 'bitter', 'red', 'hard', etc. to sense-objects.[9]

This would lead us to accept (1) explicit judgement as Plato's idea of *aisthanesthai*.

However, is it correct to interpret 185b9–c1 and 185e7 as describing perception? When Modrak and Cooper think that the activity of the mind described in these passages is perception, they rely mainly on 185b9–c1 rather than on 185e7. In fact, if it were not for 185b9–c1, they might not have thought that 185e7 describes perception, because it is possible to understand 185e7 as suggesting that the mind uses sense organs when it reflects upon sensible qualities, without implying that the reflection is identical with or involved in perception.

Because the act of considering whether something is salty or not is mentioned at 185b9–c1, it is usually supposed that perception is described here, and because it is impossible to taste a colour or a sound, the protasis at 185b9–10 is taken to state a supposition contrary to fact and is translated as such.[10] But here we must note the grammatical structure of this sentence: the optative, and not a past tense of the indicative, is used in the protasis, and the future indicative is used in the apodosis. This construction doesn't imply that the supposition of the protasis is a false one; rather it implies no opinion of the speaker as to the truth of the supposition.[11] By using the optative in the protasis, Socrates commits himself neither to the view that it is possible to consider whether a sound and a colour are salty, nor to the view that it is impossible. It may be possible or it may not. This leaves the question open whether the act of considering mentioned at 185b10 is identical with (or involved in) perception.

In interpreting the act of considering at 185b10, two ways are open to us, between which it is difficult to choose.

(i) It is identical with or involved in perception.

---

[9] Cooper, above n 1, 132.

[10] F. M. Cornford, *Plato's Theory of Knowledge* (London, 1935), 104; McDowell, above n 2, 67; A. J. Holland, 'An Argument in Plato's *Theaetetus*: 184–186', *Philosophical Quarterly*, XXIII (1973), 103; Burnyeat, above n 1, 48 n 57; Modrak, above n 1, 42.

[11] W. W. Goodwin, *Syntax of the Moods and Tenses of the Greek Verb* (New York, 1965), 168. The construction in question is a case of mixed constructions; cf. Goodwin, 188.

(ii) It is different from perception, though perception may be used in the consideration.

To help resolve this difficulty we may begin by focusing on the status of the indirect question which is used as the object of the considering: 'whether a sound and a colour are salty or not'. I wish to enquire whether the question is supposed by Socrates to be explicitly formulated and asked by Theaetetus, or not. Explicit considering where questions are specifically asked doesn't seem to be identical with or involved in perception. Accordingly, if Socrates is supposing the case in which the question is explicitly asked by Theaetetus, (i) is to be rejected and (ii) should be chosen: in order to support (i), one must have recourse to the view that the question would not be explicit to Theaetetus. Though this view may seem to conflict with the fact that the indirect question is explicitly stated in the text, the indirect question can be regarded as a formulation by an observer; it may be read by Socrates into the content of the supposed perception of Theaetetus.

We have seen just now that Socrates is ambivalent about the possibility of the act of considering whether a sound and a colour are salty or not. Interpretation (i) doesn't suit this ambivalence, because it excludes from the beginning the possibility of this act of considering. Choosing interpretation (ii), we can explain this ambivalence in the following way. Explicit consideration presupposes or involves the act of asking a question, that is, asking a question constitutes one factor of consideration. Now there are some questions the nature of which is such that one cannot engage further in their actual consideration. In fact it seems impossible to engage in the actual consideration of the question whether a colour and a sound are salty or not, for there is no way of examining the saltiness of a sound and a colour. But even so it is none the less possible to ask the question explicitly. We can suppose that Socrates' ambivalence comes from the involvement of these two stages or aspects in the act of explicit consideration.

In the question whether a sound and a colour are (*eston*) salty or not (*ou*), '*eston*' and '*ou*' are used. It is very difficult to suppose that Plato used these words unintentionally, especially in the context in which '*einai*' and '*ousia*' play such an important role. Furthermore, when at 185c6 Socrates counts as one of *koina* what is represented by '*ouk esti*' side by side with what is represented by '*estin*', he must have taken it from one of the remarks made by him or by Theaetetus before, unless it came to his mind suddenly at this point. Now it seems certain that he took it from the remark concerning Theaetetus' considering whether a sound and a colour are salty or not (185b9–c1). In fact we can regard this same remark also as the direct source of '*estin*' (185c5), although '*eston*' can be seen also at 185a9.[12] Consequently we must infer that in the act of considering whether a sound and a colour are salty or not, *koina* are clearly dealt with. But, as is said at 185e1–2, the act of considering *koina* is done by the mind itself, and not through any sense.

Then, is it still possible to maintain interpretation (i)? If we should hold the view that the act of considering is identical with or involved in perception, it follows that perception itself already involves the consideration of at least two *koina*, being and not-being, by the mind itself and not through any sense. We might be able to save this interpretation by regarding being and not-being as dealt with in the act of perceiving. This interpretation may sound plausible, especially if one holds the view that inferences and interpretations are necessary for the percipient to perceive. However, whether the text itself allows such an interpretation is another matter.

In fact nothing in the text seems to support the interpretation that for Plato perception involves the consideration of any *koina*. Let us see how in 184–6 Plato uses verbs representing the act of perceiving (*aisthanesthai, horan, akouein*), on the one hand, and verbs representing the act of judging or considering (*dianoeisthai, skepsasthai, episkopein* (or *episkepsasthai*)), on the other, and compare them to each other. Then, with a few exceptions (185a5–6, c7–8, d3–4) the former verbs are not accompanied by words representing *koina*, or by expressions which suggest the involvement of judgement or consideration, such as an object clause or an indirect question. One of the exceptions, the expression 'perceive (something) *about* (*peri*) both (a sound and a colour)' (185a5–6), may suggest that judgement is involved in perception. But we don't have to read this implication here, because Plato doesn't commit himself to the view that it is possible to perceive something about both a sound and a colour; it is stated that what is thought in common about both a sound and a colour cannot be perceived in common about both, and this statement should be understood to the effect that what is thought in common about both a

---

[12] As regards the use of '*eston* . . . *ē ou*' at 185b10, cf. Burnyeat, above n 1, 43 n 40; Kahn, above n 2, 123.

sound and a colour cannot be the object of perception.[13] As to the questions at 185c7–8 and d3–4 (Through what bodily instrument do we perceive *koina*?), it is necessary to note the rhetorical nature of these questions.[14] The use of '*aisthanesthai*' with words representing *koina* as its object here doesn't imply that *koina* can be perceived through senses. On the contrary, to these questions Plato makes Theaetetus reply at 185d7 ff that the mind considers (*episkopein*, 185e2) *koina* through itself, without making him repeat '*aisthanesthai*'. Also at 185a4, when the idea of *koina* is introduced into the argument, Plato replaces '*aisthanesthai*' with '*dianoeisthai*'. This change of expression suggests that the verb '*aisthanesthai*' is not suitable for describing the mind's dealing with *koina*, and further that Plato would never have used an expression containing '*aisthanesthai*' at 185b10–c1 in order to describe the mind's dealing with *koina* mentioned here.

In order to describe the mind's dealing with *koina*, not '*aisthanesthai*' but a different kind of verbs, such as '*dianoeisthai*' and '*episkopein*', are used. Now, let us turn to these latter verbs (*dianoeisthai*, *skepsasthai*, *episkopein*), and ask whether there is any passage in which they are used to represent a clear case of perception. By means of these verbs Socrates supposes cases in which Theaetetus is judging or considering. If we now set aside the passage in question (185b9–c1), then concerning the supposed judgement or consideration of Theaetetus we can make the following statement: when Socrates asks Theaetetus whether he thinks that they both (a sound and a colour) are, whether he considers whether they are like or unlike each other, etc. (185a8–9, 11–12, b2, 4–5), these judgements and considerations that Theaetetus is supposed to carry out are explicit judgements and considerations, accompanied by the use of the very same words we can see in Socrates' questions. This suggests that '*dianoeisthai*', '*skepsasthai*', and '*episkopein*' are used to denote explicit thinking or considering,[15] and leads us to

---

[13] It seems that 'about both' (185a5) is just a simple repetition of the same expression at 185a4.   [14] Cf. Burnyeat, above n 1, 33 n 17.

[15] '*To koinon lambanein*' (185b8) seems to be a variant of '*tauta . . . panta . . . dianoē(i)*' (185b7); then, if the cognition expressed by '*lambanein*' should be regarded as involving no explicit judgement, it follows that '*dianoeisthai*' here does not refer to the act of explicit thinking. However, the text here seems too vague for us to draw therefrom any conclusive view concerning the character of the act represented by '*dianoeisthai*'. For instance, we can take Socrates' remark at 185b7–9 as follows: after asking through what sense Theaetetus thinks *koina*, Socrates excludes in advance the view that *koina* are perceived through hearing or sight; then, we can regard '*di' akoēs . . . di' opseōs . . . lambanein*' (185b8) as representing perceiving through hearing or sight, and it's not necessary to take '*lambanein*' as a variant of '*dianoeisthai*'.

suppose that the considering referred to at 185b9–c1 (*skepsasthai, episkepsasthai*) is also explicit considering; then, if we also take account of the point established in the last paragraph (i.e. that '*aisthanesthai*' would not be suitable for describing the mind's dealing with *koina* here), we should conclude that what is described in this passage is not perception. It doesn't matter at all that a sensible quality 'saltiness' is also dealt with in this considering, because even explicit considering can deal with sensible qualities. This last point allows us to interpret also 185e7 in such a way as not to imply that the consideration here (*episkopein*) is perception.

There are three possible objections to this interpretation.

(1) At 185e7 it is stated, 'there are some things (sensible qualities) which the mind *episkopei* through the capacities of the body'. Here, the grammatical object of '*episkopein*' is not a clause but a word referring to sensible qualities. If a clause were used as the object, the activity represented by '*episkopein*' might be regarded as that of explicitly considering. However, as it is, '*episkopein*' with sensible qualities as its object, and with the capacities of the body as its means, this strongly suggests perceiving sensible qualities through the capacities of the body. In fact '*episkopein*' can mean 'look upon or at, inspect, observe', and it is often taken in the sense of direct acquaintance and translated as 'view' or 'contemplate'.[16] 'View' or 'contemplate' suggests perception.

Furthermore, '*episkopein*' at 185e7 is replaced by '*eporegetai*' (186a4). Cornford, for example, translates '*eporegetai*' as 'apprehend'.[17] This also seems to suggest that '*episkopein*' here should be understood as describing the act of perceiving.

(2) According to 185c1–3, 'the capacity through the tongue' is that with which one will consider whether a sound and a colour are salty or not. Isn't, then, 'considering with the capacity of the tongue' identical with perceiving with taste?

(3) 185b9–c3 should be considered in its context. In the part which follows 185b9–c3 Socrates asks what reveals *koina* to the mind, while at 185b9–c3 he investigates what reveals such qualities as saltiness. This

---

[16] Cornford, above n 10, 104–5; H. N. Fowler, *Plato, Theaetetus, Sophist* (The Loeb Classical Library, 1921), 163; H. F. Cherniss, 'The Philosophical Economy of the Theory of Ideas', *American Journal of Philology*, LVII (1936), 450, repr. in *Studies in Plato's Metaphysics*, ed R. E. Allen (London, 1965), 6; W. G. Runciman, *Plato's Later Epistemology* (Cambridge, 1962), 15; W. Bondeson, 'Perception, True Opinion and Knowledge in Plato's *Theaetetus*', *Phronesis*, XIV (1969), 112; Holland, above n 10, 103.

[17] Cornford, above n 10, 106. Fowler (above n 16, 163) translates it as 'grasp'.

contrast between 185b9–c3 and 185c4 ff (cf. '*de dē*' at c4) seems to be obliterated by reading the mind's act of considering *koina* into 185b9–c3.

These objections can be answered as follows.

(1) Though '*episkopein*' takes a noun as its grammatical object at 185e1–2 and e6–7, '*episkopein*' and its cognate verb '*skepsasthai*' take an indirect question as the object at 185b4–5, 10. We can compare this to the use of '*dianoeisthai*'. The grammatical object of '*dianoeisthai*' is a word representing *koina* at 185a4, b7, and a '*hoti* (that)' clause at 185a8–9, 11–12, b2.[18] The sentences at 185a4 and b7 are regarded as derived forms from the type of sentence we can find at 185a8–9, through the attraction of the subject of the subordinate clause dependent on the verb '*dianoeisthai*' into the prepositional phrase (*peri* and genitive) and the attraction of the predicate of the subordinate clause into the object of the verb.[19] As to the use of '*episkopein*', it seems possible, and perhaps more natural, to regard the sentences at 185e1–2 and e6–7 as derived from the type of sentence that we can find at 185b4–5 through the same kind of procedure. 185e1–2 and e6–7 can be considered as having an indirect question as the object in their deep structure. In fact, in all the occurrences of '*episkopein*' and '*skepsasthai*' in the *Theaetetus*, the verbs are used in the sense of 'consider a question, consider someone or something in respect to his quality, its genuineness or truth', though in many cases the verb doesn't take an indirect question as its grammatical object.[20] It seems very difficult to understand these verbs only in the sense of direct acquaintance, neglecting completely the element of considering, as far as the *Theaetetus* is concerned.

[18] Though at 185a11–12 and b2 '*dianoeisthai*' does not appear, the verb is easily supplied from 185a9.

[19] Cf. J. Lyons, *Structural Semantics* (Oxford, 1963), 107–8, and McDowell, above n 2, 188–9.

[20] What is considered are, e.g., what knowledge is (145d7), whether knowledge and perception are the same or different (163a7, 168b6, 184b5, cf. 185a11–12), the Heraclitean thesis (180c6), how many five and seven are (196a2, 5, b2, 198c5, 7, cf. 185b2), one of the things one sees or hears (191e3, in the Wax Block, in order to explain the existence of false judgements), minds in childbirth, another's judgements (Socrates' midwifery, 150b9, 160e7, 151c3, 161e7), whether someone else's judgement is correct or not (161d5), Theaetetus (in order to find whether Theodorus' praise of Theaetetus is correct or not, 145b7; in this context '*anaskepsasthai*' is also used at 145b3, cf. 144d9). As to 150b9, it may be objected that '*episkopein*' here should be taken in the sense of 'inspect, watch over'. Certainly, in the context the verb can have that sense. But in this context it should be taken also in the sense of 'consider whether the minds are giving birth to something genuine and true or falsehood', as is clear from 150b9–c3 and 151c3.

The same thing can be said about the use of *'eporegesthai'*. According to Liddell–Scott–Jones, *A Greek–English Lexicon* (Oxford, 1940), *'eporegesthai'* is used in the sense of 1. *stretch oneself towards, reach forward,* (with gen.) *reach at* a thing, 2. (with gen.) *yearn for* a thing etc. If *'eporegetai'* at 186a4 can be taken in the sense of 'reach at', it may be possible to translate it as 'apprehend', as Cornford does. However, this is not the only possibility. Here the present of the verb is used, and generally speaking, the present denotes the action of stretching oneself towards a thing, the successful performance of which results in the achievement of reaching at the thing. The aorist is used, on the other hand, to express the termination of the action (the use of terminative or resultative aorist).[21] As far as Liddell–Scott–Jones is concerned, the aorist, and not the present, is used in all the instances where *'eporegesthai'* is taken to denote the event of reaching at a thing. Besides, whenever Plato uses the present (or the imperfect) of the verbs *'eporegesthai'* and *'oregesthai'*, they denote the action or attitude of reaching after or yearning for something, which is to culminate in the achievement of grasping or reaching at it.[22] Accordingly, it is more likely that *'eporegetai'* at 186a4 is used in the sense of 'yearn for' or 'try to get hold of', as others translate it.[23]

This makes it more reasonable to take *'eporegetai'* here to represent one of the factors involved in the act of considering: when one is engaged in the act of considering, one is usually reaching after, or trying to find, something; considering starts because there is something to be found, and its finding requires the act of considering. By replacing *'episkopein'* by *'eporegetai'*, Plato seems to have intended to make us note the involvement of this factor in considering.

(2) Though it is said at 185c1–3 that the capacity through the tongue is that with which one will consider whether a sound and a colour are salty or not, the use of the dative case (*hō(i)* with, 185c1) here is not exact. If the distinction between the dative idiom and the *'dia'* idiom, which is established at 184b–e, had been followed strictly, *'di' hou'* would have been written instead of *'hō(i)'*. Only the mind can

---

[21] As to the difference of aspect between the present and the aorist, cf. Lyons, above n 19, 111 ff.

[22] *Protagoras* (*Prt.*) 326a3, *Phaedo* (*Ph.*) 65c9, 75a2, b1, *Republic* (*R.*) 437c5, 439b1, 485d4, 572a2, *Laws* 714a4, 757c7, 807c6, *Epistulae* II. 312e4. Especially, *R.* 437c5, 439b1, and 485d4 are noteworthy in that Plato uses in those contexts also *'epithumein'*, *'ephiesthai'*, *'boulesthai'*, *'horman'*, *'stergein'*, and *'erōtikōs echein'*.

[23] Cf. Liddell–Scott–Jones; McDowell, above n 2, 68; A. Diès, *Platon, Théétète* (Paris, 1967), 223.

be correctly referred to by '*hō*(*i*)', because the dative idiom expresses the subject of perception.[24] Therefore, though the grammatical subject of '*episkepsē*(*i*)' here is Theaetetus, it is legitimate to use the mind (*hē psūchē*) as the subject of the verb (cf. 185e1,6) and read 185c1–3 as if it were written, 'the mind considers through the capacity of the tongue (i.e. taste) (*hē psūchē episkepsetai dia tēs glōttēs dunameōs*, cf. 185e7) whether a sound and a colour are salty or not'. This is certainly what is meant at 185c1–3.

Then, should we still maintain that this act of considering is identical with or involved in perceiving with taste? That there is no necessity for thinking so is clear from the following passages in the *Phaedo*, in which the same kind of locution is used.

When the mind uses the body in order to consider something through seeing or through hearing or through some other sense (*skopein ti ē dia tou horan ē dia tou akouein ē di' allēs tinos aisthēseōs*)—of course considering through the body is the same as considering through sense—.(79c)

The mind is compelled to consider reality through the body as if through the bars of its prison (*hōsper dia heirgmou dia toutou skopeisthai*), and not through itself. (82e, cf. 83a–b, too)

Though the act of considering referred to in these passages of the *Phaedo* is done through sense or sense organs, it is not identical with or involved in perception. The use of sense or sense organs is only the means for the act of considering (*tō*(*i*) *sōmati proschrētai eis to skopein ti*, 79c3). The act of considering, which is described as something which is done only when a respite from the body's demands is allowed (66d), can never be regarded as identical with or involved in perception. For ordinary people the scope of the considering may be mostly limited to perceptual things. But this doesn't imply that the considering is identical with or involved in perception. As an object for which perception is used by people, the act of considering is different from perception. The passages in the *Phaedo* make it clear, I think, that at 185c1–3 of the *Theaetetus* we don't have to take the connection between perceiving with taste and the act of considering so closely as to imply that they are identical with each other or the latter is involved in the former. Perception can be taken as the means for considering whether a sound and a colour are salty or not. Although it may be impossible to use taste in this consideration (because it is impossible to

---

[24] Burnyeat, above n 1.

taste a sound and a colour), yet if it were possible to carry out the consideration, taste would be used in it.

(3) Even if the act of considering whether a sound and a colour are salty or not is understood as proper considering and not as identical with or involved in perception, it doesn't follow that the contrast between 185b9–c3 (or rather 185c1–3) and 185c4 ff has been obliterated. The contrast consists in two kinds of means through which the same act of considering is carried out, and not in two kinds of considering which have different kinds of things as their objects. The example presented by Socrates, the act of considering whether a sound and a colour are salty or not, illustrates not only the consideration through sense but also the mind's own considering in which the concepts of *koina* are used. As we have seen above, this example is the source from which Socrates took '*estin*' and '*ouk esti*' (185c5–6). In the same act of considering whether a sound and a colour are salty or not (*ar' eston halmurō ē ou*, 185b10), there are two kinds of concepts used by the mind: the concept corresponding to '*halmurō*' and the concepts corresponding to '*eston*' and '*ou (eston)*'.[25] In this act of considering the mind is using these two kinds of concepts, and dealing with two kinds of things by two kinds of means: by means of taste and by means of itself (i.e. not by means of anything else). When Socrates introduces saltiness in his illustration, naturally the attention of Theaetetus is drawn to the means necessary for dealing with saltiness. That is why his first answer is that it is with the capacity of the tongue that he will consider whether a sound and a colour are salty or not. Then, at 185c5–6 Socrates turns Theaetetus' attention to the involvement of *koina* in the same act of considering, and to the means necessary for using their concepts. The contrast expressed here is this contrast between two kinds of means through which the same act of considering is carried out. This being the case, our interpretation doesn't obliterate the contrast at all.

The same kind of contrast can be observed in 185e6–7. Suppose the mind considers whether something is red, trying to find that it is red or that it is not red; in this considering the mind deals with 'being' and 'not-being' through itself, and with 'red' through a capacity of the

---

[25] Strictly speaking, there is another kind of element, represented by the grammatical subject (a sound and a colour). However, in the question being considered it doesn't appear explicitly because of the grammatical structure of the Greek language. Accordingly, in the argument this element is not brought forward. Rather, Socrates abstains from introducing this element by saying in advance that what Theaetetus considers the question with is neither sight nor hearing (185c1–2).

body (sight). Then, on this view the contrast observed at 185e6–7 by means of *'men'* and *'de'* is the one between these two kinds of means through which the mind engages in the same act of considering, using two kinds of concepts.

Cooper thought *'ta men . . .'* and *'ta de . . .'* represent two different kinds of activity of the mind (the former represents the independent investigation of the mind, and the latter perception). Consequently, he couldn't help asking the following question.

. . . why Plato thinks that different powers of the mind are called on in deciding whether a *koinon* such as self-identity belongs to a sensed color, than are exercised in deciding whether the sensed color is, say, red. The latter operation, the classification or labelling of the data of sense, does not indeed involve the application of a concept which belongs to objects of different senses, but why should that make any difference? . . . How can Plato have thought that the application of the elementary perceptual concepts could proceed without this sort of associative activity? And even if this can be managed without the use of the *koina*, why did Plato think it involves quite a different power of the mind from that exercised in thinking about existence, similarity, and so on?[26]

However, according to our interpretation, this question is groundless. When *'ta men . . .'* and *'ta de . . .'* are correctly understood as representing two different aspects of the same activity of the mind (considering), there is nothing problematic on Plato's part. And, at the same time, contrary to Cooper, I think that deciding whether the sensed colour is red involves the use of a *koinon*, in so far as 'is' is used in the consideration.

Cooper and Modrak rely on 185b9–c3 and 185e6–7 for their contention that Plato included in the function of perception the act of considering whether something is salty, and that Plato held the view that in perceiving something the mind makes some judgements.[27] However, if 185b9–c3 and 185e6–7 are interpreted as describing not perception but the mind's own explicit considering, we cannot accept their interpretation so easily. Plato thought that in considering a question and making judgements the mind often uses perception. However, whether he thought that perception involves judgement, as Cooper and Modrak contend, is another matter. Anyway, 185b9–c3 and 185e6–7 cannot be used as evidence for the view that perception involves judgement.

[26] Cooper, above n 1, 132–3.
[27] Cooper, above n 1, 131–2; Modrak, above n 1, 42–3.

2. *Plato's idea of* aisthanesthai

At the beginning of this paper I suggested three stages of cognition as candidates for Plato's idea of *aisthanesthai*: (1) explicit judgement, (2) awareness of something as *F* (or implicit judgement), (3) feeling comparable to suffering pains. Let us define them more closely, and see which should be regarded as Plato's idea of perception.

In (1), whether someone may start from asking a question explicitly or may make his implicit judgement explicit, the judgement is clearly formulated, even when it is silently formed, and each term appearing in the judgement is not hidden to him at all. Plato has this explicit judgement and thinking in mind, when he compares thinking to carrying on a discussion, and judging to speaking (189e–190a, cf. *Sophist* 263e–264a, *Philebus* 38c–39a). The use of language and words is necessary for discussion and speaking. Accordingly, (1) requires the ability to use language and words. Through the use of words each term appearing in somebody's judgement and its concept become explicit and clear to him. For instance, in the judgement that the box is red, all the three terms 'the box' 'is' 'red' and their concepts are explicit to him. Now, in 184–6 Plato uses the verbs '*dianoeisthai*', '*skepsasthai*', '*episkopein*' on the one hand, and '*aisthanesthai*' on the other, and distinguishes between two kinds of activity. The activity represented by the former verbs involves the use of the concepts of *koina*, and includes for example the explicit judgement that the colour is red. Therefore, it is clear that in Plato's view (1) is not covered by perception.

When the awareness in (2) (e.g. the awareness of something as red) is translated into a judgement, the judgement is also formed as 'the colour is red' or 'this is red', but not by the subject of the awareness but by an observer who has read this judgement into the former's awareness.[28] The awareness has a propositional content which consists in attributing the colour red to something seen, and can be said to be an implicit judgement. However, the judgement articulating the propositional content, and the terms appearing in the judgement, are not explicit to the subject of the awareness. He is not using the word 'the colour', 'is', nor 'red'. (2) does not need the use of language and words. It may be difficult to recognize this stage clearly in the case of human beings, because their constant use of words and language in

---

[28] This includes the case in which one is the observer of one's own awareness and translates it into an explicit judgement by reflection.

thinking will change automatically their awareness of something as *F* into a corresponding explicit judgement. It is easier to recognize this stage in animals' discrimination. Though macaque monkeys may not have the concept 'red', they seem to be able to discriminate the colour red from other colours or from a background, and attribute it to something in their visual field; they can be aware of something as red.[29] Their awareness is not an explicit judgement (1). They cannot make their awareness explicit by the use of words. Neither is it an instance of feeling comparable to suffering pains (3). They are attending to some one part of the world presented to them, and discriminating it from the other, and at the same time attributing a specific character to that particular part.

In the *Sophist* (264a–b) *phantasia* is defined as 'a blend of perception (*aisthēsis*) and judgement (*doxa*)'. This definition might suggest that perception is something left after all the elements of judgement (even the element of propositional content) have been subtracted from *phantasia*. It would follow then that what Plato understands by '*aisthēsis*' or '*aisthanesthai*' is not awareness of something as *F*. However, in this definition of *phantasia* what is denoted by '*doxa*' is explicit judgement, because it contains assertion and denial (*Sophist* 263e12); this means that even after the element of *doxa* has been subtracted from *phantasia*, awareness of something as *F* can remain as an element of perception.[30]

In support of the view that awareness is involved in perception, the use of '*dēloun*' (make visible or manifest, show, make known, reveal) at *Theaetetus* 185c5 might be pointed out. Although the word referring to *koina* is used as the object of '*dēloun*', the capacity which reveals (*dēloi*) something is that of sense organs, and 'the capacity of some sense organ, *S*, *dēloi* some quality or feature, *F*, to a percipient, *P*' is equivalent to '*P* perceives (*aisthanetai*) *F* through *S*', as is clear from 185c7–8, where Socrates repeats the question of 185c4–5 in another form, mentioning sense organs explicitly. This equivalence might suggest that in perceiving a sensible quality the mind is aware of it,

[29] Cf. G. H. Jacobs, *Comparative Color Vision* (New York, London, Toronto, Sydney, San Francisco, 1981), 138 ff. According to *R.* 376a–b, dogs can discriminate between a stranger and an acquaintance.

[30] If one interprets perception's inability to attain being and truth as the inability to have a propositional content and a truth value, it follows that perception is not even awareness of something as *F*. This may also be presented as an argument against involving awareness in perception. But this interpretation of perception's inability to attain being and truth will be called into question below.

because it is made manifest (shown, made known, revealed, *dēlousthai*) to the mind. However, it is the fact of our everyday life that when something is made manifest or revealed to us, we are not aware of it unless we attend to it. The mind may not be aware of sensible qualities made manifest (shown, revealed, etc.) to it in its perceiving, unless it attends to them. So far, then, whether perception involves awareness of something as *F* is still an open question.

What I mean by (3) feeling comparable to suffering pains is the state in which a person is only passively affected, without actively attending to anything. In this state the mind is not aware of anything. In the case of pains the state in which someone is only suffering a pain is distinguishable from the state in which he is aware of a pain (aware of something being felt as a pain, or aware of something external as causing a pain). As an instance of the former state it is possible to think of the case in which someone is so absorbed in something else that he is not aware of the pain he is suffering. Later he might say, 'It was hurting me, but I didn't notice it'. His attention would be enough to make him aware of the pain. This kind of state may be very rare. As I shall show below, Plato seems to have thought that in ordinary human life, feeling pains is usually accompanied by the element of judgement, and, accordingly, by the awareness of the pains. In the same way, we can suppose the stage of cognition in which someone feels or experiences passively the sensation of a colour red without attending to it, and without being aware of its being red. Just to have something in a field of vision without attending to it may be regarded as seeing.[31] In contrast with (2), (3) lacks the factors of attending, awareness, and propositional content.

According to the *Philebus* (33d–34a),[32] some bodily affections are extinguished before they reach the mind and leave it unaffected (*apathē*), while others go through both the body and the mind, and as it were set up a disturbance in each and both together; the latter affections don't escape the notice of the mind; this state, in which the mind and the body are together in one affection and are moved together, is called '*aisthēsis*'. When the mind is perceiving a sensible quality through bodily organs, the bodily affection aroused by the

[31] Cf. G. J. Warnock, 'Seeing', *Proceedings of the Aristotelian Society*, LV (1955), 205 ff.
[32] The *Philebus* (*Phil.*) is supposed to belong to the group of Plato's later dialogues, to which the *Theaetetus* (*Tht.*) also belongs. I suppose we can use the *Phil.* in elucidating Plato's idea of perception, which is expressed mainly in the *Tht.*, as long as both dialogues present views that are compatible with one another.

sensible quality does not escape the notice of the mind. This expression 'not escape the notice of the mind' (*tēn psuchēn mē lanthanein*, 33d8–9) seems to suggest the mind's awareness. However, from this passage we cannot unreservedly infer that the mind is aware of the sensible quality in perceiving it: 33d8–10 and 33e10–34a5 seem to allow us to suppose that '*tēn psūchēn mē lanthanein*' is only another way of describing the situation in which the mind and the body are together in one affection and are moved together, without implying that the mind is aware of the affection.[33]

However, these passages of the *Philebus* indicate at least that in perceiving something the mind is affected in a certain way just as in pain it is affected in a certain way.

At 21a–c of the *Philebus* (cf. 60d and 63b, too), it is said that, if one lacked reason, memory, knowledge, and true judgement, one couldn't know whether one was enjoying oneself or not, nor remember that one had been enjoying oneself, nor judge that one was enjoying oneself when one was, nor calculate that one would enjoy oneself later on, and that such a life would not be a human life at all, but the life of a jelly-fish or some other creatures that live in shells. This suggests that pleasure or pain in ordinary human life is usually accompanied by reason, memory, knowledge, and true judgement (in short by something to do with judgement), and that the affection of pleasure or pain without any element of judgement is a product of abstraction. The same thing may be said about perception. If perception is understood as feeling comparable to suffering pains, it is only a product of abstraction, and in real life it is usually accompanied by elements of judgement. That is to say, in human life, whenever one perceives, one is aware of a sensible quality *F*, and furthermore judges that it is *F*. However, there still remains the question whether for Plato '*aisthanesthai*' covers awareness or represents only the abstracted element of feeling comparable to suffering pains.

Theaetetus 186c1–2 and *Philebus* 33d–34a suggest the passivity on the part of the mind in perceiving, while the activity of the mind is suggested at *Theaetetus* 184d8. According to this passage, in perceiving we reach (*ephiknoumetha*) white and black things through eyes.[34]

---

[33] Later I shall return to 33d8–10 and 33e10–34a5, and offer another interpretation of these passages, according to which '*tēn psuchēn mē lanthanein*' implies not only that the mind and the body are together in one affection, but also that the mind is aware of the affection.

[34] Burnyeat, above n 1, 42.

However, the apparent discrepancy between 184d8 and 186c1–2 may be resolved, if we take into account the point we raised, that in real human life, in perceiving something the element of affection is always accompanied by the element of discrimination and judgement. 186c1–2 describes the necessity of sensible qualities taking the form of bodily affections and being brought to the mind in order to be perceived, whereas 184d8 describes the fact that in actual perception the mind grasps, or tries to grasp, externally existing qualities, and not bodily affections. The mind discriminates what is given in bodily affections as externally existing qualities.

To review and summarize the results of the discussion thus far: Plato distinguishes clearly between the activity of the mind represented by '*dianoeisthai*', '*skepsasthai*', and '*episkopein*', and the activity of the mind represented by '*aisthanesthai*'. '*Aisthanesthai*' cannot cover explicit judgement with language and words;[35] it implies at least that the mind is affected in the same way as the body is affected, and in ordinary human perception, affection is usually accompanied by the elements of awareness and judgement. We have left it open whether Plato included awareness of a sensible quality in what '*aisthanesthai*' or '*aisthēsis*' denotes or he meant by these expressions only the abstracted element of being affected.

To end this section, I wish to answer the last question: I am in favour of the view that for Plato awareness of a sensible quality is covered by '*aisthanesthai*' and '*aisthēsis*'. At 179c2–4 it is said,

as to each person's present affection (*pathos*), from which there come to be his perceptions (*aisthēseis*) and the judgements (*doxai*) in accordance with them, it is more difficult to refute these latter and show they are not true.

Here Plato seems to have made a threefold distinction between *doxai*, *aisthēseis*, and *pathos*. If this distinction may be regarded as equivalent to the one we drew above between (1) explicit judgement, (2)

---

[35] Therefore, we cannot accept one of the two lines of interpretation suggested by Cooper, that at the perceptual level 'in operating through the senses the mind applies the words "bitter", "red", "hard", etc. to sense-objects' (Cooper, above n 1, 132). Because Modrak thought that 185b9–c3 and 185e7 represent perception, she also was inclined to think that the ability to make simple perceptual judgements was limited to language users (above n 1, 43–4). But at the same time, she had to add that it is 'compatible with the view that animals and infants perceive' (44) and explain how these two views are compatible with each other. If 185b9–c3 and 185e7 are understood to describe the activity of the mind different from perception, there arises no such problem at all, and the view that animals and infants perceive (186b11–c1) supports the view that perception doesn't include explicit judgement with language and words.

awareness of something as *F*, and (3) feeling comparable to suffering pains, *aisthēseis* will be regarded as equivalent to (2).

Philebus 33d–34a also seems to support this view. In this passage, '*tēn psuchēn mē lanthanein*' and '*aisthēsis*' are treated as synonymous with each other (33e8). Certainly, as we have seen above, it is possible to understand 33d8–10 and 33e10–34a5 in such a way as not to imply that in being moved by the bodily affection the mind is aware of the affection, regarding '*tēn psuchēn mē lanthanein*' simply as another way of describing the situation in which the mind and the body are moved together. However, what the expression usually reminds us of is not the mind's mere affection but the mind's awareness. Plato usually implies awareness by the expression '*mē lanthanein*' and unawareness by '*lanthanein*' (e.g. 19c3, 30e4–5). Besides, according to *Gorgias* 508a, unless someone turns his attention to something (*prosechein ton noun*), it escapes his notice (*lelēthen*). This suggests that the situation described by '*mē lanthanein*' necessarily involves the element of attention, and that when something *mē lelēthen* a person, the person has attended to, and is aware of, it. Then, we can understand 33d8–10 and 33e10–34a5 in a way different from the one suggested above: when the mind is affected and moved by the bodily affection, the mind never fails to attend to the affection it has received from the body and to be aware of it, and this awareness is denoted by the word '*aisthēsis*'. This is why the state of the mind's being affected and moved by the bodily affection is called '*aisthēsis*'. This interpretation of these passages seems more acceptable than the other one in that it allows us to understand the expression '*tēn psuchēn mē lanthanein*' in its usual sense which implies 'awareness'.

Here, it is necessary to distinguish between the mind's being affected and the person's being affected. According to *Philebus* 43b, not everything that affects living beings (*hoposa paschei ti tōn empsuchōn*) is perceived, but most of such affections escape their notice. A person, a living being, has both the mind and the body, and even when the person is affected, the mind is not necessarily affected. That is, a person's affection doesn't necessarily lead to perception. There is a distinction between a person's affection and his perception. This distinction is observed also in the distinction between each person's affection and his perceptions at 179c2–3 of the *Theaetetus* (cf. *hekastō*(*i*), c3). When a person is affected, he (or his mind) is not necessarily aware of the affection, whereas when the mind is affected by the bodily affection, it is at the same time attending to the affection, and is aware of it as an external sensible quality. And this act or state of the mind is called by Plato '*aisthanesthai*' or '*aisthēsis*'.[36]

Finally, however, the following objection may be raised. Certainly at 179c each person's present *pathos* and *aisthēseis* arising therefrom are distinguished from each other. But how about 186d–e? At 186d10–e3 Socrates asks Theaetetus, 'What name do you give to that (*ekeinō (i)*): to seeing, hearing, smelling, feeling cold, feeling hot?' Theaetetus answers, 'Perceiving (*aisthanesthai*), of course'. Socrates then asks whether Theaetetus calls all of that, taken together, perception (*aisthēsis*), and Theaetetus replies in the affirmative. Now, '*ekeinō (i)*' (186d10) and '*ekeino*' (186d7) seem to refer back to the thing represented by '*pathēmasin*' (affections, 186d2). If so, it follows that Plato thought '*aisthanesthai*' and '*aisthēsis*' represented the state of being affected, and not awareness. It may be that Plato used '*pathēmasin*' (186d2) instead of '*aisthēsei*' simply because he regarded them as interchangeable with each other.

I wish to answer this objection as follows: firstly, it is not so certain whether '*ekeino*' and '*ekeinō (i)*' (186d7,10) refer just to affections (*pathēmasin*, d2). The fact that '*ekeino*' and '*ekeinō (i)*' are used in the singular neuter makes us suspect that they refer more vaguely to what has been contrasted with the act of reasoning or considering, that is, the act of perceiving sensible qualities (186b2–4) or the act of perceiving the affections that stretch through the body to the mind (186c1–2) (cf. '*men*' and '*de*' at 186b2, 6, 11, c2). This suspicion is confirmed further by the use of the plural form '*tosautas diaphoras*' ('such great differences' or 'so many differences', 186d7–8). More than one difference is referred to by Socrates here, for they include not only the one mentioned at 186d2–5 but also the one mentioned at 186b11–c6, and this, in turn, suggests that '*ekeino*' (186d7) refers to the perceiving mentioned at 186b11–c2.

Then, why did Plato use the expression '*pathēmasin*' at 186d2? He used '*pathēmata*' also at 186c2, as the grammatical object of '*aisthanesthai*'. Whatever reason there is for the use of the word at 186d2 must be the same as the reason for its use at 186c2. Now, as the

---

[36] We cannot know for certain whether Plato thought that the mind's attention triggers the mind's being affected by the bodily affection or that the mind's affection triggers the mind's attention. Plato might have accepted both views. For instance, we are usually unaware of the ticking sound of a clock, but become aware of it by our attention. This can be regarded as an example of the former alternative. On the other hand, the sound of a thunderclap arouses our attention and notice. This can be regarded as an example of the latter alternative.

reason for its use at 186c2 we can think of two possibilities: it is either (1) in order to emphasize the non-propositional (affection-like) character of perceiving, or (2) in order to make it explicit that in perceiving one cannot help being affected by various conditions and doesn't necessarily grasp facts or states of affairs. If (1), then we should suppose that perceiving is nothing but being affected, and that '*pathēmata*' or '*paschein*' is interchangeable with '*aisthēsis*' or '*aisthanesthai*'. If (2), we don't have to suppose that they are interchangeable with each other; though in perceiving one is always affected in some way, one may be at the same time aware of some sensible quality, and this awareness may be represented by '*aisthanesthai*'. For reasons that will be shown below (cf. 70), I think we should choose (2). (2) should be chosen at 186d2–5 as well.

Rejecting (1) and adopting (2) makes it possible for us not to suppose that for Plato '*pathēmata*' is interchangeable with '*aisthēsis*'. However, it is still an undeniable fact that '*aisthēsis*' or '*aisthanesthai*' does not appear at 186d2–5, although in this passage some ground on which to deny perception's claim to be knowledge must be stated. How can we regard this passage as contributing to the refutation of perception's claim to be knowledge? We can answer this question by noting the use of the preposition 'in' (*en*) in the expression 'knowledge is not in (*en*) the *pathēmata* . . .' (186d2–3). The preposition '*en*' can be used in the sense of 'within one's reach or power', and 'something *A* is *en* another thing *B*' can mean that *A* depends on *B*. *B* is the means through which to achieve or acquire *A*.[37] This is supposed to be the use of '*en*' at 186d2–3, and this passage is understood as being to the effect that knowledge does not depend on the *pathēmata* but on the reasoning about them, or that in order to acquire knowledge one cannot depend on the *pathēmata* but on the reasoning about them. This notion of the necessary or appropriate means is certainly to be read into 186d3–5, though the adverbs '*entautha*' and '*ekei*', and not the prepositional phrase with '*en*', are used there. That passage means that in order to attain being and truth one cannot depend on the *pathēmata* but on the reasoning about them. The means of *pathēmata* and that of reasoning are contrasted at 186d2–5, and it is declared that the former means alone does not enable one to attain being and truth and to obtain knowledge, and that for this purpose it is necessary to exercise the ability to reason and to reflect on the *pathēmata*.

[37] Cf. *Prt.* 324e1, 354e7, 356d1, e5, 357a6, *Gorgias* 470e8, etc., and also Liddell–Scott–Jones, '*en*' A, I, 6.

Then, when one depends on perception, understood as awareness of some sensible quality by our interpretation, on which means is one regarded as depending? Whenever one is aware of some sensible quality in the act of perceiving, the sensible quality is brought to the mind in the form of some bodily affection. This means that in the act of perceiving one is always dependent on the *pathēmata* that are brought to the mind, whereas at this stage one has not yet exercised the ability to reason. If one relies merely on perception in the attempt to attain being and truth and to obtain knowledge, one is after all dependent on the *pathēmata* and not on the reasoning about them. Thus, even though '*aisthanesthai*' or '*aisthēsis*' does not appear at 186d2–5, the description there implies that perception as awareness of a sensible quality cannot be knowledge. Because of this implication Plato could easily refer to the act of perceiving by means of '*ekeino*' (186d7) and '*ekeinō(i)*' (d10), and declare at 186e that perception and knowledge cannot be the same thing.[38]

II 'Being' in 186A–E

The results of the preceeding section have a close connection with the interpretation of 186a–e. Here, perception's claim to be knowledge is rejected on the ground that one cannot attain being and truth in perception, while attaining being and truth is a necessary condition for having knowledge. This argument requires that what Plato understands by 'attain being and truth' is something that cannot take place in perception. The ability to attain being is sometimes understood as the ability to have a propositional content or to frame a propositional structure. This interpretation would make our view of '*aisthanesthai*' less likely, because according to this interpretation perception understood as awareness of something as *F* would be regarded as

---

[38] It is possible to understand the *pathēmata* at 186d2 not as *pathēmata* in general but more specifically as the *pathēmata* that extend through the body as far as the mind (186c1–2), and to regard them as present to the mind's awareness by extending as far as the mind and moving it. On this view the *pathēmata* at 186d2 are what the mind is aware of in the act of perceiving, and it is stated there that knowledge does not depend on such *pathēmata*. Thus, when we take into account the force of the qualifying phrase 'that extend through the body as far as the mind' (186c1–2), the contribution of 186d2–5 to the refutation of perception's claim to be knowledge becomes clearer. The possibility of understanding the *pathēmata* (186d2) in connection with 186c1–2 has been suggested to me by Professor Lloyd. Concerning 186d2–5 I shall have more to say in the following sections.

having already attained being.[39] On the other hand, if our view is correct, there seems to be some defect in that interpretation of 'attain being'.

My contention is that 'attain being' should be taken in the sense of attaining objectivity or finding how things are in the world; perception's claim to be knowledge is rejected on the ground that perception lacks the means necessary for attaining objectivity, that is, the act of considering.

In order to support this contention it is necessary to engage in a detailed analysis of 186a–e. But before starting the analysis, I wish to ask this question which I think is crucial to the correct understanding of 184–6. What is the target of the criticism at 184–6? It is certain that Theaetetus' definition that knowledge is perception is criticized. The criticism begins by repeating this definition (184b5–7). However, how it is to be understood is not so clear. As we have seen above, the word '*aisthanesthai*' itself allows of various interpretations. Accordingly, the definition can be understood in various ways. If Theaetetus' definition should be taken to the effect that knowledge is a kind of feeling comparable to suffering pains, it will be possible to refute it by showing that perception understood in this way has no propositional content. On the other hand, if the definition is to be taken to the effect that knowledge is judgement by means of perception, it will not work as a refutation to point out that to have a propositional content or structure is necessary for knowledge.

1. *The target of the criticism*

When Theaetetus presented his definition that knowledge is perception, his position was at once regarded as equivalent to that of Protagoras, and '*aisthanesthai*' was said to denote the same as '*phainesthai*' (151e–152c). This means that at the beginning of the dialogue Theaetetus' definition was understood as being to the effect that

---

[39] It may be necessary to distinguish between having a propositional content and framing a propositional structure, because perception taken in the sense of awareness of something as F (implicit judgement) seems to have a propositional content and not a propositional structure, i.e. a propositional structure of thought modelled on language. If this distinction holds and 'attain being' is to be understood in the sense of 'frame a propositional structure' and not of 'have a propositional content', our interpretation of '*aisthanesthai*' can be maintained. However, for the reason that will be stated below (cf. 60 ff), I reject even the possibility of understanding 'attain being' in the sense of 'frame a propositional structure'.

knowledge is *phantasia*. According to *Sophist* 263e–264b, *phantasia* is a blend of perception and judgement, and judgement in turn is explicit judgement, which contains assertion and denial. We can say that *phantasia*, in the *Sophist*, is explicit judgement by means of perception. It seems that also in the *Theaetetus* '*phantasia*' is understood in this sense, and that Theaetetus' definition claims that knowledge is explicit judgement by means of perception; in the exposition of the Protagorean thesis the definition is described as the claim that whatever anyone judges (*doxazē(i)*) by means of perception is true for him and is knowledge (161d3).[40]

At 160d–e Socrates says that Theaetetus' definition, the Protagorean thesis, and the Heraclitean thesis coincide. It is not until then that something is explicitly stated to be Theaetetus' new-born child and the product of Socratic midwifery; before this Theaetetus was still described as being in travail (157c–d). From this we can infer that Theaetetus' definition or thesis that knowledge is perception is nothing but what has been explained in the argument lasting until 160, that is, part of the Protagorean thesis. The Protagorean thesis in its most general form claims concerning any quality or feature that any judgement is true for the person who forms it. Theaetetus' thesis deals with sensible qualities, and not with all kinds of qualities or features, but its contention is not substantially different from that of the Protagorean thesis. Theaetetus' thesis claims concerning sensible qualities that (explicit) judgement by means of perception is true for the percipient and that it is knowledge. Otherwise the definition would not be regarded as equivalent to the Protagorean thesis, nor would Protagoras try to defend the definition in his defence (166b).[41]

---

[40] Cf. 161e8, too, where *phantasia* and *doxa* are mentioned side by side.

[41] At 166a2–b1 Protagoras distinguishes himself from Theaetetus and says that from the fact that Theaetetus has been refuted in an eristic manner it doesn't follow that Protagoras himself has been refuted. This may suggest that Theaetetus' position should not be identified with the Protagorean thesis nor with any of its parts. Cf. E. N. Lee, ' "Hoist with His Own Petard": Ironic and Comic Elements in Plato's Critique of Protagoras (*Tht.* 161–171)', *Exegesis and Argument, Studies in Greek Philosophy presented to Gregory Vlastos* (*Phronesis*, supp vol I), ed E. N. Lee, A. P. D. Mourelatos, and R. M. Rorty, (Assen, 1973), 230 ff and n 12. However, Protagoras' remark at 166a2–b1 doesn't necessarily imply that Protagoras distinguishes the position expressed in Theaetetus' definition from his own. Though Theaetetus has been refuted in an eristic manner, it's one thing for Theaetetus as a young person to be refuted or defeated, and quite another for the position expressed in his definition to be refuted or defeated. Theaetetus required the explanation of his definition in order to be regarded as having given birth to his child (his definition), and it is very likely that even afterwards his understanding of the definition was not complete, and because of the lack of full

Though Theaetetus gave his definition at 151e, what is meant by this definition was not clear, even to Theaetetus himself, and he needed its clarification in order to be regarded as having given birth to his child at 160e. Theaetetus' thesis claiming that (explicit) judgement by means of perception is true for the percipient and is knowledge is the target of the criticism of 184–6.[42]

Before starting the criticism of Theaetetus' thesis, Socrates criticizes the Protagorean thesis in its most general form by means of the *peritropē* argument and the argument concerning things in the future (170–9). Through them the area in which the Protagorean thesis holds is narrowed down, and finally at 179c we find the following remark, which we have already quoted:

> as to each person's present affection, from which there come to be his perceptions and the judgements in accordance with them, it is more difficult to refute these latter and show they are not true.

The position expressed in this passage, which claims that judgements in accordance with perceptions are true, is that of Theaetetus' thesis.[43]

understanding he couldn't defend his definition. Protagoras' remark at 166a2–b1 can be understood to the effect that though a young man Theaetetus was refuted, the position expressed in his definition, which is equivalent to the Protagorean thesis, has not been refuted, because Theaetetus didn't give such answers as Protagoras would have given. Theaetetus didn't fully understand the significance of the Heraclitean thesis that backs up the Protagorean thesis and Theaetetus' position. That is why at 168b Protagoras demands Socrates to consider firstly the Heraclitean thesis and the Protagorean thesis, and go on from there to consider whether knowledge and perception are the same or different.

[42] This doesn't imply that in Plato's view '*aisthanesthai*' or '*aisthēsis*' represents *phantasia* (explicit judgement by means of perception), or that when *aisthēsis* is declared to be different from knowledge at 186e9–10, '*aisthēsis*' is used in the sense of *phantasia*. It has become clear through the examination of the previous section that what Plato understands by '*aisthanesthai*' (or '*aisthēsis*' at 186e9) is not explicit judgement, and, therefore, is not *phantasia*. When Plato identifies *aisthēsis* and *phantasia* at 151e–152c, his purpose is to relate Theaetetus' definition to the Protagorean thesis, and not to express his own view. Even if we suppose that what Plato understands by '*aisthanesthai*' in 184–6 and by '*aisthēsis*' at 186e9 is not *phantasia*, it is still possible to read 184–6 in such a way as to imply that *phantasia* is denied to be knowledge there, and I think 184–6 should be read in such a way in order that it really constitute the criticism of Theaetetus' definition.

[43] In formulating Theaetetus' thesis I have used above the expression 'judgement by means of (*dia*) perception' (cf. 161d3), and now use 'judgements in accordance with (*kata*) perceptions' (cf. 179c3). The former expression and the latter might be supposed to differ from each other in that the former allows, and the latter may not allow, the possibility of the judgement's disagreeing with the content of perception, though based on it. However, as I shall show below (64), both expressions should be taken in the same sense, as meaning 'judgement as exact articulation of the content of perception, conforming completely to perception'.

I understand this passage in the following way. After the narrowing down of the area where the Protagorean thesis holds, one part of it, Theaetetus' thesis, is left still intact; it is difficult to refute the Protagorean thesis in this area of sensible qualities; but in spite of the difficulty Socrates and Theaetetus go on to refute it, and the refutation is completed at 184–6. Thus, the refutation at 184–6 can be regarded as the final step in the general criticism of the Protagorean thesis.

However, 179c is sometimes differently interpreted, which in turn leads to a different view on the target of the criticism at 184–6. For instance, Modrak interprets Socrates' remark just quoted as if Plato accepted there the view that perceptions are infallible and true.[44] A similar interpretation is suggested by Cooper concerning the next remark by Socrates (179c4–5). There Socrates says, 'Perhaps I am talking nonsense, when I say "more difficult". Because it may be that they are impossible to refute (*analōtoi*)'. Cooper understands '*analōtoi*' in the sense of 'not open to criticism or correction' and reads here the implication that 'perception is purely subjective, because it is not open to criticism or correction.'[45]

The following consideration seems to underline their interpretation. If perceptions and judgements in accordance with them are to be expressed in such a sentence as 'This appears red (to me)' or 'This seems sour (to me)', they will be regarded as true or not open to criticism or correction. This affects the interpretation of the criticism of 184–6. If its target is the claim that the type of judgement expressed in such a sentence as 'This appears red (to me)' is always true and is knowledge, it seems impossible to refute this claim by contending that one cannot attain truth and states of affairs by this type of judgement. By forming this type of judgement one can be considered to have attained truth and states of affairs, at least, concerning one's own affections or experiences.[46] Then, it seems better to reject our

---

[44] Modrak, above n 1, 52 n 12, 53 n 15. Note 12 is given to support the view that according to Plato's phenomenalist theory, one cannot refute the claim that perception is knowledge by pointing out that we sometimes have false perceptions ('179e2–4' in n 12 is a misprint for '179c2–4').

[45] Cooper, above n 1, 142.

[46] According to Cornford, above n 10, 'I judge that this wine seems sour to me. No one can challenge the truth of such a judgment [i.e. judgment which is supposed merely to register the fact of a present sensation: my note]' (73), and 'Plato has now shown why he will not accept the Protagorean position as extended by its author to judgments which go beyond the individual's immediate and private experience of his present sensations. But within this narrower field he has himself accepted the position, and built it into his own account of the nature of perception' (92).

interpretation of 184–6: the target of the criticism may not be the claim that judgements in accordance with perceptions are always true and are instances of knowledge, or it may be that 'attain being' should not be understood in the sense of 'find states of affairs'. This consideration leads to interpretations other than ours; for instance, it is possible to suppose that perception without any element of judgement is denied to be knowledge by the criticism, and that 'attain being' means 'attain propositional structure'. According to another interpretation, 'attain being' means 'attain true reality', and Plato hints at Forms by this expression.

However, I cannot accept the interpretation of Modrak and Cooper concerning 179c. Firstly, at 179c4 Socrates says only that it is *more difficult* to refute the claim that perceptions and judgements in accordance with them are true, and not that it is *impossible* to do so. Certainly, at 179c5 Socrates uses '*analōtoi*' ('impossible to refute'), but at the same time he weakens the force of his assertion by using '*ei etuchon*' ('it may be that'): it is not so certain that perceptions and judgements in accordance with them are *analōtoi*.[47] If judgements in accordance with perceptions are to be expressed in such a sentence as 'This appears red (to me)' they can be regarded as always true or not open to correction. However, my contention is that this type of

---

[47] After the remark of 179c4–5 Socrates continues, 'and the people who assert that they are quite clear and are instances of knowledge may be saying things which are, and Theaetetus here was not beside the mark when he laid it down that perception and knowledge are the same thing.' Concerning this passage Shea says, 'Socrates clearly utters the second possibility for strictly dialectical purposes, and surely this is the motivation for the first, also. This view is further supported by the fact that these claims are put forward in the optative mood' (J. Shea, 'Judgment and Perception in *Theaetetus* 184–6', *Journal of the History of Philosophy*, XXIII (1985), 4). I agree with him in this point. However, as to 179c5 Shea seems to have neglected the force of '*ei etuchon*'. He thinks that here 'Socrates owns . . . that a person's perceptions are *analōtoi*, impregnable', and in order to avoid attributing to Socrates the view that perceptions are true or infallible, he takes Socrates to be making a point about human psychology, i.e. that people are not usually willing to disbelieve sensory reports, and not that perceptions are necessarily revelatory of truth (4 and 11 n 29). But it is doubtful whether '*analōtoi*' refers simply to a psychological fact about people's unwillingness to disbelieve. '*Haliskomai*' from which '*analōtos*' comes is often used as the passive of '*haireō*', and this verb is used at 179c4 in order to say that it is more difficult to refute perceptions and judgements in accordance with them and show that they are not true (*helein hōs ouk alētheis*). This suggests that 'something is *analōtos*' means that it is impossible to refute it and show that it is not true. Accordingly, when something is *analōtos*, it is necessarily true, whether people are willing to disbelieve it or not. But it doesn't follow from this that by using the expression '*analōtoi*' Socrates commits himself to the view that perceptions are necessarily true or infallible, because he seems to refrain from committing himself by adding '*ei etuchon*'.

judgement is not the typical case of judgements in accordance with perceptions. Most of them are expressed in such a sentence as 'This is red', and assert that there is some objectivity or state of affairs, corresponding to the statement that this is red. In this case judgements in accordance with perceptions are not incorrigible.

As we have seen above, Theaetetus' thesis is not substantially different from the Protagorean thesis, except in respect of the area covered by them. The type of judgements dealt with by them is the same. Now, the Protagorean thesis maintains that judgements made by ordinary people, and not merely by those versed in his thesis, are true (for them). It is not the case that Protagoras persuades ordinary people to reduce their claim in their judgements and to form only a certain type of judgements applying to appearances alone, in order that they may get rid totally of the danger of making mistakes. Rather Protagoras claims that judgements made by ordinary people are, as they are, true (for them). let us take examples of judgements made by them and regarded as true according to the Protagorean thesis. When they think that the Protagorean thesis is mistaken, their judgement is not that Protagoras is mistaken for them nor that he seems mistaken to them, but that he is simply and flatly mistaken (170c ff);[48] people who are mad or dreaming think that they are gods or they are flying (158a–b). These examples show that Protagoras admits as true (for the one who judges) any judgement asserting that such and such is the case (*simpliciter*).

If we follow these examples, we should conclude that Theaetetus' thesis claims that perceptual judgements asserting something in the world is such and such are true (for the percipient) and are instances of knowledge: when ordinary people see something red, they usually say, not 'This appears red', but 'This is red' (unless the conditions under which they see it are very unfavourable), and they mean that there is something red in front of them (in the world). As the Protagorean thesis claims to apply to any judgement of any person, so does its part, Theaetetus' thesis, claim to apply to any perceptual judgement of any person.

At 152b5–8 it is said that we should not say that the wind is itself cold, but that it is cold for the one who shivers. This doesn't imply that

---

[48] Cf. S. S. Tigner, 'The "Exquisite" Argument at *Tht.* 171a', *Mnemosyne*, XXIV (1971), 368; McDowell, above n 2, 171; Lee, above n 41, 244–5; M. F. Burnyeat, 'Protagoras and Self-Refutation in Plato's *Theaetetus*', *The Philosophical Review*, LXXXV (1976), 184–5.

Protagoras forbids anyone to judge that the wind is cold (*simpliciter*). The judgement that the wind is not itself cold but is cold only for the one who feels so is made by Socrates and Theaetetus (cf. '*phēsomen*', 152b6) in order to establish the view that the judgement formed by the one who shivers to the effect that the wind is cold (*simpliciter*) is true (for him).

However, we may still wonder why Socrates said at 179c that it was more difficult, and might be impossible, to show that perceptions and judgements in accordance with them are not true. If judgements in accordance with perceptions assert that something in the world is such and such, and not that something appears such and such, isn't it easy to show that they are not necessarily true? A hint to the answer is given by the following request of Protagoras:

Consider what we mean when we declare that all things change and that what seems to any private person or state is for that person or state. And you'll go on *from there* to consider whether knowledge and perception are the same or different. (168b4–7)

'From there' indicates that it is necessary to examine (and refute) the Heraclitean thesis and the Protagorean thesis beforehand in order to refute Theaetetus' thesis. The Protagorean thesis in its most general form has been disposed of in 169d–171d and 177c–179b. But the Heraclitean thesis has not yet been examined prior to 179c. The Heraclitean thesis has been supported by all wise men except Parmenides (152e) and its power to pull Theaetetus and Socrates on its side is strong (180e–181a). The Heraclitean thesis with many supporters and much persuasiveness must be very difficult to refute, and this is supposed to lend difficulty to the refutation of Theaetetus' thesis. At 179d1–4, after admitting the difficulty of the refutation, Socrates continues:

So we must go in closer, as our argument on behalf of Protagoras enjoined, and consider that being which is in motion, striking it to see whether it rings sound or flawed.

'As our argument on behalf of Protagoras enjoined' refers back to the passage we have just seen (168b4–7). This makes it clear that Socrates and Theaetetus launch the criticism of Theaetetus' thesis at 179d, starting by examining the Heraclitean thesis.

It is necessary to examine the Heraclitean thesis before Theaetetus' thesis, because the latter is backed up by the former: when Theaetetus' thesis claims that a perceptual judgement to the effect that something is such and such is true for the percipient, 'is true for someone' doesn't mean the same as 'seems true to someone' or 'is believed by someone', but as 'is true in someone's world'.[49] To quote Burnyeat:

> To speak of how things appear to someone is to describe his state of mind, but to say that things are for him as they appear is to point beyond his state of mind to the way things actually are, not indeed in the world *tout court* (for Protagoras there is no such thing), but in the world as it is for him, in his world.

The Heraclitean thesis denies that there is in a common world such a stable pattern as a judgement should reflect in order that it be true, on the ground that there is only flux in the common world. As long as this Heraclitean thesis holds, there can be no genuine disagreement or conflict between perceptions or judgements in accordance with them.[50] They all reflect what comes to be through the interaction of two kinds of change (156–7), and what comes to be is objectivity in each person's world: what one is experiencing is always true (167a–b).

In 181–3 the Heraclitean thesis is examined, and it is shown that it cannot back up Theaetetus' thesis. It is not simply the case that Theaetetus' thesis cannot rely on it, though the Heraclitean thesis itself stands. The Heraclitean thesis itself cannot be accepted, because it annihilates completely the possibility of meaningful use of language and words. This means that when the criticism of Theaetetus' thesis is carried out, some stable patterns identifiable and expressible by words and language have been admitted in the common world. This already implies that the position that judgements in accordance with perceptions are always true and instances of knowledge cannot be maintained, because stable patterns in the common world will be regarded as standards according to which to decide whether judgements are true or not. However, this point is not yet explicit at the end of the refutation of the Heraclitean thesis. I think that the criticism of 184–6 is carried out both by developing this point and by establishing another point that is not admitted by Protagoras (the mind's act of considering). This will be explained more in detail below.[51]

Henceforth I shall call Theaetetus' thesis 'Tht-Prt thesis' in order

---

[49] Burnyeat, above n 48, 181.   [50] Burnyeat, above n 48, 181–2.

[51] Cf. 63–5, 80–1, 68–9. At 183c1–3, after the refutation of the Heraclitean thesis and before the refutation of Theaetetus' thesis, Socrates says, 'Also, we are not going to concede that knowledge is perception, *at least* according to the theory that all things change.' 'At least' (*ge*) also suggests that they have still to examine what will become of Theaetetus' thesis when the Heraclitean thesis has been rejected.

to make it clear that it is part of the Protagorean thesis and defended by him.

2. *Considering and attaining being*

Let us return to the question of how to interpret 'attain being'. According to Kahn,

'being' represents (a) the facts in the world, *ta onta*, the way things really are, and (b) the assertion of these facts in (true or false) judgements to the effect that things are so (*hōs esti*) or not so (*hōs ouk esti*), as a short-hand expression for the propositional structure of thought.[52]

Kahn chooses (b), though he later wavers between (a) and (b).[53] However, against (b) we can raise the following objections.

First objection: if the target of the criticism at 184–6 is, as we have seen, the claim that judgements in accordance with perceptions to the effect that something is such and such are instances of knowledge, then this claim cannot be refuted simply by arguing that such judgements cannot attain propositional structure. They certainly have propositional structure. Interpreters who understand 'being' in the sense of the assertion of facts in judgements contend that the criticism of perception's claim to be knowledge is carried out by pointing out that perceiving is different from judging, and that judging is necessary for knowledge. This point is certainly established in the criticism. But to what does this refutation amount? Although the target of the criticism is the claim that judgements in accordance with perceptions are instances of knowledge, according to this interpretation what is refuted would become simply the position that perception understood as something that lacks the factor of judging is knowledge. In this case, Protagoras would be still able to defend Tht-Prt thesis: he would feel no reluctance in admitting that the words '*aisthanesthai*' and '*aisthēsis*' should be used to denote an episode which lacks the factor of judging, while still claiming that judgements in accordance with perceptions are true for the percipient and are instances of knowledge. For him it would not matter at all how '*aisthanesthai*' and '*aisthēsis*' are used.

However, against this objection of ours it may be argued that judgement is brought up for discussion in Part II of the *Theaetetus*, and that judgements in accordance with perceptions are outside the scope of Part I. But we can offer the following answer: when true

---

[52] Kahn, above n 2, 119.   [53] Kahn, above n 2, 119–20, 126.

judgement's claim to be knowledge is refuted at the end of Part II (200e–201c), one of the criteria used for the refutation is directness in experience. Though direct experience is necessary for knowledge (201b8), it is not necessary for true judgement. Accordingly, it is difficult to suppose that the refutation at Part II disposes of judgements in accordance with perceptions. Besides, we should not think that Part II deals with all kinds of judgements; when 'judgement' (*doxa*) or 'judging' (*doxazein*) is introduced in Part II, 'judge' is said to be the word representing the mind's busying itself about the things which are (187a) and 'the mind's busying itself' is supposed to refer to the mind's own considering, reviewing and comparing, and reasoning, etc., all of which are mentioned in 186 (186a10, b8, c2–3, d3). This suggests that Part II deals with the kind of judgement that results from considering. At 189e–190a also, 'judgement' (*doxa*) is described as resulting from considering. Then, we should conclude that the kind of judgement whose formation doesn't presuppose the act of considering is outside the scope of Part II. This kind of judgement is supposed to be dealt with in Part I, and I take it that judgements in accordance with perceptions belong to this kind.[54]

Second objection: according to 186d2–5, it is impossible to attain being and truth in the *pathēmata* (affections, experiences), but it is possible to do so in the reasoning about these *pathēmata*.[55] This remark is most naturally understood as follows: reasoning is necessary for attaining being and truth, but the *pathēmata* alone do not constitute this necessary means; therefore, it is impossible to attain being and truth in the *pathēmata*. Now, if 'attain being' meant simply 'judge that things are so', making one's *pathēmata* explicit in propositional structure would be sufficient for attaining being, and reasoning (*sullogismos*), which involves the act of reflecting and considering, would not be necessary for it. Besides, according to 186c, calculations (*analogismata*) about one's *pathēmata* with respect to (*pros*) being and usefulness are acquired as the result of difficult and troublesome education. It is not certain how 'with respect to' (*pros*) should be interpreted. Calculations *pros* being may be calculations which aim at

[54] I shall explain below (63 ff) what I mean by 'considering' and 'the kind of judgement whose formation doesn't presuppose the act of considering'.

[55] As to '*ekeinōn*' at 186d3 McDowell says, 'we should understand *ekeinōn* at 186d3 to have a different reference from *tois pathēmasin* at 186d2' and 'In fact *ekeinōn* does, in any case, seem exceedingly weighty to refer back only one line' (above n 2, 111). But Plato's use of '*ekeinos*' seems to be more flexible. Cf. *Ph.* 68e6, where '*ekeinōn*' refers to the same thing as '*heterōn hēdonōn*', which appears in the same line.

attaining being or calculations which are done in accordance with being.[56] But in whichever way '*pros*' may be interpreted, if '*ousia*' represented simply the assertion of the facts in judgements, calculations *pros* being would not be so difficult as to require troublesome education.

I take 'being' to represent facts or states of affairs in the world, and 'attain being' in the sense of 'find how things are in the world'.[57] According to this interpretation, if our *pathēmata* don't necessarily reflect states of affairs in the world, reasoning is certainly needed in order to attain being (find how things are); it must be also difficult to calculate in such a way as to allow one to aim at being and find facts, and very difficult to calculate in accordance with facts.

Let me present here a preliminary summary of the argument at 186a ff, as understood by this interpretation. At 185e6–7 as the result of the preceding section Socrates draws attention to two different means used in considering. One is the means of sense organs, through which the mind can deal with sensible qualities and gain information about them. The other is the means of considering itself, through which the mind can entertain the concepts of *koina*, without any use of sense organs. Now, according to Tht-Prt thesis what one is experiencing is always true, and in perception one always grasps the way things are (cf. 167a–b); in order to find the way things are, it is enough to articulate what is grasped in perception and form judgements, and it is unnecessary to engage in considering. But Socrates here asks in which class Theaetetus puts being (objectivity, the way things are), in the class of things which can be dealt with and found by means of sense organs or in the class of things the dealing with which requires the mind's own considering (186a2–3). Theaetetus puts objectivity in the latter class, and replies that the mind yearns for being on its own (186a4). This means that he has chosen a position directly contrary to Tht-Prt thesis. Accordingly, in order to see whether Theaetetus is right in putting being in the latter class, Socrates begins to examine several types of qualities or features: (1) like, unlike, the same, different, (2) beautiful, ugly, good, bad, (3) hard, soft; he asks concerning each of these types whether it is through its own considering that the mind tries to find the way things are, and in each case Theaetetus replies in the affirmative (186a5–b10). The necessity of the mind's own considering (reviewing and comparing) is admitted

---

[56] This latter possibility is suggested to me by Professor Burnyeat.
[57] Kahn (above n 2, 127) admits this possibility.

even in the case of sensible qualities (3), contrary to Tht-Prt thesis. Then, Socrates hammers in the distinction between perceiving and considering, by referring to the former's easiness and the latter's difficulty (186b11–c6). Finally he concludes that it is in considering (reasoning) and not in one's *pathēmata* given in perception that one can attain being and truth and have knowledge; therefore, perception cannot be the same as knowledge (186c7–e10). Let us keep in mind that this criticism is carried out in such a way as to dispose of Tht-Prt thesis and show that judgements in accordance with perceptions are not instances of knowledge. At 186d2–5 it is said that in our *pathēmata* it is impossible to attain being and truth, but in our reasoning about them it is possible. We can understand this remark to the effect that as long as one depends on what one is experiencing in perception, and doesn't go beyond that by putting the mind's own considering into action, one cannot attain being and truth, even if one articulates one's experiences in the form of judgements.

As is clear from this brief summary, this interpretation attaches great importance to the mind's own considering, and distinguishes it from the articulation of one's *pathēmata* in the form of judgements. Here let me explain what I mean by 'considering'. The ability to consider is not limited to a small number of people, such as philosophers, scientists, or experts, but ordinary people can engage in considering. In order to consider, one doesn't need such a thing as theory or intelligible standard; considering is not theorizing. Considering is also different from direct, unreflective articulation of what is given in the form of judgements in that it involves or presupposes the act of asking (in speech or silently) and seeking for the answer.

To emphasize this act of considering in interpreting 184–6 has an advantage of making the connection between Part I and Part II smooth. As we have seen, at the beginning of Part II 'judge' (*doxazein*) is presented as a word denoting the mind's busying itself, or the act of considering, reasoning, etc., and the main topic of Part II is considering and the judgement which results from it. Now, the judgement dealt with in Part II is not the judgement resulting from theorizing, nor the judgement as unreflective articulation of what is given. For instance, the jury's judgement mentioned as an example of the true judgement, which is the candidate for knowledge in Part II (201a–c), doesn't result from theorizing or intelligible standards:[58] in

---

[58] Professor Burnyeat drew my attention to this example.

Athens all the citizens above thirty years of age could become jurors, unless they were in debt to the state and under the sentence of *atimia* (Aristotle, *Athēnaiōn Politeia* 63. 3); they also seem to have been easily persuaded by appeals to passion, such as a defendant bringing children into court (Plato, *Apology* 34d, 35b). Neither is their judgement the unreflective articulation of what is given to them, for in judging they asked themselves whether the crime on trial had been really committed by the defendant.

It is usually the case that when ordinary people make perceptual judgements, considering has already been involved. For example, when they see a stick half submerged in water, they usually judge that it is straight, by taking into consideration various conditions. If considering is one of the natural characteristics of human beings, it is rather difficult to find a case where one doesn't consider at all in articulating one's *pathēmata* in the form of judgements. However, it is possible to suppose such a case, and in order to support Tht-Prt thesis Protagoras must allow its possibility and indeed accept it alone.

Protagoras' position is expressed at 167a–b:

(1) it is possible to have in one's judgements only what one is experiencing,

(2) what one is experiencing is always true.

(1) is necessary for Tht-Prt thesis in that if it were possible to have in one's judgements anything other than what one is experiencing, from (2) it would follow that it is possible to have in one's judgements something that is not true. However, one cannot adopt (1) without denying the possibility of considering, for if it were possible to consider, it would become possible to refuse what one is experiencing and accept something else in judging. Thus, in order that Tht-Prt thesis be maintained, the possibility of the mind's own considering must be completely negated or neglected.

Contrary to this complete negation or neglect of the act of considering by Protagoras, the refutation of 184–6 is built on its acceptance. Its acceptance is carefully prepared for in the argument by the introduction of *koina*: the existence of *koina* makes us notice that there are concepts which are not derived from experiences and perceptions, and that there are acts of the mind (thinking (*dianoeisthai*), considering (*skepsasthai, episkopein*)) in which such concepts are used and which are independent of experiences and perceptions. I take it that in 186 considering, which is neglected by Protagoras and just admitted through the introduction of *koina*, plays a very important role as an act without which one cannot attain being and truth and have knowledge.

However, when we look at the text more closely, can this interpretation be still maintained? Against it the following objections can be raised.

(1) The suggested interpretation requires that 'being' should be treated as having a different status from other features mentioned in 186a5 ff, that is, 'like', 'unlike', 'the same', 'different', 'beautiful', 'ugly', 'good', 'bad'. But if Socrates' elliptical question (186a5–6) is made into a full sentence, it becomes 'Do you put (not only "being" but) also "like", "unlike", "the same", "different" in the class of things which the mind yearns for on its own by considering or in the class of things which the mind can perceive through sense organs?' '(Not only "being" but) also . . .' suggests that Socrates treated 'being' as on the same level as 'like', 'unlike', etc. Moreover, the remark at 186a2–3, 'Because that is above all something that goes with everything' has been understood in connection with the expression '*to t' epi pasi koinon*' (185c4–5)[59] and taken to be a recapitulation of the point already admitted, that is, that 'being' as a *koinon* is thought about objects of different senses. This leads us to conclude that 186a2–7 is simply a recapitulation of 'some concessions made by Theaetetus in the course of 185c4–186a1',[60] and that 'being' is picked up by Socrates simply as one of *koina*, and no such importance as the suggested interpretation required is attached to 'being'.

(2) The suggested interpretation requires that the contrast expressed by '*men*' and '*de*' (186b2,6) should be the one between perceiving some quality as hardness and the mind's own considering carried out in order to find whether the quality perceived as hardness is in fact hardness. However, what first occurs to us as the contrast here observed is the one between the episode in which the mind doesn't use the concepts of *koina* (i.e. perceiving) and the episode in which the mind uses the concepts of *koina*, such as 'being' and 'oppositeness' (i.e. the mind's own considering), irrespective of the purpose of the considering. This seems to be the contrast established in 185. If, as objection (1) has pointed out, no special importance is attached to

[59] L. Campbell, *The Theaetetus of Plato*, 2nd edn (Oxford, 1883), 162.
[60] McDowell, above n 2, 190.

'being' at 186a2 ff, 186b2–10 can be understood simply as a repetition of this established contrast.

These objections make us suppose as an interpretation of 186a2 ff that at 186a2–b1 Socrates obtains Theaetetus' agreement on the impossibility of perceiving 'being' by counting it in the list of *koina*, and at 186b2–10 makes Theaetetus reconfirm that the concepts of *koina*, especially that of 'being', are not used by the mind in perceiving. This interpretation of 186a2–b1 is further strengthened by taking Socrates to be adding new items to the list of *koina* at 186a8.[61] In fact, 'beautiful', 'ugly', 'good', 'bad' there have been regarded as *koina* by many interpreters.[62] However, what is the point of making a list of *koina* and counting 'being' in it?

In the context of the refutation of Tht-Prt thesis, it is unlikely that Plato is interested in making the list itself. It may be supposed that the list is made in order to make it easy for Theaetetus to reconfirm at 186b2–10 that the mind cannot use the concept of 'being' in perceiving. However, if this were the purpose, making a list would not be necessary at all, and 186a2–b1 would be gratuitous.[63] Theaetetus has already counted 'being' among *koina* (185c9) and noted that *koina* in general are not available to the mind in perceiving. Besides, if Socrates' remark 'Because that is above all something that goes with everything' (186a2–3) should be understood in the way suggested in objection (1), it would follow that Socrates made this remark in order to hint to Theaetetus that he should choose the class of *koina* as the class in which to put being. However, in order to make this choice, Theaetetus doesn't need such a hint at all, because he has already counted 'being' as a *koinon*. Also against the view that Socrates is adding new items to the list of *koina* at 186a8–b1, we can make the following objection. At 186a9–b1 Theaetetus says,

---

[61] McDowell, above n 2, 190.

[62] H. Jackson, 'Plato's Later Theory of Ideas, IV *The Theaetetus*', *The Journal of Philology*, XIII (1884–5), 257, 270–1; J. Burnet, *Greek Philosophy* (Macmillan, 1914; repr 1978), 200; A. E. Taylor, *Plato, The Man and his Work* (London, 1926; repr 1977), 339; W. D. Ross, *Plato's Theory of Ideas* (Oxford, 1951), 103; N. Gulley, *Plato's Theory of Knowledge* (London, 1962), 85; Cornford, above n 10, 106; McDowell, above n 2, 190; W. K. C. Guthrie, *A History of Greek Philosophy*, vol. V (Cambridge, 1978), 101–2; Modrak, above n 1, 37.

[63] 'Hold on' (*eche dē*, 186b2) is taken by McDowell as an expression 'intended to indicate that Theaetetus . . . is in danger of missing the point of the present section' (above n 2, 190). Then, to regard 186a2–b1 as gratuitous is supposed to contain no difficulty. However, 'hold on' should be taken rather as an expression used to draw attention to what was just said by the interlocutor. Cf. 77 ff below.

They, too, seem to me to be pre-eminently things whose *being* the mind considers in relation to one another, calculating in itself things past and present in relation to things in the future. (tr. McDowell, with my underlining)

Here it is said that their being, and not they themselves, is considered by the mind on its own. The fact that the being of something is considered by the mind on its own does not imply that the something is a *koinon*, as is clear from 186b6–9 where the being of 'hardness' and 'softness' is described as considered by the mind on its own. Of course, if asked, Plato might have counted 'beautiful', 'ugly', 'good', and 'bad' among *koina*: they might be thought about objects of different senses. However, there is no independent evidence in the text that allows us to regard them as *koina*, and we must say that the supposition that new items are added to the list of *koina* at 186a8–b1 is groundless. These points make us suppose that at 186a2 ff Socrates does not list *koina* in order to make Theaetetus reconfirm that 'being' cannot be perceived; he must have some other intention.

At 186a9 Theaetetus adds '*kai*' and says that 'beautiful' etc., *too*, seem to be things whose being the mind considers on its own. This suggests that in his answer at 186a7 he was thinking that the being of 'like', 'unlike', etc., and not 'like', 'unlike', etc. themselves, is considered by the mind on its own.[64] This supports our interpretation of giving a special status to 'being'. But how about Socrates' question at 186a5–6? As we have seen, in this question 'like', 'unlike', etc. seem to be treated as on a par with 'being'. However, when we examine more closely what it is for the mind to yearn for or reach after (*eporegetai*, 186a4) 'being' and 'like', 'unlike', etc. by its own considering, it will become clear that the mind's reaching after 'like' etc. is only one case of the mind's reaching after 'being'. In reaching after 'being' by its own considering, the mind considers whether something *is* such and such. Just as the mind thinks that something is such and such when it entertains the concept of 'being' in thinking (cf. 185a9),[65] so does the mind consider whether something is such and such when it entertains the concept of 'being' in considering. On the

---

[64] The expression '*kai toutōn . . . skopeisthai tēn ousian*' allows of two interpretations. (1) The mind considers not only 'like', 'unlike', etc., but also the being of 'beautiful' etc. (2) The mind considers the being of not only 'like' etc. but also 'beautiful' etc. The expression '*tēn ousian*' occurs just after '*skopeisthai*' and is very distant from '*kai toutōn*'. This suggests that '*kai*' connects 'like' etc. and 'beautiful' etc., and not 'like' etc. and the being of 'beautiful' etc., and supports interpretation (2).

[65] Even if '*eston*' at 185a9 should be read as existential, it is pregnant with the incomplete copula, as Kahn says (above n 2, 122–3).

other hand, in reaching after 'like', 'unlike' by its own considering the mind considers whether something is *like* or *unlike* some other thing. An example of this considering can be found at 185b4–5. When Theaetetus replied definitely in the affirmative at 186a7, he must have had the remarks at 185a11–12 and b4–5 in mind.

Now, let us compare the mind's reaching after 'being' and its reaching after 'like' etc. In the latter the mind considers whether something is *like* some other thing whereas in the former the mind considers whether something *is* such and such. Though the verb 'are' (*eston*) is not explicitly used at 185a11–12 and b4–5, it is to be supplied from 185a9 in order to make the sentences complete.[66] Then, the propositional content expressed by '*hoti amphoterō eston*' ('that they both are', 185a9) is regarded as the general pattern whose instances are the propositional contents that involve the use of 'like', 'unlike', 'the same', 'different' (185a11–12, b4–5). Just so should the act of reaching after 'being' be regarded as the general pattern whose instances are the acts of reaching after 'like', 'unlike', 'the same', 'different'.

The fact that Theaetetus replied at 186a9–b1 that 'beautiful' etc. are things whose being the mind considers indicates that he realized that Socrates' question concerned the mind's reaching after 'being', and understood him as asking through which means the mind tries to find whether something *is* beautiful, through the mind's own considering or through sense organs. At 186a5–7 'being' is not explicit. However, from 186a2 on the argument has been centring on the mind's reaching after 'being', that is, trying to find whether something *is F*, where '*F*' stands for a feature or quality, and Socrates has been asking concerning each type of feature or quality whether the mind's reaching after 'being' is carried out through its own considering or through sense organs. If this interpretation is correct, Socrates' question at 186a5–6 should be taken to the following effect: take as the value of '*F*' such a feature as 'like', 'unlike', 'the same', 'different'; then what means is used for the mind's reaching after the being of each.[67]

[66] Kahn, above n 2, 122.

[67] It may be also possible to read '*ē kai*' at 186a5 so as not to imply that 'like' etc. are treated as on the same level as 'being', since sometimes '*ē kai*' has the force of enquiring with a certain eagerness. Cf. Jebb's note on Sophocles, *Electra* 314 (R. C. Jebb, *Sophocles Part VI, The Electra* (Cambridge, 1924)) and J. D. Denniston, *The Greek Particles*, 2nd edn (Oxford, 1954), 285. We may be able to understand Socrates to be asking with a certain eagerness whether the general point just established concerning 'being' applies

According to the view that Socrates begins to count *koina* at 186a2, Socrates' remark 'Because that is above all something that goes with everything' (186a2–3) loses its point, except as a hint which Theaetetus himself didn't need at all. Our interpretation can make its significance clear. As is shown by the fact that Socrates is going to deal with the being of each type of feature or quality (ranging from *koina* to sensible qualities) at 186a5, 'being' goes with whatever feature or quality it is. It goes with every feature or quality in the sense that for every feature or quality there exists some state of affairs in which the feature or quality is realized. It is because of this importance of 'being' that the question of the class in which to put it has to be asked.[68]

'Being' is going to play a very important role at 186c when the ability to attain being is used as a criterion to distinguish between perception and knowledge. We should suppose that 186a2 focuses on 'being', as it is the concept which will play such an important role at the final stage of the argument. This general picture of the argument would become out of focus if Socrates were simply counting *koina* at 186a2 ff.

However, it may still be argued that even if we admit a special status to 'being', it is possible to understand the argument at 186 in a way different from the way we interpreted it. For instance, Kahn admits a special status to 'being', but at the same time he doesn't understand 'being' in the sense of objectivity or the way things are in the world, but in the sense of 'propositional structure capable of carrying a truth claim'.[69] Thus on this interpretation, the contrast at 186b2–10 becomes the one between perceiving of sensible qualities through senses (which is only passive feeling and has no propositional content) and the identification or labelling of a perceived quality as for example 'hard' or 'soft'.[70] This interpretation claims that in the latter and not in

to each feature. The reason for the eagerness is supposed to lie in the fact that the general point just established to the effect that the mind's own considering is necessary for finding 'being' is directly contrary to Tht-Prt thesis, the target of the criticism here. This point will be further explained below.

[68] Cf. Denniston, above n 67, 60, '*Gar* gives the motive for saying that which has just been said: "I say this because . . .".'

[69] Kahn, above n 2, 123–4.

[70] Kahn, above n 2, 125; McDowell, above n 2, 191. As far as Kahn is concerned, this is only one of the possible interpretations suggested by him concerning 186b6–10. Besides, though he is inclined to interpret 'being' at 186b6 as 'propositional structure as a representation of reality' or 'intentional being-so', he also leaves open the possibility that it is 'how the world is' or 'objective being-so' (134 n 42). Anyway, he cannot help admitting that at 186c 'being' represents objectivity or how the world is (126 and 134 n 42), and thinks that Plato slides at 186c3 from the intentional to the objective being-so (126).

the former the mind uses the concepts of *koina*, especially that of 'being'.

I don't intend to deny that we can read in 186b2–10 the contrast between the episode in which the mind doesn't use the concepts of *koina* and the episode in which the mind uses them. I wish to contend that this does not exhaust the contrast expressed there. What is the contrast observed there? It is repeated at 186b11–c6, again by the use of *'men'* and *'de'*, as the contrast between perceiving *pathēmata* and reasoning (or calculating) about these *pathēmata* with respect to being and usefulness. Plato's intention in using *'pathēmata'* here might be either to emphasize the non-propositional (affection-like) character of perceiving or to make it explicit that what is directly given to the mind in perceiving is nothing but affections and that the mind doesn't necessarily grasp correctly states of affairs in the world in the act of perceiving.

To ask why 'usefulness' (*ōpheleian*, 186c3) is mentioned here will (I think) help us to choose between these two possibilities. It may be supposed that 'usefulness' is mentioned here because it is a *koinon*. But as we have seen above, it is not so clear that 'useful' or 'good' represents a *koinon*,[71] and even if it were clearly the case that 'usefulness' is a *koinon*, this wouldn't explain why 'usefulness', and not some other *koinon*, is mentioned here. Rather, a hint about the reason for mentioning 'usefulness' here can be found in 178–9. There it has been established that 'usefulness' has to do with the future, and experts are needed to find how things will be in the future: even Protagoras had to admit at least 'usefulness' is something whose finding requires experts. In order to find whether something is useful or not, one cannot rely on what is given at present. It is necessary to go beyond things in the present to things in the future. When we take into account this necessity of going beyond what is given in the attempt to find whether something is useful, the mention of 'usefulness' at 186c3 leads us to suppose that *'pathēmata'* is used here to make it explicit that in perceiving the mind does not necessarily grasp states of affairs in the world. Just as what is given at present is not reliable in the attempt to find whether something is useful or not, so what is directly given to the mind in perceiving (i.e. *pathēmata*) is not reliable in the attempt to find how things are in the world. From these considerations we should conclude that the contrast observed at 186b11–c6 is the one between

[71] At 177d 'useful' (*ōphelimos*) and 'good' (*agathos*) are used as synonyms.

the inability of perception and the ability of the mind's own considering to go beyond *pathēmata* and to find how things are in the world and how things will be in the future. This leads us to take the contrast at 186b2–10 to be concerned with the finding of objectivity and not with the presence of propositional content.

In 185–6 various cases in which a person has the concepts of *koina* in mind and is using them are presented. By using them a person forms a proposition and entertains it. At the same time, he does perform some act: he thinks or considers. When a person thinks by using the concepts of *koina* (especially that of 'being'), he thinks that (*dianoeisthai hoti*, 185a9) *p* (where *p* is a proposition in forming which the concepts of *koina* are used), thereby asserting that *p*, and committing himself to the existence in the world of the state of affairs specified by *p*.[72] When a person considers by using them, he asks and considers whether (*episkepsasthai eite, skepsasthai ara*, 185b4–5, 10) the state of affairs specified by *p* obtains in the world and tries to find how things are.

In 185 Plato draws attention to the fact that the mind cannot obtain the concepts of *koina* through perceiving, in order to distinguish perceiving from other acts of the mind in which it can entertain the concepts of *koina* (i.e. thinking and considering). Thus an emphasis is placed here on the way the mind can obtain or entertain the concepts of *koina*. This emphasis may turn our attention from the fact that the mind performs these acts by using them, and that in these acts it is directed at states of affairs in the world. In the considering (reviewing and comparing carried out in order to decide) described at 186b6–9, too, this feature of the mind's being directed at states of affairs in the world must be involved, and states of affairs or the way things are, at which the mind is directed, can be represented by '*ousia*' ('being').

When 'be' (*einai*) is used in a clause introduced by '*dianoeisthai hoti*' (185a9), the way things are is asserted in judgements to the effect that things are such and such, and accordingly it can be said that 'being' represents the assertion of the facts in (true or false) judgements. However, in 185–6 expressions other than '*dianoeisthai hoti*' are also used, such as '*episkepsasthai eite*' (185b4–5, cf. c1), '*skepsasthai ara*' (b10), '*eporegesthai*' (186a4), '*analogizesthai*' (a10, cf. '*analogismata*' c2–3), '*epaniousa kai sumballousa pros allēla krinein peirasthai*' (b8–9), all of which represent acts or attitudes of the mind that are different from

---

[72] With such exceptions as imagination or telling lies.

that which is represented by '*dianoeisthai hoti*'. In these acts the way things are is not asserted: in the act represented by '(*epi*)*skepsasthai ei* or *ara*', the mind doesn't assert but asks and tries to find how things are in the world by considering. This act presupposes or involves various acts or attitudes of the mind, such as that of trying to find, and that of engaging in considering or reasoning. I take it that the attitude of trying to find is represented by '*eporegesthai*' and '*peirasthai krinein*', and the act of engaging in considering or reasoning by '*analogizesthai*', '*analogismata*' and '*epaniousa kai sumballousa*'. All these acts presuppose the mind's asking, which is clearly distinct from asserting. When 'being' (*ousia*) is used as the grammatical object of these verbs, or when 'be' (*einai*) is used in a clause introduced by one of these verbs, the way things are is not asserted but is asked, considered, and yearned for.

Now, suppose perception doesn't enable the mind to decide whether the qualities it has perceived and is aware of as hardness and softness are in fact hardness and softness, and the mind tries to decide and find the facts concerning the qualities it has perceived (whether they are in fact hardness and softness), by reviewing and comparing them to each other, and in comparing them to each other it considers whether they are opposite to each other (because their oppositeness is a necessary condition for the one being hardness and the other being softness), and, because its judgement that they are opposite to each other may be mistaken, it tries to decide in turn whether the relation between them, identified as oppositeness, is in fact oppositeness. I suppose 186b6–9 to be a compact Greek expression of this process of considering. '*Tēn* . . . *ousian*' (186b6) can be understood as an expression for 'the fact concerning the qualities the mind has perceived and is aware of as hardness and softness', or 'the way the qualities perceived as hardness and softness are', or 'the existence in the world of the hardness and the softness grasped in perception'. '*Hoti eston*' (b6) can be understood as an expression for 'that the qualities perceived as hardness and softness are (in fact) hardness and softness', or 'that the hardness and the softness grasped in perception (really) exist (in front of the percipient)', or to read '*ho ti*' instead of '*hoti*', 'what are the qualities perceived as hardness and softness?'[73]

---

[73] At 186b6 we don't find the word to qualify '*tēn ousian*' nor the subject of '*eston*'. Here, as what qualifies '*tēn ousian*' and as the subject of '*eston*' I took the qualities perceived as hardness and softness or the hardness and the softness grasped in perception, and not their possessors, because 'it is the qualities rather than their possessors which are naturally spoken of as opposite to each other' (McDowell, above n 2, 191). If the possessors should be thought of as qualifying '*tēn ousian*' and as the

The position Theaetetus endorses at 186b2–10 is that in perception one cannot find how things are in the world (even if one articulates one's *pathēmata* in the form of judgements), and that one has to consider (i.e. review and compare the qualities one perceives) in order to decide whether the fact is as it is grasped in perception. As we have pointed out above, this position is directly contrary to the position of Tht-Prt thesis. When we survey Socrates' successive questions in 186, it becomes clear that Socrates leads Theaetetus to this conclusion step by step, examining different types of qualities or features one after another.

After obtaining Theaetetus' agreement to the effect that 'being' is yearned for or reached after by the mind on its own (i.e. by its own considering) and not through any sense organ, Socrates begins to ask whether this general principle can apply to the following types of qualities or features: (1) 'like', 'unlike', 'the same', 'different', (2*a*)

subject of '*eston*', we can regard the former as representing 'the state of affairs which obtains concerning the perceived things' and the latter as representing 'that the perceived things are hard and soft'. It is not certain how '*kai*' connecting '*tēn . . . ousian*' and '*hoti eston*' should be taken, in the sense of 'i.e.' or as adding a new item, and the text here is too underdetermined for us to draw any definite conclusion from it. However, for our present purpose, it is enough to show that it is possible to understand the passage in such a way as to allow our interpretation, because we have already seen other evidences which support it.

At 186b6–7 Socrates refers to 'their oppositeness to each other' and 'the being of their oppositeness' as things to be decided. Now, according to our interpretation of this passage we can explain this reference as follows. Firstly, Socrates refers to 'the oppositeness to each other', because this is a necessary condition for the qualities perceived as hardness and softness being really hardness and softness: if the mind finds that they are not opposite to each other by reviewing and comparing (*epaniousa kai sumballousa*), this proves that they are not hardness and softness, respectively. Secondly, concerning '*au*' (186b7) Kahn says, 'The expression "in turn" (*au*) suggests that the *ousia* of their opposition is related to that opposition itself just as the *ousia* of the two tactile qualities is related to these qualities' (above n 2, 125). Now, according to our interpretation, when the two tactile qualities are perceived, the mind is aware of these qualities as hardness and softness, and when the being (*ousia*) of the two tactile qualities is decided, the mind reflects on the perceived qualities and decides whether the fact is as it is grasped in perception. Though in perception the mind is aware of the tactile qualities as hardness and softness, this awareness may not correspond correctly to states of affairs obtaining in the world, and this is why the mind tries to decide the being of the tactile qualities. This is what our interpretation takes to be the way the being (*ousia*) of the tactile qualities is related to the qualities themselves. Now, if, as '*au*' suggests, according to this relation we should understand the relation between the being of their oppositeness and that oppositeness itself, we can say as follows: though in deciding their oppositeness to each other the mind is aware of the relation between the perceived qualities as oppositeness, this awareness may not correspond correctly to states of affairs obtaining in the world, and this is why the mind further tries to decide the being of their oppositeness (i.e. whether their oppositeness obtains in the world, or whether the relation between the two qualities is really oppositeness).

'beautiful', 'ugly', (2*b*) 'good', 'bad', (3) 'soft', 'hard'. (1) is the group of *koina*, which have been just introduced into the argument at 185. (2*a*), (2*b*), and (3) also have been treated in the *Theaetetus*, that is, in the argument concerning the Protagorean thesis. And (1), (2), and (3) exhaust all the types of qualities or features that have appeared in the *Theaetetus*. We have already rejected the view that Socrates refers to qualities of group (2) in order to add new items to the list of *koina*. Now we can offer our own interpretation instead: Socrates refers to 'beautiful' etc. because he intends to exhaust all the types of qualities or features that have appeared in the argument so far, and to examine whether the general principle admitted by Theaetetus can apply to each type. He examines it because it is directly opposite to the Protagorean thesis, and this examination leads to the establishment of the position contrary to Tht-Prt thesis.

The reason why I have divided (2) into (2*a*) and (2*b*) is as follows. Plato has already criticized the Protagorean thesis in its most general form in such a way that the area in which the Protagorean thesis may stand is narrowed down. As the result of the *peritropē* argument, it has been claimed that concerning (i) 'healthy', 'unhealthy', 'advantageous', 'disadvantageous', people's judgements do not necessarily reflect facts, which obtain irrespective of their judgements, whereas concerning (ii) 'hot', 'dry', 'sweet', and other sensible qualities, and concerning (iii) 'beautiful', 'ugly', 'just', 'unjust', 'holy', and 'unholy', there may be no objectivity by nature, and everything is for each person as it appears to him (171e–172b). At 177d 'good' and 'useful' are mentioned instead of 'advantageous' as examples of group (i). Later through the argument concerning things in the future, the area in which the Protagorean thesis may stand is further narrowed down: the measure doctrine cannot hold concerning things in the future. But as far as judgements concerning things in the present go, what is given as the summary at 171E–172b describes exactly in what area the Protagorean thesis can and cannot hold. This is the point reached before 184–6. The comparison of this distinction with the distinction mentioned above makes it clear that (i) corresponds to (2*b*), (ii) to (3), and (iii) to (2*a*) and (2*b*) should not be grouped together without any distinction.

Let us now look at each group, following the text of 186, in order to see how each type conforms to the general principle that one cannot find being (facts or states of affairs) through perceiving, but through the mind's own considering.

(1) 'like', 'unlike', 'the same', 'different'

It has already been established in 185 that the question of whether something is like some other thing, etc., is considered by the mind on its own, and not through sense organs. Thus, it is needless to say that in the case of these features the mind has to have recourse to its own considering in reaching after being.

(2a) 'beautiful', 'ugly', (2b) 'good', 'bad'

Theaetetus admits that the mind considers the being of these qualities in relation to one another, calculating in itself things past and present in relation to things in the future (186a9–b1). Concerning this remark interpreters unanimously refer to the argument against Protagoras (177c–179b or 166d ff).[74] However, the following problem arises when we see a reference to this argument. As is clear from our subdivision of (2) into (2a) and (2b) there is a difference: although concerning (2b) people's judgements do not necessarily reflect facts and the mind's own considering is necessary in order to find facts, concerning (2a) there may be no objectivity by nature and it may be that if someone or something seems, for example, beautiful to a person, the someone or something is in fact beautiful for him, and the mind's own considering is not necessary in order to find whether the someone or something is beautiful. Thus, if Theaetetus had in mind only the argument against Protagoras when he answered at 186a9–b1, his answer would be regarded as lacking exactness and mistaken in that he treats (2a) and (2b) in the same way. But this would not be an answer of the person who was praised by Socrates as beautiful and good (185e). Rather, we should suppose that in his reply Theaetetus enlarged the area in which the finding of facts requires the mind's own considering as far as (2a), without simply repeating the results of the argument against Protagoras. Then, was he right in expanding the area? I think that he was not necessarily wrong. He may not have had sufficient grounds for the enlargement, but he is considered to have noted in the course of the discussion with Socrates such points that allow one to enlarge the area. Firstly, as we have seen above, the criticism of Tht-Prt thesis is carried out on the basis of the refutation

---

[74] Campbell, above n 59, 162; Cornford, above n 10, 107 n 1; Cooper, above n 1, 142. McDowell (above n 2, 190) sees a reference to 177c–179b, whereas Kahn (above n 2, 124, 133 n 39) sees a reference to 166d ff.

of the Heraclitean thesis, and it has already been admitted that there are some stable patterns in the world which obtain irrespective of people's judgements. Of course, it has not been shown that objectivity has to be admitted concerning (2a). But in Socrates' digression (172d–177b) Socrates treated a quality 'just', which belongs to group (2a) (cf. 172a), as having objectivity. He does so by saying that a god is as just as it's possible to be, and that the best way to become like a god is to become as just as possible (176b–c).

Secondly, as a thing which was occupying Theaetetus' mind at 186a9–b1 I would like to suggest Socrates' praise of him, though he may have had also the argument against Protagoras in mind as far as 'good' and 'bad' are concerned. The praise begins at 185d5 with an unprecedented remark, 'exceedingly well' (*hupereu*). This expression appears only once here in Plato's texts. And after Theaetetus' next remark Socrates continues:

> Because you are beautiful (*kalos*), Theaetetus, and not ugly (*aischros*), as Theodorus was saying. For someone who speaks beautifully (*kalōs*) is beautiful (*kalos*) and good (*agathos*).

In three lines of Greek text here, three of the four words focused on in Socrates' question at 186a8 are used. At 143e Theodorus said that Theaetetus was not beautiful (*kalos*). At first glance he may not seem beautiful. But Socrates, midwife, has been considering (*skopeisthai*) Theaetetus (145b7, cf. 150b9, 151c3, 160e7, 161e7), and has found that Theaetetus is in fact beautiful. That Theaetetus is in fact beautiful (i.e. the being of 'beautiful' in the case of Theaetetus) could be found only through the mind's own considering on Socrates' part. Socrates' praise must have remained in Theaetetus' mind when he replied at 186a9–b1, and he must have been encouraged in his answer by the fact that Socrates himself had been considering in his attempt to find whether Theaetetus is beautiful.

By using the being of 'beautiful' in the case of Theaetetus as an example, we can give a concrete sense to Theaetetus' answer (186a9–b1). Whether Theaetetus is beautiful or not is a thing which the mind considers, calculating in itself things past and present (his past and present deeds and remarks) in relation to things in the future (what kind of person he will become, and what kind of thing he will say and do in the future). After the discussion with Theaetetus, Socrates told Eucleides what kind of person Theaetetus would become (142c4–5). In fact Socrates' judgement about Theaetetus was correct.

By the time he died, he had been regarded as *kalos* and *agathos* by everybody (142b6–7).

(3) 'hard', 'soft'

In the argument at 186 the area in which the finding of facts needs the mind's own considering has been enlarged as far as (2*a*). It may be just because of this enlargement that Socrates stopped Theaetetus, saying 'hold on' (*eche dē*, 186b2). Concerning this expression McDowell says,

> Socrates' 'Hold on' may be intended to indicate that Theaetetus, in recalling the argument of 177c–179b, is in danger of missing the point of the present section.[75]

McDowell seems to think that 'hold on' plays the role of getting the discussion back on the right track, because Theaetetus strayed from the main point. However, when we examine other passages in which Plato uses 'hold on' (*eche dē*), we can find that Plato never uses this expression in order to stop the digression of Socrates' interlocutor and turn the topic of conversation from what the interlocutor has been talking about, or in order to make him forget what he has just said. This would destroy discussion (*dialogos*). On the contrary, in most cases Plato uses the expression in order to draw attention to what the interlocutor has just said and to make it the topic of conversation. For instance, in *Protagoras* 349d–e, when Protagoras said that there are many people who are unjust, unholy, intemperate, and ignorant, but outstandingly courageous, Socrates said, '*Eche dē*,' stopped him, and continued, 'What you say deserves consideration. Do you call the courageous confident, or in any other way?' In *Gorgias* 460a, after Gorgias' remark about the art of rhetoric, Socrates says, '*Eche dē*, because you're speaking well,' and continues the examination of Gorgias' remark. We can see a similar use of '*eche dē*' in *Hippias Minor* 366a2, *Cratylus* 435e6, *Gorgias* 490b1, *Republic* 353b14, etc.

Plato uses '*Eche dē pros Dios*' at *Cratylus* 439a1, exceptionally, in the case where Socrates tries to show that there is another possibility, because his interlocutor Cratylus agreed with him too easily. But in this case, too, '*eche dē*' is not used to make the interlocutor forget what he said. In some cases it can be used as equivalent to '*age dē*'. But in most cases where '*eche dē*' is used in the sense of 'hold on', it plays the role of drawing attention to what was just said by the interlocutor,

---

[75] McDowell, above n 2, 190.

whether what he said may be developed further or an antithesis may be presented against it. It never plays the role of diverting the interlocutor's attention from what he said. Accordingly, contrary to McDowell's interpretation, I think that by saying 'hold on' Socrates is noting a good point Theaetetus made. Theaetetus is regarded as right in extending the area in which the finding of being or facts requires the mind's own considering, and Socrates is now going to examine the possibility of further enlargement with the example of hardness and softness. We have already stated our interpretation of how to understand 186b2–10. Here the area is extended as far as sensible qualities: it is necessary for the mind to engage in its own consideration, by reviewing and comparing the qualities perceived as hardness and softness, in order that it may decide whether the fact is as it is grasped in perception, and further it is necessary to consider even whether the perceived qualities are opposite to each other in order that it reach a firm decision. The position finally admitted here is contrary to that of Tht-Prt thesis.

As we have noted above, the refutation of the Heraclitean thesis has admitted in the world stable patterns, which are distinct from *pathēmata*. As the use of '*pathēmata*' as the object of the verb '*aisthanesthai*' (186b11–c2) indicates, in perception stable patterns or states of affairs in the world are not presented as such to the mind, but in the form of *pathēmata*. This gives rise to mistakes in the attempt to find how things are in the world. In order to find states of affairs in the world, it is necessary to consider. As long as one doesn't exercise one's ability to consider but depends on the *pathēmata*, it is impossible to attain being and truth and to have knowledge (186d2–5). Now the state in which one is regarded as depending on the *pathēmata* includes the state in which one is aware of a sensible quality as F without considering and the state in which one articulates what is given in perception in the form of a judgement without considering. This means that as long as one doesn't consider, one cannot attain being and truth even if one is aware of a sensible quality, or even if one judges that something is F. Thus, Tht-Prt thesis is rejected by the argument of 184–6.

From our interpretation of the argument of 184–6 it follows that as long as one doesn't consider, one cannot attain truth even if one judges that such and such is the case on the basis of perception. However, against this point the following two objections may be raised. I wish to conclude this paper by answering them.

(1) At 182a–b and 156c–157b such words as 'hotness' and 'whiteness' seem to denote what come to be in the course of perception, and not qualities existing independently of perception. If this is the position Plato adopts himself, it follows that even without the act of considering one can correctly use such words and identify something by, for example, 'hardness'. This means that one doesn't need the act of considering in order to attain truth, contrary to our interpretation.

We can answer this objection by reminding ourselves that Tht-Prt thesis, which is the target of the criticism, claims that perceptual judgements of ordinary people are, as they are, true for them. It doesn't demand that in making perceptual judgements ordinary people should restrict their usage of words representing sensible qualities. When ordinary people use such words as 'hard', it is not usually the case that they attribute qualities represented by these words to things which come to be only in the course of perception. They judge, for example, that something in front of them (in the common world) is hard, and Tht-Prt thesis claims that such judgements are always true. Therefore, the question of whether such words as 'hardness' should be used to refer to things which come to be only in the course of perception is irrelevant to Plato's objective in the criticism of Tht-Prt thesis. Against Tht-Prt thesis, which claims that people's judgements that things are such and such in the world are always true, Plato points out that their judgements don't necessarily correspond to states of affairs in the world, and that the mind's own considering is necessary for finding them.

(2) A second objection: it sometimes happens by chance that judgements formed by articulating one's *pathēmata*, without considering, are true, even if one is not sure about their truth. This suggests that perceiving and articulating one's *pathēmata* in the form of judgements do enable one to attain truth, even if one has not engaged in considering, contrary to our interpretation.

Now, although I can concede that judgements as simple articulation of *pathēmata* sometimes happen to be true, I doubt that in such a case one is regarded as having attained truth and being in the sense of 'attain' in which it is used in 186. The Greek verbs *'tuchein'* and *'hapsasthai'*, which we have translated as 'attain', are used when a target or a goal is set in front of someone, in the sense of 'hit the target' or 'arrive at the goal' (cf. *Laws* 717b, *Symposium* 211b). Of course, '*tuchein*' can be used in the sense of 'hit upon', 'light upon', 'fall in with', even when a thing one hits upon has not been regarded as one's target or goal. However, in the context of 186 'being' is considered to be the goal to arrive at, as the expression '*eporegesthai*' (yearn for, reach after, 186a4) indicates, and the latter use of '*tuchein*' is irrelevant here. Then, when a target or a goal is set in front of someone, there must be appropriate means for hitting the target or arriving at the goal; without using these means it is impossible to hit the target or arrive at the goal. In the context of 186 the appropriate means is the mind's own considering or reasoning. Accordingly, just as it is impossible to arrive at a destination without travelling, it is impossible to attain being and truth without considering.[76]

As we have seen above, Tht-Prt thesis has two bases: (*a*) it is possible to have in one's judgements only what one is experiencing, (*b*) what one is experiencing is always true (167a–b). In the criticism of 184–6 (*a*) is undermined by drawing attention to the existence of *koina*. The use of their concepts in forming judgements shows that one cannot but have in one's judgement something that does not come from one's experiences. Accordingly, if (*a*) is understood to the effect that nothing but concepts derived from experiences can be used in judgements, then the introduction of *koina* is taken to have already disposed of (*a*). But (*a*) allows of another interpretation, too, to the effect that only to assent to one's experiences is possible, and to oppose them is impossible. Then, the introduction of *koina* itself doesn't constitute the disposal of (*a*). However, what Plato does in 184–6 is not simply to call attention to the concepts of *koina*. The introduction of *koina* enables him to bring the act of considering to the fore. The act of considering presupposes or involves the act of asking, and asking

---

[76] Let me explain what I mean more fully by comparing 'being' and 'truth' to 'a destination', 'attain being and truth' to 'arriving at the destination', and 'considering' to 'travelling and other means for arriving there'. Suppose a person, *A*, has promised another, *B*, to give a prize if *B* has arrived at some destination, and *A* has taken *B* to a place and told *B* to start from there; though this place is in fact the destination, *A* knows this fact, and *B* doesn't. This case is similar to the case in which one's judgement in accordance with perception happens to be true. In this case, *B* may be regarded in a sense as having arrived at his destination. But in another sense *B* is not regarded as having arrived there: *A* will not give the prize to *B* just because *B* happens to be at the destination; *A* will give it to *B* only when *B* has done various things, e.g., consulted a map, walked around, and has found that from the start he had been at the destination. Similarly, when someone's judgements in accordance with perceptions happen to be true, he will not be given credit for having attained his destination, being and truth, unless he has arrived there as the result of his considering.

consists in abstaining from assenting automatically to what is given or suggested to the mind. In asking, it is possible even to suppose things contrary to facts. It is possible to ask whether a colour and a sound are salty (185b10). This is a very clear example contrary to (*a*).[77] By the introduction of *koina* a door has been opened for the mind's own considering, which is totally independent of one's experiences and perception. As to (*b*) the refutation of the Heraclitean thesis has already undermined it. In 186 Socrates asks Theaetetus through which means the mind can attain being, through sense organs or through the means just admitted in 184–5, that is, the means of considering. Taking account of the latter means as a possibility has its point because (*b*) has already been disposed of.

When the criticism of Tht-Prt thesis is widely taken, it starts at 179d, following the order stipulated by Protagoras at 168b. In the course of the criticism the two bases of Tht-Prt thesis, (*a*) and (*b*), are undermined. At the same time, the disposal of (*a*) prepares for the topic of Part II, that is, judgement resulting from considering. What is to be emphasized in interpreting 184–6 is the mind's act of considering, and not propositional content or structure.[78]

Kyoto University, Japan

---

[77] In the first section we criticized the view which takes 185b10 to describe perception. This criticism was necessary in order to obtain a correct understanding of Plato's idea of perception. It's now clear that it serves also the purpose of placing a due emphasis on the mind's considering.

[78] This paper arose from my study as a research student at King's College, Cambridge in 1983–5. I am especially grateful to Professor G. E. R. Lloyd and Professor M. F. Burnyeat for their helpful criticisms and encouragement, which have given me a concrete idea of Socratic midwifery, and indeed without which this paper could not have come into being. I am also grateful to the British Council for a scholarship in 1983–4 and to King's College for a studentship in 1984–5. Finally, I thank the editor of *Oxford Studies in Ancient Philosophy* for giving me the benefit of comments by the referee.

THE ORIGIN OF THE STOIC THEORY
OF SIGNS IN SEXTUS EMPIRICUS*

THEODOR EBERT

IN his critical discussion of the dogmatic philosophers Sextus
Empiricus expounds a Stoic doctrine which has conveniently been
labelled 'the theory of signs'. This chapter of Stoic philosophy offers a
blend of logic and epistemology, a mixture bound to attract the interest
of present-day 'ancient philosophers'. Hence, with the growing
discussion focusing on the philosophy of the Hellenistic period, this
part of Stoicism was to get a fair share of attention.[1] Controversy has
been flourishing over the merits and weaknesses of this theory; it has
been compared with tenets about the topic of signs held by earlier and
later philosophers, yet in these discussions it has almost universally
been taken for granted that there is a *single* theory of signs and that it
can be attributed unqualifiedly to *the* Stoics.[2]

Part of what I want to do in this paper is to challenge this
assumption. I shall argue that the material relating to the theory of
signs which is preserved in Sextus does *not* reflect Chrysippan
teaching, but goes back to Stoics antedating Chrysippus. To have a
convenient term, I shall refer to the pre-Chrysippan Stoics as 'early

---

* © Theodor Ebert 1987

[1] Cf. G. Verbeke, 'La philosophie du signe chez les Stoiciens', in *Les Stoiciens et leur
logique*, ed J. Brunschwig (Paris, 1978), 401–24; J. M. Rist, 'Zeno and the origins of stoic
logic', *ibid.* 387–400; M. Baratin, 'Les origines stoiciennes de la théorie augustinienne
du signe', *Revue des Etudes Latines*, LIX (1981), 260–8; M. F. Burnyeat, 'The Origins of
Non-deductive Inference', in *Science and Speculation: Studies in Hellenistic Theory and
Practice*, ed J. Barnes *et al.* (Cambridge/Paris, 1982), 193–238; D. Sedley, 'On Signs',
ibid. 239–72; D. Glidden, 'Skeptic Semiotics', *Phronesis*, XX (1983), 213–55. For
discussions in the older literature cf. R. Philippson, *De Philodemi Libro qui est περὶ
σημείων καὶ σημειώσεων et Epicureorum doctrina logica* (Berlin, 1881); P. Natorp,
Forschungen zur Geschichte des Erkenntnisproblems im Altertum (Berlin, 1884), 127 ff; W.
Heintz, *Studien zu Sextus Empiricus* (Halle, 1932), 42–51; G. Preti, 'Sulla dottrina del
σημεῖον nella logica stoica', *Rivista Critica di Storia della Filosofia*, XI (1956), 5–14.

[2] The only exception known to me is D. Sedley who wants to 'put into abeyance the
widespread belief that Stoic doctrine is under discussion by Sextus Empiricus
throughout *M* VIII. 141–298 and *PH* II. 97–133' (Sedley, above n 1, 241).

Stoics'.[3] I shall further argue that the theory of signs of the early Stoics was a harvest not grown in the fields of Stoic philosophy, but that it originated from the 'Dialecticians', a group of philosophers confused for a long time with the Megarians and rediscovered as a group in its own right by David Sedley.[4] I shall further try to point out some modifications which this theory underwent as it was integrated into the epistemology of the early Stoics. I shall not discuss the doctrine of signs advocated by the opponents of the Epicureans in Philodemus' *de Signis*—almost certainly Stoic philosophers—a doctrine which has been ably discussed by David Sedley in a recent paper.[5]

I

What we find in Sextus is, roughly speaking, a definition and a division. The definition of sign (*sēmeion*) is stated and explained in two passages (*Outlines of Pyrrhonism* (*PH*) II 104–6; *adversus Mathematicos* (*M*) VIII. 244–56), and so is the division of all signs into two sorts, the indicative and the commemorative (*PH* II. 99–101; *M* VIII. 149–55). The theory of signs thus holds a place in either of the two extant Sextonian discussions of logic (i.e. *PH* II, *M* VII and VIII). Yet whereas *M* discusses the two topics in two separate passages, *PH* offers us an exposition in a continuous stretch of text. For both topics, the exposition in *PH* is considerably shorter than the one in *M*.

I shall first discuss the material relating to the definition of sign. Here is a translation of the relevant bit of text from the *PH*:

Now the sign, judging by the statements of the Dogmatists about it, is inconceivable (*anepinoēton*). Thus, for instance, the Stoics, who seem to have defined it strictly, meaning to establish the conception (*ennoia*) of the sign, state

---

[3] The traditional division of Stoicism puts Chrysippus' Stoic predecessors together with his own school into the Old Stoa, separating it from middle Stoicism inaugurated by Panaetius. This classification seems to be based on Stoic ethics, and understandably so. After all, it was their moral philosophy which, beginning with Cicero, made the Stoics so immensely influential, and here the affinity between Zeno and Chrysippus is clearly stronger than the one between Chrysippus and Panaetius. Yet in logic and epistemology, there is no similar relationship between Chrysippus and his predecessors. Here the great break comes about with Chrysippus, and we should group Stoic philosophers in this field accordingly.

[4] Cf. D. Sedley, 'Diodorus Cronus and Hellenistic Philosophy', *Proceedings of the Cambridge Philological Society*, CCIII, N S 23 (1977), 74–120.

[5] Cf. D. Sedley, above n 1.

that 'a sign is a proposition which forms the pre-antecedent (*prokathēgoumenon*) in a sound conditional, and which reveals the consequent'.[6]

(PH II. 104)

Since this is the only text where the Stoics are explicitly credited with an account of signs, it is worth noting how Sextus introduces them here. Notice that the Stoics are chosen as an instance. This is made clear by the Greek *autika* at the beginning of the second sentence (for this use of *autika* cf. Liddell–Scott–Jones, s.v. *autika* II; this usage is not uncommon in Sextus cf. *M* VIII. 251, IX. 30). Sextus (or his source), that is, has picked the Stoics out of a larger group of dogmatic philosophers all dealing with the notion of sign.

Who else may have to be included in this group? At first sight, the Epicureans seem to qualify as likely candidates. As we learn from *M* VIII. 177, they also have something to say about the sign, claiming that it belongs to the sensible realm, in opposition to the Stoics for whom the sign is something intelligible. However, at second glance this suggestion looks rather implausible. For, in his critical discussion of sign Sextus aims at proving that sign is 'inconceivable' (*anepinoēton*). This is made clear at the start of the passage quoted above (*PH* II. 104) and is repeated twice afterwards (*PH* II. 118, 123). Yet, this aim of his overall argument makes it quite implausible that Sextus should want to include philosophers who deny that the sign is intelligible (*noēton*) in the group of Dogmatists which is the target of attack in this passage. Moreover, it seems unlikely that Sextus would have the Stoics represent a group of philosophers which also includes their greatest rivals among the Dogmatists. Thus, we should leave the Epicureans out of the picture.

The Peripatetics seem to be a more plausible guess. They were, at least in Sextus' eyes (cf. *M* VII. 217), prepared to allow for sensible as well as for intelligible things. Aristotle has a chapter of his *Prior Analytics* (II. 27) devoted to the discussion of signs, and in the list of Theophrastus' writings there is a treatise *On Signs* (cf. Diogenes Laertius (D.L.) V. 45). Yet the treatment of signs in the *Analytics* would hardly prove that this topic is of more than minor importance for Aristotle. As for Theophrastus, he keeps a conspicuously low profile in Sextus; his name occurs only three times in the (extant) writings of Sextus and he is credited only once with a tenet of his own (cf. *M* VII. 218). (In *M* VII. 217, Sextus refers to 'the school of Aristotle and Theophrastus

---

[6] My translation does not lay claim to originality. I have borrowed from existing translations and I shall do so on other occasions.

and the Peripatetics in general'; in *M* I. 258, Theophrastus is mentioned as the teacher of a grandson of Aristotle's.) Now these observations will certainly not be sufficient to put the Peripatetics on a par with the Epicureans; they may after all still qualify as candidates for the group of dogmatic philosophers the Stoics are meant to represent at *PH* II. 104. Yet even if they do, we may be well advised to reckon with the possibility of there being other philosophical companions of the Stoics who held views similar to those expounded and explained in this passage.

The definition of sign as reported by Sextus will look strange to a modern reader: a sign is an antecedent proposition in a conditional of a certain type. We are inclined to treat the trail of an animal, a traffic light or a gesture as signs, not something that corresponds to statements about such things or events. To understand the rationale of this Stoic definition of sign we should pay heed to a specific feature in the concept of sign. 'Sign', like many other words (e.g. 'tool', 'material', 'premiss') is an expression indicating a specific *function*; it can be used to fill the gap in 'to be used as . . .'. This, in turn, means that it is not the mere capacity of being such and such a thing or such and such an event which makes something qualify as a sign. Whatever is a sign is so only with respect to a (maybe potential) user. The concept of sign entails that of an interpreter of signs.[7]

It is a consequence of this feature in the concept of sign that something can be a sign for one person, but not for another. Incidentally, this point is noticed by Sextus: in *M* VIII. 204, he states that 'blushing and swelling of the vessels and thirst' are signs of diseases, and then goes on to explain that it is the doctor who is able to tell your disease from bodily symptoms 'which the uninstructed person does not apprehend as signs' (ibid). It is a similar consequence that something can be *discovered* to be a sign of something. Functions can be discovered.

Although this feature constitutes an essential and basic character of signs, it tends to be overlooked particularly when it comes to artificial signs, that is, things or events that are meant to be signs and are made

---

[7] For this feature of signs, cf. in particular the pragmatist theories of sign by Peirce and by Morris: Ch. S. Peirce, *Collected Papers*, vol II, ed Charles Hartshorne and Paul Weiss (Cambridge, Mass., 1931), 134, 156; Ch. W. Morris, *Foundations of the Theory of Signs* (Chicago, 1951), 5 f, 29 ff. It should be noticed that there is an important difference between 'using' and 'using as': not every word that can be used to fill the first phrase can also be used to fill the second one. You can use your hand, but you cannot use something as your hand. 'Hand' is not a function word.

for this purpose. Their use is normally restricted to situations where the active and the passive user (e.g. speaker and hearer, writer and reader) have a common knowledge of the signs used. It is difficult to imagine a situation where an artificial sign is discovered to be a sign (although you may well discover of what it is a sign, e.g. in the case of a code). Hence, the use of artificial signs strengthens the tendency to equate signs with those things and events that function *as* signs. However, doing this is leaving out the interpretation needed to turn the thing or the event into a sign.

Now I take it that the rationale lying behind the definition of sign as reported by Sextus is the attempt to catch the functional character of signs and to contravene the tendency of identifying signs with things or events as such. By tying the sign, taken to be an antecedent in a conditional of a certain type, to the consequent of this conditional you have built the notion of interpretation of some phenomenon as sign right into the very notion of sign. (I do not want to deny that this treatment of sign as an antecedent has also grave defects, e.g. the lack of a clear distinction between implication and inference. What I want to do for the moment is to point to the problem that may have given rise to this construal of signs as antecedents.)

Let us go back to Sextus' exposition. After having outlined the definition of sign, Sextus goes on to explain four terms used in it: proposition (*axiōma*), sound conditional (*hugies sunēmmenon*), pre-antecedent (*prokathēgoumenon*), and revealing the consequent (*ekkaluptikon tou lēgontos*). Sextus' aim in providing these explanations is *not* to help his reader to a proper understanding of the definition quoted, but to provide himself with a basis for attack on the notion of sign. All four explications are used successively as starting points for criticisms in the subsequent discussion (proposition: *PH* II. 107–9; sound conditional: 110–15; pre-antecedent: 115–16; revealing the consequent: 117–18). Thus, we should read these four explanations against the polemical background of Sextus' overall strategy.

Sextus first explains what the upholders of the definition of sign consider to be a proposition: 'a *lekton* which is complete in itself and declarative as far as its being so depends on itself' (II. 104). We need not go into the technicalities of this account for our purpose.[8] It will be sufficient to retain two points in connection with it. The first concerns its origin. We find it attributed to Chrysippus in Diogenes Laertius

---

[8] Cf. the discussion of this definition in M. Frede, *Die stoische Logik* (Göttingen, 1974), 32–7.

VII. 65 (with minor differences which need not concern us here), and Aulus Gellius quotes it *verbatim* (refusing to give a Latin translation of the Greek) as what seems to be a standard definition of *axiōma* from his 'Greek books' (*Noctes Atticae* XVI. viii. 4). This fact also points to Chrysippus, for by the time of Aulus Gellius (2nd century AD) Stoic logic was identical with the logic of Chrysippus and his followers.

The second point to be noted is the absence of this account of proposition in the parallel passage in *M* VIII. 245–56. This absence is conspicuous, for all the other explications found in the *PH* passage have counterparts, though less systematic ones, in the passage in *M*. Hence, it seems, Sextus who, in the *PH* passage, has just given us what he declares to be a Stoic definition of sign, allows himself to import other Stoic material as well. There is of course ample reason for him to do so: Since this account classifies a proposition as a *lekton*, Sextus is able to deploy his battery of arguments against the Stoic *lekton* against the sign as well, and we find him doing just this when it comes to the critical discussion (cf. II. 107–8).

The explanation of the sound conditional which Sextus adduces next is based on the truth-functional interpretation of the conditional. As is well known, this interpretation of the conditional was advocated by Philo who was a prominent member of the Dialectical school. The sound conditional, Sextus tells us, is the one that 'does not begin with truth and end with a falsehood' (II. 104). This definition of the sound conditional is attributed *verbatim* to Philo a little later in the text (cf. II. 110). It is also attributed to Philo in *M* VIII. 113–14, a passage where we find the very same examples used as in our passage (II. 105) for all those cases which yield the truth-value true (*TT*, *FF*, *FT*). We learn from Diogenes Laertius (cf. VII. 16) that Zeno, the founder of Stoicism, studied logic with Philo. Yet Philo certainly was not a Stoic himself. So why does Sextus, who is after all explicating a definition of sign attributed to the Stoics, bring in the Philonian criterion of a sound conditional? Why does he not use the criterion of cohesion (*sunartēsis*) which is mentioned later in the text (cf. II. 111) and which, for all we know, was the standard Stoic account of the sound conditional (cf. D. L. VII 73) and, thus, may be safely attributed to Chrysippus? After all, he did use an account of proposition which seems to be Chrysippan.

We find the answer to this question when we come to the third term explained in Sextus' report: pre-antecedent (*prokathēgoumenon*). This word may have sounded as unusual to Greek ears as the term I have coined may sound to English ones. As a technical term of logic, *prokathēgoumenon* does not occur outside Sextus, and in Sextus it is used only in the definition of sign just quoted by Sextus and in passages that comment upon this definition (II. 106 and 115).[9] Hence, *prokathēgoumenon* is definitely tied to this definition of sign. This term now is paraphrased as 'the antecedent (*hēgoumenon*) in a conditional which begins with truth and ends in truth' (II. 106). It is patent that this account presupposes the Philonian, truth-functional interpretation of the conditional; actually, the wording of this account relating to the conditional corresponds exactly to the description of the *TT*-case as given in the exposition of truth-functional implication some lines earlier (II. 105).

This now explains why Sextus brings in Philonian implication when reporting the criterion of a sound conditional. He has to. Only the truth-functional interpretation of the conditional ties in with the account of *prokathēgoumenon* which Sextus has found in his source. This, I think, is an important finding if we want to assess the nature of Sextus' source. The bare fact that Sextus attributes to the Stoics (cf. the *phasin* in the last line of II. 105) the Philonian interpretation of the conditional is not sufficient to establish the conclusion that the Stoics under discussion antedate Chrysippus, for we find Sextus using the Chrysippan definition of proposition in the same passage. Hence, these two pieces of evidence would only lead us to a sceptical equipollence of arguments. Yet the fact that the explication of the term *prokathēgoumenon*, which is the hallmark of the definition of sign discussed in this passage, ties in only with Philo's position in the debate about conditionals, tips the balance definitely against Chrysippus.[10] The Stoics discussed in this passage are early Stoics.[11]

---

[9] The occurrence of *prokathēgoumenon* in the text of Pseudo-Galen, *Historia Philosopha*, in H. Diels, *Doxographi Graeci* (*Doxogr. Gr.*) (Berlin, 1879). 605, 11, is due to a correction by Diels of the *kai hēgoumenon* in the manuscripts. Yet, as M. Burnyeat convincingly argues (cf. Burnyeat, above n 1, 222 n 70), *kathēgoumenon* is a much more likely emendation, since it does not augment the number of letters. The term *kathēgoumenon* is used in the relevant sense in *M* VIII. 245, 248.

[10] It has been suggested by D. Sedley that it 'seems entirely possible' that our passage (as well as the parallel one in *M* VIII) represents 'an early Stoic account of signs, one presumably antedating Chrysippus' authorisation of *sunartēsis* as the correct criterion' (sc. of a sound conditional) (Sedley, above n 1, 256). I take it that the observation just made warrants a stronger claim: it is not only possible but certain that Sextus' report ultimately goes back to the early Stoics.

[11] A possible objection to this conclusion might still be based on the fact that Cicero (cf. *de Fato* VIII, 15) attributes to Chrysippus the view that certain conditionals should be reformulated as negated conjunctions. As Cicero tells us, Chrysippus wants the diviners to restate a conditional like 'If someone was born at the rising of the dogstar he will not

Let us come to the fourth and final term: revealing the consequent. For this phrase we do not get, as we did for the other three terms, a general account. What we get instead is an explanation by way of an example. The example is: 'If this woman has milk, she has conceived' and here the antecedent is said to be revealing the consequent because it seems to be 'disclosing' (*dēlōtikon*) the consequent (II. 106). This does not sound very illuminating. To see why this substitution of 'disclosing' for 'revealing' can be supposed to have any explanatory force at all, we ought to consider an important distinction in the epistemology underlying the theory of signs, a distinction explained in the paragraphs preceding the passage under discussion, that is the distinction between things pre-evident (*prodēla*) and things non-evident (*adēla*) (cf. *PH* II. 97–9).

The non-evident things are divided into three groups: some are altogether non-evident (*kathapax adēla*), that is those things 'which are not of a nature to fall within our apprehension (*katalēpsis*)' (II. 97); the example given is the question whether the stars are even in number (II. 97). Some are occasionally non-evident (*pros kairon adēla*), that is, things 'which, though patent (*enargē*) in their nature, are occasionally rendered non-evident to us owing to external circumstances (*peristaseis*)' (II. 98), for example a town in a distant country. Finally, some are naturally non-evident, that is, 'those which are not of such a nature as to fall within our clear perception (*enargeia*), like the intelligible pores' (II. 98).

die at sea' in the form 'It is not the case both that some person was born at the rising of the dogstar and that that person will die at sea'. This clearly amounts to a material implication view of the conditional in question. Hence, it is argued, Chrysippus recognized Philo's truth-functional criterion besides his own criterion of 'cohesion' (*sunartēsis*) (cf. D.L. VII. 73) and, it is further argued, he wants us to construe all empirical laws in this way (cf. S. Sambursky, *Physics of the Stoics* (London, 1959), 79; M. Frede, *Die stoische Logik* (Göttingen, 1974), 86 ff). Yet, following R. Sorabji on this point (cf. R. Sorabji, 'Causation, Laws, and Necessity', in M. Schofield *et al.* (eds), *Doubt and Dogmatism* (Oxford, 1980), 250–82, esp. 266 f), I do not think that this passage from Cicero can be used to attribute to Chrysippus such an extensive adoption of the truth-functional criterion of the conditional. For first of all, the context of the Ciceronian passage clearly shows that Cicero is reporting a Chrysippan proposal which in his (i.e. Cicero's) eyes amounts to a makeshift for a special case. Secondly, the subsequent arguments adduced by Cicero against Chrysippus imply that the latter does not want to extend his reformulation to medical or geometrical cases. The first example which, according to Cicero, Chrysippus could not want to reformulate in the way proposed for the diviners is the following: 'If a person's pulse is so and so, he has got a fever'. This, it should be noticed, would certainly count as a sign relation on the account given by Sextus. Hence, if the theory of signs reported in Sextus was shared by Chrysippus, we should expect this example to be a straightforward candidate for the truth-functional reformulation, contrary to what we find in Cicero.

Having set forth these distinctions, Sextus is then in a position to circumscribe the role of signs according to the Dogmatists; to use the Stoic terminology of Sextus' text: signs provide us with an apprehension (*katalēpsis*) of things in the latter two classes of the non-evident, that is, of things which are not, as the *prodēla*, apprehended of themselves and neither, as things altogether non-evident, excluded from apprehension once and for all (cf. II. 99). It is the job of signs to bridge the gap between things pre-evident and things non-evident and this job is mirrored in the word *dēlōtikon*, disclosing, since its etymology connects it to the *prodēla* and the *adēla*. This seems to be the reason why substituting *dēlōtikon* for *ekkaluptikon* can be taken to amount to an explanation: in opposition to *ekkaluptikon*, the word *dēlōtikon*, because of its etymology, reminds us that the last requirement in the sign definition is to be understood against the epistemological background of the *prodēla/adēla* distinction. Although this may plausibly explain why the Stoics want to bring in the term *dēlōtikon*, it will not explain why they choose *ekkaluptikon* in the first place, that is, in the defining formula quoted in II. 104. *If* the sign definition attributed to the Stoics in this passage was not only held but also worked out by the Stoics, it is hard to understand why the supposedly Stoic authors of this definition did not use *dēlōtikon*, a term which fits in so nicely with their epistemology, in lieu of *ekkaluptikon* in the sign definition itself. Hence, we may have reason to doubt the truth of the antecedent.

II

Let us turn to the parallel passage in *M* (VIII. 245–56). Although we find essentially the same doctrine expounded here as in *PH*, the *M* passage on the whole is inferior. Points explained in a concise way in *PH* are dealt with in a rather long-winded fashion in *M*. Thus, for example, *PH* needs 11 lines (in the edition of Mutschmann/Mau) for its account of the sound conditional, *M* takes 19 for the same job. Whereas *PH* starts off with a precise statement of the criterion ('a sound conditional is one that does not begin with truth and end in a falsehood' *PH* II. 104), *M* treats us first to the list of the four possible combinations of truth-values, each illustrated by an example, then repeats the four combinations once again and only after that—we have been dragged through 13 lines of text—are we told that the first three combinations, again listed in the subsequent lines, make the conditional true (*alēthes*), the *TF* combination makes it false (*pseudos*) (cf. *M* VIII. 245–7). Thus, where *PH* offers a concise general account, all we get in *M* is a list. We may note another point in passing: *M* uses 'true' and 'sound' ('false' and 'unsound') interchangeably for the conditional, *PH* sticks to 'sound' (*hugies*) ('unsound' (*mochthēros*)), reserving 'true' and 'false' for the antecedent and the consequent.

As for the requirement that a sign ought to be a true antecedent in a sound conditional, *PH* states it in a brief definition of a technical term (*prokathēgoumenon*), using 3 lines of text (cf. II. 106); *M* settles the same point in a tiresome exposition of 19 lines (cf. VIII. 248–50). Moreover, it is worth noticing that the author of the source used in *M* not only fails to give a proper definition of *kathēgoumenon* as the true antecedent in a sound conditional, but also seems to use this term eventually in the broader sense of 'antecedent'. The exposition leads to the following conclusion:

> Thus when the sign is said to be 'a proposition which forms the pre-antecedent (*kathēgoumenon*) in a sound conditional', we shall have to understand that it is a pre-antecedent (*kathēgoumenon*) in that conditional only which begins with truth and ends in truth.
>
> (*M* VIII. 250)

The explication contained in the apodosis of this sentence is meant to provide a *specification* circumscribing the meaning of *kathēgoumenon* in the protasis. This in turn means that *kathēgoumenon* when it occurs in the apodosis is used as a generic term in a formula specifying the sense of *kathēgoumenon* in its first occurrence. Hence, we should expect *hēgoumenon*, the standard term for 'antecedent' (cf. *PH* II. 106 and *M* VIII. 251, 252). The use made of the term *kathēgoumenon* in the apodosis of the sentence quoted is hardly justified if the job of *kathēgoumenon* as used in the sign definition at *M* VIII. 245 is that of a technical term denoting the *true* antecedent in a sound conditional. It should be obvious that it in fact has this technical sense in that definition (and, therefore, performs the same job as the *prokathēgoumenon* at *PH* II. 104). If it were otherwise, the sign definition would not warrant the requirement that a sign has to be a *true* antecedent.[12]

---

[12] What has been said above (cf. 89) concerning the term *prokathēgoumenon*, i.e. that it seems to be tied to the definition in which it occurs, holds also for *kathēgoumenon*: as noted by M. Burnyeat (above n 1, 221), this expression 'occurs in Sextus *only* when he is reporting or referring directly to this very definition' (i.e. the one stated in *M* VIII. 245). The relevant passages as given in Janáček's index are the following: *M* VIII. 248, 250, 256, 265, 268, 269, 271, 272.

The conclusion to be drawn from this observation about the use of a term in M may sound disappointing and paradoxical: It seems that the author of M's (ultimate) source in his attempts to explain the definition of sign is not quite up to the mark in respect to his explanandum.

The account of the last part of M's definition of a sign, stipulating that a sign ought to be 'revealing the consequent', takes up as much as 20 lines in M (cf. M VIII. 250–3). *PH* needs 4 lines for the same work (cf. *PH* II. 106). Again we may notice some confusion about a point of logic in our unknown author. He first explains that not every (antecedent) proposition in a sound conditional that begins with truth and ends in truth (cf. M VIII. 250, overlooking the somewhat redundant characterization) would count as a sign, since this criterion would still allow in cases like 'if it is day, it is light', cases, that is, where antecedent and consequent are equally evident (cf. M VIII. 251). Then he comes up with the following conclusion:

The sign, therefore, must not only be the antecedent (*hēgoumenon*) in a sound conditional—that is (*toutesti*), in one that begins in truth and ends in truth—but must also possess a nature which serves to reveal the consequent.

(M VIII. 252)

Our unknown author here identifies the sound conditional with one of the three combinations of truth-values that yield, under Philo's criterion, a sound conditional. This is all the more remarkable since this misleading, not to say false, statement might easily have been avoided: it would have sufficed to say 'The sign, therefore, must not only be the antecedent in a conditional that begins in truth and ends in truth, but etc.'.

In the text immediately subsequent to the passage just quoted, we are offered two conditionals whose antecedents comply with the 'revealing' requirement (cf. M VIII. 252–3). The first of these two conditionals is a slightly longer version of the corresponding example in *PH* (c. II. 106). M, no more than *PH*, does offer a general explanation of the term *ekkaluptikon* nor does it offer, as the *PH* version did, a paraphrasing term (*dēlōtikon* in *PH*) for the one used in the definition. What we get instead, is a statement concerning the sign/significatum relation as a whole: 'For by observing (*prosballontes*) the former (i.e. the sign) we come to an apprehension (*katalēpsis*) of the latter (i.e. the significatum).' (M VIII. 253).

As an account meant to explicate a term of a defining formula this statement suffers from a grave defect: it catches only a necessary condition of the revelatory character of a sign, but fails to give us a sufficient one. For although it is a feature of every sign (as understood in the theory under discussion) that, by observing it, we become aware of some other thing, this feature is by no means restricted to signs. Take the case where you look at the mirror image of a person that you could also observe directly (he/she is in the same room as you). The mirror image would not count as a sign. What is implied in assigning a revelatory character to signs is the contention that the significatum, either in principle or in the prevailing circumstances, can *only* be known by way of a sign (not necessarily only by way of that particular sign). If *a* is able to reveal *b*, *b* must in some sense be hidden away. The defect in the above explication consists in the failure to catch this feature in the revealing character of signs.

I said at the beginning of the discussion of the *M* version (above p. 91) that we find in *M* 'essentially the same doctrine' as in *PH*, and I can now use the room this 'essentially' leaves for qualification. A qualification is needed, for the *M* version, in the passages subsequent to the text just discussed, now brings in material which has no counterpart in *PH* (cf. *M* VIII. 254–6). The unknown author of *M*'s (ultimate) source introduces something which he, as is shown by the résumé in VIII. 256, takes to be a further requirement in the sign definition: a sign, it is claimed, 'must be the present sign of a present thing' (*paron parontos dei einai sēmeion* VIII. 254). The way Sextus introduces this further material in his report—'further, they say . . .' (*eti, phasi . . .*)—may suggest that it had the character of a supplement also in his source.

Our unknown author grants that some people 'erroneously' (*exapatōmenoi* VIII. 254, cf. the equally high-handed *agnoousi dē hoi ta toiauta legontes* VIII. 255) think that there are signs of past things ('If this man has a scar, he has had a wound') as well as of future ones ('If this man is wounded in the heart, he will die') (cf. VIII. 254). Yet he is convinced he has an easy reply to this objection. He defends his additional criterion by claiming that, although the wound is past and death will come about in the future, the *propositions* about the past wound and about imminent death are things present (cf. VIII. 255).

This vindication will hardly stand scrutiny. First of all, the proposed addition would be superfluous as a further specification in the definiens since this requirement is met by any conditional with a true antecedent and a true consequent, and hence, also by those examples which have been shown not to qualify as signs a few paragraphs earlier (cf. VIII. 251). Secondly, the justification offered makes this further requirement inconsistent with the 'revealing' requirement. For if the significatum of a sign is indeed the consequent proposition itself (and not the fact stated in this proposition), then there is nothing left for the sign to reveal. After all, the consequent proposition is as evident as is the antecedent. The 'revealing' requirement presupposes a different degree of evidence between sign and significatum, and this essential difference is levelled out if the significatum is identified with the consequent *proposition* of the sign conditional. Among the many shortcomings we noticed in what *M* has to say about the sign definition this last point is by far the grossest blemish.[13]

To sum up: the observations made about the material preserved in *M* amply justify the conclusion that Sextus here is working from a source much inferior to the one used in *PH*. *M* is lacking in conciseness and precision, it is careless in its use of terminology, it is confused in a point of elementary logic, and it expands the sign definition to include a point which makes the resulting formula inconsistent.

What can be inferred from Sextus' report as to the historical position of his source in *M*? A first point that is pertinent here concerns the chronological relation of the (ultimate) sources used in *M* and *PH* respectively. As Myles Burnyeat has correctly observed, the term *prokathēgoumenon* used in *PH* presupposes the *kathēgoumenon* of *M*, and since both terms are tied to the context of their respective definitions, we may safely conclude that the *PH* source is posterior to the one used in *M*.[14] Other observations will corroborate this finding: with one exception (to be explained soon) all examples illustrating points in the *PH* version also turn up in *M*, and on the whole, the *PH* author seems to have trimmed the material contained in *M*'s source, improving on points of detail, cutting back its long-winded accounts, and silently dropping the unfortunate expansion of the sign definition which we find introduced at the end of the version in *M*.

The source Sextus is drawing from in *M* thus precedes the one used in *PH*. Is it also Stoic? Sextus does not mention a Stoic philosopher or the Stoic school in *M* VIII. 244–56, but there is sufficient evidence to answer this question in the affirmative. The *M* passage is prefaced by a remark stating that the doctrine expounded in what follows belongs to philosophers who hold that the sign is something intelligible, in

---

[13] *contra* Burnyeat, above n 1, 221 n 68.　　[14] Burnyeat, above n 1, 222.

opposition to people taking the sign to be something sensible (cf. *M* VIII. 244). The two groups were opposed already at *M* VIII. 177, and there they have been identified as Stoics and Epicureans respectively. This alone would be sufficient to warrant the Stoic character of the material reported in *M*.

Yet we find also in the text of *M* VIII. 244–56 itself evidence for the Stoic origin of this doctrine. At VIII. 253 the term 'apprehension' (*katalēpsis*) is used for the kind of cognition brought about by the sign. Now this term is definitely Stoic: Cicero (cf. *Academica* (*Acad.*) I. 41 and II. 145) tells us that Zeno of Citium introduced this word as a technical term of epistemology. The verb *prosballein* used in the same sentence (VIII. 253) also points to the Stoics. This technical use of the word as a term of epistemology is attested in another text reporting Stoic doctrines (*M* VII. 252), but does not seem to be recorded for any earlier philosophers.

Moreover, there is a quite telling example used in the illustration of truth-functional implication (cf. VIII. 246). Whilst the examples meant to furnish an instance for the *FF* and *FT* combinations are identical with the ones used by Philo (cf. *M* VIII. 113–14)—stealing examples from other authors' logic books seems to have a venerable tradition—the unknown author exploited here by Sextus has rejected Philo's examples for the *TT* and the *TF* case ('if it is day, it is light' and 'if it is day, it is night' respectively). The new illustration for the *TF* case is not of interest, but the *TT* combination has been chosen to bring in an edifying bit of Stoic natural theology: 'If there are gods, the world is ordered by the gods' providence (*pronoia*).' The doctrine of divine providence is Stoic teaching beginning with Zeno (cf. D.L. VII. 133, 138; Cicero, *de Natura Deorum* (*ND*) II. 74; for attribution to Zeno see Cicero, *ND* II. 58). This, incidentally, is the only instantiation not adopted by the author of the source used in *PH*; wisely enough, he has chosen to reinstate Philo's example (cf. *PH* II. 105).

We may therefore safely ascribe the material used in *M* VIII. 245–56 to a Stoic author. Since the source exploited in this passage precedes the source used in the *PH* version and since we had reason to hand over the *PH* source to the early Stoics, *a fortiori* we ought to put the unknown author of *M*'s (ultimate) source among the early Stoics.

III

What does Sextus tell us about the second ingredient in the theory of signs, the division of signs into commemorative and indicative ones? A report of this part of the doctrine is given in *PH* II. 99–101 and in *M* VIII. 149–55, and in both passages it follows upon a classification of evident (*prodēla*) and non-evident things (*adēla pragmata*) (cf. *PH* II. 97–8; *M* VIII. 141–8). We had occasion to refer to this latter classification when discussing the account offered in *PH* for the 'revealing' requirement, and it seems appropriate to take a closer look at it now, for the epistemological distinctions it contains (and in particular the subdivision of things non-evident) in some sense seem to form the background to the division of signs. After all, the exposition and the account of these distinctions are immediately subsequent to the announcement of the sign discussion in *PH* (II. 96) as well as in *M* (VIII 140).[15]

If we compare the two passages dealing with these divisions, the *PH* version again seems to have the advantage of greater conciseness and clarity. So I shall use it as the starting-point for my discussion. *PH* first divides things (*pragmata*) into evident (*prodēla*) and non-evident (*adēla*) things, subdividing non-evident things further into three classes, the altogether non-evident (*kathapax adēla*), the occasionally non-evident (*pros kairon adēla*), and the naturally non-evident things (*phusei adēla*) (cf. *PH* II. 97). This classification which Sextus attributes to the 'dogmatic philosophers' (II. 97) is obviously meant to be exhaustive and mutually exclusive.

Next Sextus gives us, still reporting on the Dogmatists, a general account and an example of each one of these four groups, that is, of things evident and of the three classes of things non-evident (cf. *PH* II. 97–8). The evident things are those 'which come to our cognition of themselves' (*ta ex heautōn eis gnōsin hēmin erchomena*, II. 97), as the fact

---

[15] Unlike the *definition* of sign reported by Sextus, the *division* of signs into commemorative and indicative ones is denied to be a part of Stoic doctrine by a number of authors: so Philippson, above n 1, 66; Heintz, above n 1, 48 n 1; Preti, above n 1, 10; most recently Sedley, above n 1, 241; and Glidden, above n 1, 218 *passim*. I shall try to show that both ingredients go back to the Dialecticians but were taken over into Stoic doctrine by the early Stoics. I shall not comment on the problem connected to Sextus' criticism of the theory of signs—is his criticism, as he explicitly claims (cf. *PH* II. 102; *M* VIII. 156–8), directed only against the indicative sign or else is it, as suggested by the arguments Sextus actually employs, an attack on the notion of sign in general?

that it is day. The altogether non-evident things are those 'which are not of a nature to fall within our apprehension' (*ha mē pephuken eis tēn hēmeteran piptein katalēpsin*, II. 97), as the fact that the stars are even in number. Occasionally non-evident are things 'which, though patent in their nature, are, for the time being, rendered non-evident to us owing to certain external circumstances' (*haper tēn phusin echonta enargē para tinas exōthen peristaseis kata kairon hēmin adēleitai*, II. 98), 'as the city of Athens is now to me' (II. 98). Finally, the naturally non-evident are those things 'which are not of such a nature as to fall within our clear perception' (*ta mē echonta phusin hupo tēn hēmeteran piptein enargeian*, II. 98), as the intelligible pores (i.e. the pores in the skin). For the latter, it is explained, never appear of themselves but are inferred from other things, for example from perspiration.

It is not clear how we are to understand the 'things' (*pragmata*) which this classification is meant to divide. Does *pragma* stand for an object or a state of affairs? The first two examples tell in favour of the latter alternative: the *pragmata* used for illustration are of a propositional structure; the that clause in the English rendering corresponds to an infinitive construction in the Greek. The *pragmata* in the latter two examples, as it seems, are objects: the city of Athens and the pores in the skin. Yet in spite of its grammatical outlook the last illustration again can only represent a fact, not an object. For what we become aware of in this case is not the pores themselves, but their existence, the fact that there are these little holes in the skin. This is all you can learn about them when taking perspiration as your starting-point. However, the city of Athens example will not lend itself to such a propositional interpretation. For the city of Athens, in opposition to the invisible pores, is an object of knowledge by acquaintance and is taken to be such in this example. So in the end we have to concede that the unknown author of this classification very probably was confused about the fact/object distinction and in any case did not pay attention to it. Hence, I shall continue to render *pragmata* by 'things', exploiting the ambiguity of the English word in this respect.

Let us take a quick glance at the parallel version of this division in *M* (VIII. 141–8). *M* offers two accounts of things evident (cf. VIII. 141, 144) each of which has attached to it an explanation of non-evident things in general. *PH* was content with one criterion for evident things, leaving aside a general circumscription of things non-evident (cf. *PH* II. 97). *M*'s account of the class of evident things at VIII. 144 agrees *verbatim* with the definition in *PH*: the evident things are 'those which come to our cognition of themselves', the non-evident things, *M* continues, are those 'which are not of this character'. This is no proper definition but merely a characterization by way of negation. As for the other passage (VIII. 141), the picture is no better: the account of evident things given there—'those which fall of themselves within the senses and the mind'—leaves it unclear as to whether falling of itself within the senses (or, alternatively, within the mind) counts by itself as a sufficient condition for something's being an evident thing, or whether the two requirements have to be taken together to form a sufficient condition. This sort of amphiboly should be avoided in a proper definition. In the same passage, the non-evident things are said to be those 'which are not apprehensible of themselves' (*ta mē ex hautōn lēpta*). This is misleading, not to say false. For the negation here applies only the qualification 'of themselves' (*ex hautōn*) and, hence, this account does not include in the class of non-evident things those that are not apprehensible at all, that is, the altogether non-evident things.

The explications found in *M* for the things occasionally and those altogether non-evident agree—apart from minor stylistic differences— with those in *PH*. Yet *M* disagrees from *PH* in its account of the naturally non-evident things (cf. *M* VIII. 146). The latter are characterized as 'the things which are everlastingly hidden away and are not capable of falling within our clear perception' (*ta di' aiōnos apokekrummena kai mē dunamena hupo tēn hēmeteran pesein enargeian*, VIII. 146). The first half of this formula is simply superfluous for the purpose of the definition. It is quietly dropped in *PH* (cf. II. 98).

Thus where *M* disagrees from *PH* in its account of the different divisions of evident/non-evident things, it is always to the disadvantage of *M*. The (ultimate) source used in the *M* version seems to be inferior to the one exploited in *PH*. Other observations confirm this assessment. The exposition in *M* is long-winded where *PH* is concise. The recapitulation at *M* VIII. 148, for example, could be dropped without any loss for the overall argument. The author of *M*'s source thinks it necessary to explain the example offered for the occasionally non-evident things, that is, the (far-away) city of Athens (cf. *M* VIII. 145), *PH* takes this example to be self-explaining (cf. *PH* II. 98). On the other hand, *M* fails to give an explication where it would have been more appropriate to deliver one and where, in fact, we find one in *PH*: when it comes to the example of the things naturally non-evident (cf. *M* VIII. 146 and *PH* II. 98). Hence our comparison between *PH* II.

97–8 and *M* VIII. 141–8 confirms our findings about the parallel treatment of the sign definition in *M* and *PH* respectively: the source used in *PH* is superior to the one underlying *M*.

We may extend this similarity also to the point of chronology: the source exploited in *PH* is not only better, but also later than the one used in *M*. Here, as in the treatment of the sign definition, the *PH* version is the result of trimming and correcting the work of the unknown author of *M*'s source. Thus all examples used in *PH* also turn up in *M*, but wherever *M* uses two examples to illustrate one and the same point, as it does on most occasions, *PH* leaves out one of the two. Now this sort of economy could also be attributed to a later compiler, for example Sextus himself. Yet the omission of a superfluous bit in *M*'s account of things naturally non-evident which we find effected in the parallel version in *PH* cannot possibly be the work of a compiler. This correction is very strong evidence to the effect that the unknown author of the source used in *PH* was working with the material reported in *M* in front of him.

There is also sufficient evidence to support ascription of both the *PH* and the *M* source to Stoic philosophers. The Stoic terms 'apprehend' (*katalambanesthai*) and 'apprehension' (*katalēpsis*) occur in *PH* II. 97–9 and the latter term is found in two passages in *M* (VIII. 147, 149). We may add a further observation: the word *peristasis* which is used down to Epicurus in a local sense only (cf. D.L. X. 106, 109), occurs in the sense of 'circumstance' when we come to the explanations of things occasionally non-evident (cf. *PH* II. 98; *M* VIII. 145, 150). This expression is used in the same sense by two pupils of Zeno: by Herillus (cf. D.L. VII. 165) and by the heterodox Stoic Ariston (cf. *M* XI. 65).

Let us then turn to our main topic, the division of signs into commemorative and indicative signs. In both the *PH* and the *M* version, this distinction is introduced in intimate connection to the classification just discussed. In both versions we are told that evident things do not need a sign; they are, after all, perceived directly. Things altogether non-evident cannot be known at all, *a fortiori* they cannot be known by means of a sign: they are removed from apprehension altogether (cf. *PH* II. 99; *M* VIII. 149). *PH* then continues as follows:

Such things as are occasionally or naturally non-evident are apprehended by means of signs—not of course by the same signs, but by commemorative signs in the case of the occasionally non-evident and by indicative signs in the case of the naturally non-evident.

(*PH* II. 99)

This seems to be a rather neat picture. Each of the two types of sign has a class of things non-evident allotted to it. Since there can be no objects of signs outside these two classes (this is warranted by the completeness of the division of *pragmata* together with the exclusion of things evident and things altogether non-evident from being significata), each of the two types of sign can find its significata only within the allotted class of things.

Hence we would expect that a definition of the commemorative and of the indicative sign would refer to these classes of things non-evident, stating for example that something is a commemorative sign if and only if it reveals something occasionally non-evident. Surprisingly however, when Sextus, in the text following immediately upon the passage quoted, reports a definition of each of the two sorts of sign, no mention is made of the two sorts of non-evident things corresponding, as we have just been told, to the two sorts of sign. Here is the definition of the commemorative sign according to *PH*:

They call that a commemorative sign which, having been observed together with its significatum (*sēmeiōton*) in a clear manner at the time of perception, brings to our mind that which has been observed together with it, when this thing is not evident and is not clearly perceived at the moment.[16]

(*PH* II. 100)

The formula used in this definition reappears *verbatim* at *M* VIII. 152. In both passages it is illustrated by the example of smoke as a sign of fire.

As for the indicative sign, *PH* reports the following definition:

An indicative sign, they say, is that which, not having been observed together with its significatum in a clear manner, signifies (*sēmainei*) that of which it is a sign by its own nature and construction (*ek tēs idias phuseōs kai kataskeuēs*).

(*PH* II. 101)

The example illustrating this kind of sign is 'the bodily motions which are a sign of the soul'. The example also appears in *M* (cf. VIII. 155),

---

[16] For the translation of *sumparatērēthen* (participle of the present tense) by 'having been observed' cf. Kühner and Gerth, *Grammatik der griechischen Sprache* (Hannover/Leipzig, 1890), § 382, 4.a. Notice also that *sumparatērēthen* is used together with *proteron* in Pseudo-Galen, *Historia Philosopha* cap. 9 (= Diels, *Doxogr. Graeci* 605, 16).

but in *M* we do not find a definition proper of the indicative sign. What we get instead is an explication of this type of sign by contrasting it with the commemorative one (cf. *M* VIII. 154). Unlike the latter, the indicative sign

does not admit of concomitant observation (*sumparatērēsis*) with its significatum— for the naturally non-evident thing (*to phusei adēlon pragma*) is in principle imperceptible (*anhupoptōton*) and therefore cannot be observed together with one of the things apparent (*phainomena*)—but entirely by its own nature and construction (*ek tēs idias phuseōs kai kataskeuēs*), all but uttering its voice aloud, it is said to signify that whereof it is indicative.

(*M* VIII. 154)

Now notice first that this account in *M* differs from the one in *PH* in an important respect. Where *PH* tells us that the indicative sign *has not been observed* together with its significatum, *M* states that it *does not admit of being observed* together with its significatum and it explains why: because the naturally non-evident is in principle imperceptible and, *a fortiori*, cannot be observed together with an apparent thing. Hence *M* establishes a connection between the indicative sign and the class of things naturally non-evident. Yet notice secondly that this connection only occurs in an explanation added to what seem to be the *disiecta membra definitionis* in *M*. Neither in *M* nor in *PH* is any attempt made to use the classification of things non-evident for the definitions (of commemorative and indicative sign) themselves. We can go a step further: of the terms used in both *PH* and *M* for the definitions proper, none is unmistakably Stoic. In particular, Stoic talk of 'apprehension' (*katalēpsis*) and 'apprehend' (*katalambanein*) is conspicuously absent from these sentences. As noted above, both terms have been used in the preceding paragraphs in *PH*, and *katalēpsis* twice turns up in *M*'s two accounts of things altogether non-evident (cf. *M* VIII. 147, 149).

As for the division of signs into commemorative and indicative, we thus have to state a strange discrepancy. Both the passages reporting the accounts of the two classes of signs are preceded by a classification of things (*pragmata*) into evident and three subdivisions of non-evident things, a classification leading up to the statement that signs can find their significata in two of the subdivisions of non-evident things only (cf. *PH* II. 99; *M* VIII. 149–50). Yet oddly enough, when it comes to actually stating the defining criteria of the commemorative/indicative sign respectively, no use is made of these divisions for this task. Even in M, where what is reported of the *definiens* of the indicative sign sets a stricter criterion of this type of sign in comparison to *PH*, reference to the class of things naturally non-evident, which could have been used to establish the definition, is found only in an explication added to a defining criterion (cf. M VIII. 154).

The discrepancy noted on material grounds is further strengthened by our observations as to the terminology used. Stoic influence is obvious in the *pragmata* classification (cf. use of *katalēpsis, katalambanein*, and *peristasis*), but it is conspicuously absent in the accounts of the indicative/commemorative signs themselves. What are we to infer from these observations? We should *not* conclude that Sextus (or some other compiler) has introduced the distinction of indicative/ commemorative sign into (Stoic) source material which was unaware of this distinction. For in one passage (cf. *M* VIII. 154) we find the class of things naturally non-evident—which, I take it, has good Stoic credentials—intimately linked to the account of the indicative sign. I doubt very much that this addition of an explication could be the work of someone piecing together disparate sources. So what then are we to conclude? For the moment, I think, we can infer no more than a plausible possibility, namely, that the accounts of the indicative and commemorative sign, wholly or in part, may go back to a pre-Stoic source. However, to reach a more definite conclusion, we have to leave Sextus.

IV

The next address on our way is of course Diogenes Laertius. It is in Diogenes that we find the most systematic exposition of the philosophy of the Old Stoa. As is well known, Diogenes' report is based on Diocles the Magnesian who seems to have been an older contemporary of Cicero and, hence, comparatively close to the philosophers he is reporting. Yet strangely enough, at least at first sight, in Diogenes' exposition of Stoic logic (D.L. VII. 42–83) there is not a single sign of a Stoic theory of signs. This may sound disappointing. However, this fact can be made to lend support to one of our tentative results, if we pay attention to the nature of the source material used by Diogenes.

Among the nine Stoic authorities quoted or referred to by name in this report of Stoic logic (VII. 42–83) there is not a single early (i.e.

pre-Chrysippan) Stoic.[17] Notice also that middle Stoicism keeps a very low profile. Panaetius is not mentioned at all, and Posidonius who is mentioned in three passages (cf. VII. 54, 60, 62) is allowed only once to bring in something he has to say about logic: his account of dialectic (VII. 62) which is different from that attributed to Chrysippus.[18] At VII. 60 his definition of a poem is referred to, and at VII. 54 he is used as a source for the older Stoics' view of the criterion.[19] The Stoics used in Diogenes' logic report are Chrysippus and his followers. Notice that this restriction is in sharp contrast to the policy followed in the reports on Stoic ethics (VII. 84–131) and physics (VII. 132–59) where the names of Zeno and Cleanthes hold a prominent place.[20]

It hardly needs mention that Chrysippus was not the first Stoic to take an interest in logic.[21] After all, it was their proclivity towards dialectic which made the founders of Stoicism part company with the Cynics. Even Diogenes testifies to this interest in logic shown by the early Stoics: Zeno as well as Cleanthes are said to have made logic a part of philosophy (cf. VII. 39 and VII. 41 resp.), and Zeno's interest in dialectic is confirmed by his studies with the Dialecticians Philo and Diodorus Cronus (cf. VII. 16 and 25).

Hence, when we find the cast of the logic chapter in Diogenes restricted to Chrysippan personnel, the reason for this must be that Stoic logic as established by Chrysippus superseded its Stoic forerunners in a radical and definite way. This, of course, is amply confirmed by what we are told about the logic of Chrysippus in ancient

---

[17] Here is a list of the names of Stoic philosophers mentioned in D.L. VII. 42–83 together with the number of occurrences: Chrysippus 11, Diogenes 6, Antipater 5, Crinis 4, Posidonius 3, Apollodorus 2, Archedemus 2, Boethus 1, Athenodorus 1 (cf. VII. 68, probably to be deleted, cf. U. Egli, *Zur stoischen Dialektik* (Basel, 1967), 37). Notice also the frequent coincidences between the terminology used in Diogenes' report and the terms occurring in Chrysippan titles (D.L. VII. 189–202).

[18] At VII. 42 the same account is attributed to the Stoics, this time without mentioning Posidonius' name.

[19] R. D. Hicks, the translator of the *Vitae* in the Loeb edition, unfortunately mistranslates the passage: what is meant to be a *reference* to a source (*hōs ho Poseidōnios en tōi peri Kritēriou phēsi* = 'as Posidonius says in his treatise *On the Standard*'), is turned into a further testimony ('so also does Posidonius in his treatise *On the Standard*').

[20] Here is a list of early Stoics mentioned in the two other reports in D.L. Ethics-report: Zeno 8, Cleanthes 5, Persaeus 1; Physics-report: Zeno 11, Cleanthes 4, Sphaerus 2.

[21] M. Frede has rightly emphasized that a Stoic logic in the proper sense of the word (i.e. a logic worked out by Stoic logicians) did not exist before Chrysippus (cf. Frede, above n 11, 26). Yet this is compatible with there being Stoic logicians and a logic adopted by Stoic philosophers well before the time of Chrysippus.

authors (e.g. D.L. VII. 180).[22] The famous dictum quoted by D.L. (VII. 183) that 'but for Chrysippus, there had been no Porch', if anywhere, applies to the field of Stoic dialectic. This, in turn, accounts for the absence of early Stoics and their logical doctrines in Diogenes' exposition of Stoic dialectic. Thus, when the Stoic theory of signs, so well attested in Sextus, is nowhere mentioned in D.L., this amounts to an argument from silence to the effect that this theory can only be part of early Stoic doctrine.

I think we can even find evidence in D.L. to show that the absence of this theory cannot be due to a simple omission on the part of Diogenes or Diocles, but that it cannot possibly have been part of the Stoic epistemology as reported by D.L. The reason for this has to do with the account of proof (*apodeixis*) attributed to the (i.e. Diogenes') Stoics in D.L. VII. 45. However, to see the implications of this bit of Stoic doctrine, we first have to bring in some material from Sextus again.

Proof, we are told several times in Sextus' reports, is a kind of sign (cf. *M* VIII. 180, 277, 299, 301; *PH* II. 96, 122, 131, 134). The accounts of proof reported by Sextus all make it a requirement of proof that it *reveals* a non-evident (*adēlon*) conclusion (cf. *M* VIII. 314, 385, 422–3; *PH* II. 135, 143, 170). Hence, we also find the milk example used to illustrate the revealing character of proof (*M* VIII. 423), not only of sign (as in *M* VIII. 252; *PH* II. 106). The claim that proof (which is an *argument* cf. *M* VIII. 134; *PH* II. 135) is a kind of sign (which is a *conditional proposition*, cf. *M* VIII. 245; *PH* II. 104) is highly problematical indeed, since it blurs the distinction between asserted and non-asserted proposition. Yet for the moment we may ignore this. What is important for our purpose is the fact that, as far as Sextus is concerned, sign (the genus) as well as proof (the species) rely on the opposition between things evident and things non-evident. For this clear-cut opposition is watered down to a merely gradual difference when we come to the Stoic (Chrysippan, I take it) definition of proof in Diogenes' exposition:

Proof is an argument (*logos*) inferring by means of what is better apprehended (*dia tōn mallon katalambanomenōn*) something less well apprehended (*to hētton katalambanomenon*).

(D.L. VII. 45)

Whoever may have supported this account of proof, he cannot also

---

[22] For references see Frede, above n 11, 27 f.

have made both proof a kind of sign and sign an antecedent revealing the consequent. For the concept of something less well apprehended is more comprehensive than the concept of something non-evident. It is, of course, not logically excluded that the author of the proof definition preserved in D.L. cancelled only the relation of species to genus between proof and sign. Yet it is far more likely that the considerations which have prompted the new definition of proof reported in D.L. also have had consequences for its epistemological relative, the concept of sign. This in turn means that it is quite unlikely that the theory of sign which we find attributed to the Stoics in Sextus Empiricus has been part of the logical doctrines of Chrysippus and his followers.[23]

Thus, it is not only the absence of early Stoic philosophers in Diogenes' exposition of Stoic logic which, together with Diogenes' silence on a Stoic theory of signs, lends plausibility to the claim that this theory was part of early Stoic doctrine. We can also draw support for this claim from the Stoic definition of proof as reported in D.L.

V

Because of the Chrysippan material used, the report on Stoic logic in D.L. (VII. 42–83) can confirm our ascription of the theory of signs to the early Stoics only in a negative respect: by excluding it from Stoic logic as established by Chrysippus and his school. After all, no early Stoic is mentioned in this report. Yet outside this exposition, D.L. contains a lot of information on early Stoics which is also quite pertinent to our problem. D.L., for most of the early Stoics, includes lists of their writings in his report.[24] Although these inventories cannot tell us anything about particular doctrines advocated in the writings

---

[23] O. Rieth, in an excursus ('Die stoische σημεῖον-Lehre') to his excellent monograph on *Die Grundbegriffe der stoischen Ethik* (Berlin, 1933), has tried to show that the Stoic theory of signs must belong to Chrysippus. He bases his claim on two passages (i.e. Cicero, *ND* II. 16; Alexander, *de Mixtione* 216 f, ed I. Bruns) where we find arguments attributed to Chrysippus which infer things unobservable from observed phenomena (Rieth, loc cit, 187–9). Yet even if these arguments (or certain premisses used in them) would qualify as *sēmeia*, this does not warrant the conclusion that Chrysippus also adheres to the interpretation given of such *sēmeia* in the theory of signs as expounded in Sextus. His use of *sēmeia* commits him to this theory as little as the use of an argument of the form *Barbara* commits an arguer to Aristotle's syllogistic theory.

[24] D.L. supplies the following Stoics with lists of their writings: Zeno (VII. 4), Persaeus (VII. 36), Aristo (VII. 163), Herillus (VII. 166), Dionysius (VII. 167), Cleanthes (VII. 174–5), Sphaerus (VII. 178), Chrysippus (VII. 189–202).

registered, they provide valuable information about topics of discussion among the early Stoics.

First and foremost, we learn that Zeno has written a treatise *On Signs* (*peri sēmeiōn* VII. 4). This title is listed in a (probably incomplete) catalogue of nineteen Zenonian works.[25] D.L. does not offer any information as to the content of this treatise, but I think it is a fair guess that one of the sources used by Sextus ultimately goes back to Zeno's book *On Signs*. Secondly, we learn that the founder of Stoicism got his knowledge of logic from members of the Dialectical school: from Philo (cf. VII. 16) and from Diodorus Cronus (cf. VII. 25). D.L. also relates the story that Zeno, being offered a logical treatise by a Dialectician, was prepared to pay double the price he was asked for (VII. 25). Moreover, there is evidence showing that not only Zeno but other early Stoics as well were influenced by the logic of the Dialecticians. Among the titles of logical works attributed to early Stoics there are four that have counterparts in titles (or topics) of writings attributed to members of the Dialectical school.

Clinomachus who seems to have been the founder of the Dialectical school is said to have written 'on propositions, predicates, and the like' (D.L. II. 112).[26] Even if this is not an enumeration of titles, but of topics, it is quite telling that in the list of writings attributed to Cleanthes and to his pupil Sphaerus respectively (cf. D.L. VII. 175, 178) we meet with a title *On Predicates*. Cleanthes' work *On Forms of Argument* (*peri Tropōn*, cf. VII. 175) is matched by a treatise carrying the same title written by Philo to which Chrysippus bothered to write a refutation (cf. VII. 194). Again in the long inventory of Chrysippus' works there is a treatise arguing against a book *On Ambiguities* (*peri Amphiboliōn*) produced by the Dialectician Panthoides (cf. VII. 193; for Panthoides as a Dialectician see D.L. V. 68). The same title turns up

---

[25] This catalogue is discussed by K. v. Fritz, 'Zenon von Kition', in *Pauly-Wissowa's Realencyclopädie*, vol X A (1972) col 90. As for the content of this treatise, v. Fritz argues that its place in the list of writings suggests that its topic was signs of future events whose discussion was part of physics. I do not think that this argument carries any weight: the title preceding the one under discussion indicates a physical treatise (*peri tou Holou* = *Of the Whole World*), but the subsequent one (*Puthagorika* = *Pythagorean Questions*) would hardly be suitable for a work on physics. Moreover, the fact that *sēmeion* is used already by Aristotle (*Analytica Priora* (*APr*) II. 27) as a technical term in epistemology tells against this suggestion. Since there is, as we have seen, sufficient evidence to attribute the theory of signs reported by Sextus to early Stoics, it is reasonable to assume that Zeno's book contributed to the epistemological discussion on signs.

[26] On Clinomachus cf. K. Döring, *Die Megariker: Kommentierte Sammlung der Testimonien* (Amsterdam, 1972), test. 32A, 34, 35.

in the list of writings by Sphaerus (VII. 178). Given the extremely meagre evidence we have for any writings of the Dialecticians, and in view of the fact that among the titles attributed to early Stoics, hardly more than a dozen testify to a logical topic, these parallel titles are quite impressive. They show that, as far as logic is concerned, the early Stoics follow in the wake of the Dialecticians.[27] It seems reasonable to assume that what holds for pre-Chrysippan Stoic logic in general will also hold for the theory of signs: that it goes back to the Dialecticians. After all, the use of Philonian implication in the account of a technical term used in the sign definition strongly points in this direction. I shall attempt to strengthen this suggestion in what follows next.

In the list of Chrysippus' writings we find a title: *pros to peri Sēmasiōn Philōnos, A Reply to the Work of Philo On Sēmasiai* (D.L. VII. 191). The Greek term which I have only transliterated, *sēmasia*, is rendered by translators of this list as 'meaning'.[28] Philo then would have written a treatise *On Meanings*. I shall try to show that this was in fact a work *On Signs*.

The word *sēmasia* in the sense of 'meaning' (of a word) is frequent in Apollonius Dyscolus (2nd cent. AD); it does not seem to occur in other grammarians.[29] The earliest evidence for the use of *sēmasia* in this sense seems to be a passage in the *de Signis* (XXXIV. 2) written by the Epicurean Philodemus of Gadara around the middle of the first century BC or a little later.[30] In all earlier occurrences this term has the meaning 'sign' or 'signal'. It is used in this sense on several occasions in the *Septuagint*, the Greek translation of the Old Testament produced in between 300 and 150 BC.[31] It turns up in this sense in

---

[27] Frede has noticed the dependence of pre-Chrysippan Stoic logicians upon the pre-Stoic logicians mentioned above (cf. Frede, above n 11, 22). Frede, however, does not yet distinguish the Dialecticians from the Megarians and, thus, takes this influence to be one of Megarian logicians; cf. also Rist, n 1 above, 390 ff.

[28] In the Loeb edition of the *Vitae* (London, 1925), R. D. Hicks translates this title as *On Meanings*; the German translation by O. Apelt and K. Reich (Hamburg, 1967), has *Von den Bedeutungen*.

[29] cf. Apollonius Dyscolus, *de Pronominibus*, ed R. Schneider (Leipzig, 1878), 14 l 3, 39 l 21, 44 l 16, 56 l 13, 62 l 13, 161 l 13, 171 l 22, 178 l 5; *de Adverbiis*, ed R. Schneider (Leipzig, 1878) 154 ll 2 and 4, 205 l 14. Further instances of this usage: Iamblichus, *Protrepticus*, ed H. Pistelli (Leipzig, 1888), 4; Aelianus, *Tactica*, ed H. Köchly and W. Rüstow (Leipzig, 1855), 24 l 4.

[30] Thus P. H. and E. A. de Lacy (eds), *Philodemus: On Methods of Inference* (²Naples, 1978), 163 f.

[31] The word occurs 25 times in the Septuagint (18 of these occurrences are to be found in the Leviticus and in the Numeri). The full list of the references in the Septuagint was kindly provided by Dr Larry Schrenk, using the Ibycus Computer of the University of Texas at Austin. The Greek word is used to translate Hebrew expressions

Diodorus Siculus (II. 54) and in Strabo (VIII. 6. 5), both active in the first century BC. And the only occurrence of *sēmasia* in the Corpus Aristotelicum, the passage 919b36–7 of the Pseudo-Aristotelian *Problemata*, clearly demands the rendering 'sign': 'the deeds are a *sēmasia* of character'. The *Problemata* were probably not written before 250 BC.[32] Philo's title, incidentally, seems to be the earliest recorded use of this term. Hence, we have very good reason to translate the title preserved in the list of Chrysippus' writings as *A Reply to the Work of Philo On Signs*.

We can get further corroboration of this result if we take into consideration the context of the Chrysippan title. It occurs in a group of altogether eight titles, the 'second series' (*suntaxis deutera*), within a larger class of Chrysippus' logical writings (cf. D.L. VII. 190–3). These 'series' are arranged according to a systematic aspect. The first series of this class collects titles dealing with propositions in general, with conjunction, and with several kinds of simple (non-complex) propositions (cf. VII. 190). Four types of simple propositions among those discussed in D.L. VII. 69 have counterparts in this list. The third series specifies titles of works whose topics seem to be sentences which are *not* propositions: imperatives, questions, enquiries, investigations, answers (cf. D.L. VII. 191).

The second series, that is the group containing our title, is an inventory of writings which seem to discuss complex propositions and parts of such propositions. The first two treatises listed are about the true disjunctive and the true conditional proposition respectively (cf. VII. 190 *ad fin*). The work whose title is listed in the fourth place discusses the *akoloutha*, that is, the apodoseis in complex propositions introduced by 'since' (*epei*) or 'because' (*dihoti*) (cf. VII. 74). This title, however, seems to be mutilated. The formula of the title indicates that this Chrysippan writing is directed against (*pros*) another author's treatise *peri akolouthōn*. Yet unlike the four other titles with the same

---

having a somewhat technical sense: scab (Lev. 13: 2, 6, 7, 8; 14:56); signal of a trumpet (Num. 10:5, 6, 7; 29, 1; 1 Para. 15:28; 2 Para. 13:12; 2 Esd. 2:12, 13); signal for the jubilee (Lev. 25:10, 11, 12, 13). For further references see Liddell–Scott–Jones, s. v. *sēmasia*. The references given in LSJ should be completed by Galen, *Opera*, vol xix, ed C. G. Kühn (Leipzig, 1830), 205, 539, 551, 561, 571. In all these Galenian passages, *sēmasia* means 'seizure' of a disease.

[32] For the date of this Pseudo-Aristotelian treatise, cf. H. Flashar (ed), *Aristoteles: Problemata physica*, transl H. Flashar (Berlin, 1962; 2nd edn 1975), 357. Flashar states that the earliest texts of this treatise could hardly have been written before the middle of the third century.

initial formula in the list of Chrysippus' works,[33] this one does not mention the name of the author criticized. We may, therefore, suspect a lacuna in the text, perhaps due to a mechanical damage in a manuscript.

This observation about a textual problem may also prove helpful when we come to the third title in this list: *Hairesis* (VII. 191 *ad in*). For several reasons, this word is bound to arouse suspicion. First of all, of the two meanings of the Greek word none fits the title of a logical treatise: neither 'choice' nor '(philosophical) sect'. Secondly, whenever the first word of a title in this list is not a preposition but a substantive, these substantives when used in the singular invariably indicate the formal character of the respective work, e.g. 'abridgement' (*epitomē*), 'treatise' (*technē*), 'outline' (*hupographē*), 'comparison' (*sugkrisis*). Substantives specifying the content of a work are consistently used in the plural. Finally, Gorgippides, the addressee of this treatise, on all other occasions where his name occurs in this list (cf. 190–1, 198, 200) is related to the title of a logical work. So his name also makes it rather implausible that this might be the title of an ethical treatise. Hence, we have good reason to suspect a textual corruption here as well as in the subsequent title, and possibly for a similar reason: a damage in a manuscript.[34] Title number five joins its two predecessors in arousing suspicion: *peri tou dia Triōn palin pros Gorgippidēn*, translated by Hicks as *On the Argument which employs three Terms, also addressed to Gorgippides*. It should be noted that 'argument' as well as 'terms' have no counterpart in the Greek; they are supplemented by the translator. The translation thus supplemented takes the treatise to be about a type of argument. Yet the Chrysippan writings on the topic of arguments are collected in another section of this inventory (cf. VII. 194–8) and a work dealing with this topic would hardly fit into a group of writings whose overall theme is propositions. Thus, one might contest the completion as effected by Hicks and look out for a better one. As far as I can see the only possible supplement after *dia Triōn* which can, perhaps, be based on textual evidence is *Tropikōn*. We learn from a passage in Galen that the Stoics recognized syllogisms called *dia Duo*

---

[33] i.e. VII. 193, 194, and 196 as well as the title in our passage which mentions Philo's treatise.

[34] A possible conjecture would be: *peri aitiōdous*. This is a complex proposition containing the conjunction 'because' (*dihoti*). The Stoic criteria for this proposition are reported at D.L. VII. 74.

Tropikōn and also *dia Triōn.*[35] In that case, we would have to correct Hicks' 'terms' into something like 'premisses'. Yet this would still leave us with a work of syllogisms and, hence, not calm our main misgivings.

Let me raise two further objections against this title. First of all, it seems to be over-elliptical even for a Greek author. It certainly would be unique in this respect among the titles of this rather long list. Secondly, the 'again' (*palin*) preceding the addressee's name looks strange. For although we quite often meet with the name of one and the same addressee in succession (e.g. Zeno 5 times, VII. 195; Aristocreon 3 times, VII. 197; Metrodorus 4 times, VII. 199), there is never again a *palin* (or an equivalent expression) preceding one of these names. So all these observations taken together strongly suggest that the wording of this title again is the outcome of textual corruption.[36]

Titles number six and eight (number seven is the one mentioning Philo's treatise) do not seem to offer any problems. Both confirm our claim that this group contains titles of works dealing with propositions. This is clearly so in the case of the last one: *On the Question what are False Propositions*, even though the 'propositions' has to be added in the translation. For according to Stoic theory, only propositions can be bearers of (truth and) falsity (cf. D.L. VII. 65). The title *On Possibles* (*peri Dunatōn*) also refers to a writing about propositions: the *dunaton*, as we are told in Diogenes' report (cf. VII. 75), is a proposition 'which admits of being true, there being nothing in external circumstances to prevent it being true'.[37]

Hence among the seven titles contained in this group besides the one that made us embark on this digression, there are only two (i.e. numbers 3 and 5) which are not clearly dealing with propositions and both of them offered strong reasons to suspect a textual corruption.

---

[35] Cf. Galenus, *De placitis Hippocratis et Platonis*, ed I. Mueller (Leipzig, 1874), 182; the reading *ē triōn* is not very well attested and, unlike Mueller, the latest editor of this Galenian treatise did not adopt it, cf. P. H. de Lacy (ed), *Galenus on the Doctrines of Hippocrates and Plato*, vol I (Berlin, 1978) 114.

[36] A possible conjecture for this title would be: *peri tou Diasaphountos pros Gorgippidēn.* For the type of complex proposition called *diasaphoun* by the Stoics see D.L. VII. 72–3.

[37] One might ask why a type of modal proposition occurs in this catalogue of titles referring to complex propositions or parts of such propositions (title no. 4). A tentative answer can perhaps be suggested on the following lines: certain propositions that are parts of complex propositions may sensibly be required to be though not true, yet admitting of truth, e.g. antecedents and consequents in non-counterfactual conditionals. The concept of 'admitting of truth' (*epidektikon tou alēthes einai*) is central to the Stoic definition of possibility (cf. D.L. VII. 75). Hence the discussion of the concept of the possible (proposition) may have involved a discussion of (parts of) complex propositions.

Thus the context of the Chrysippan title which has preserved a mention of Philo's *peri Sēmasiōn* strongly tells against the supposition that this Philonian treatise was a work about meanings. We ought to translate its title as *On Signs*.[38]

Furthermore, the occurrence of this title of Philo's in the group of Chrysippan titles just discussed also suggested that Philo may have established some connection between signs and (complex) propositions, a connection which we also have met with in the Stoic theory of signs as expounded in Sextus. There is at least some reason to assume that this Stoic doctrine owes some of its outlook to the Dialectician Philo. Can we go any further than this, or will the answer to the question of how much the Stoic theory owes to the Dialecticians remain an *adēlon* for ever? In the rest of this paper I shall try a further thrust into the non-evident by attempting to bring out what can be known about the Dialectical theory of signs and to compare it to the theory of signs as held by the Stoics.

VI

For this purpose I have to bring in a passage of text which I have so far left out of the picture: chapter IX of Pseudo-Galen's *Historia Philosopha*. Its title is *On Sign* (*peri Sēmeiou*). Here is the Greek text together with a translation:

Σημεῖον τοίνυν οἱ μὲν διαλεκτικοί φασιν ἀξίωμα ἐν ὑγιεῖ συνημμένῳ καθηγούμενον ἐκκαλυπτικὸν τοῦ λήγοντος. τῶν δὲ σημείων τὰ μέν ἐστιν ἐνδεικτικά τὰ δὲ ὑπομνηστικά. ὑπομνηστικὸν μὲν οὖν ἐστιν, ὅπερ συμπαρατηρηθὲν τῷ σημειωτῷ ἅμα ⟨τῷ⟩ φανῆναι τὸ σημεῖον καὶ τοῦ σημειωτοῦ εἰς γνῶσιν ἡμᾶς ἄγει, ὁποῖόν ἐστιν ἐπὶ τοῦ καπνοῦ. τοῦτον

---

[38] Still it seems to be rather odd that Philo, in using *sēmasia* for 'sign', falls back on a very rare word (this Philonian title would in fact be the earliest extant evidence for a use of *sēmasia*) in order to denote something for which a well established technical term is at hand at least since Aristotle, i.e. *sēmeion*, a term also used by the Stoic sources exploited by Sextus. The context in which this Philonian treatise is mentioned suggests that for Philo the concept of sign is in some way connected to an analysis of propositions, a connection well apparent in the Stoic discussion of sign reported by Sextus. Notice too that Aristotle classifies signs as propositions (cf. *APr* II. 27. 70a6–7). This broad agreement between Aristotle, Philo, and the early Stoics reported by Sextus makes Philo's switch to a new term all the more strange. This together with the above observations concerning textual corruptions in this list may lend a certain plausibility to the supposition that *peri Sēmasiōn* may be a corrupted reading for *peri Sēmeiōn*, even if the text handed down in D.L. is the *lectio difficilior*.

γάρ ἰδόντες εὐθὺς γινώσκομεν, ὅτι εκ πυρὸς γεγονώς ἐστιν. ἐνδεικτικὸν δέ ἐστι σημεῖον τὸ μὴ πρότερον συμπαρατηρηθὲν τῷ σημειωτῷ, οὗ δὲ φανέντος εἰς γνῶσιν ἀφικόμεθα τοῦ σημειωτοῦ, ὥσπερ ἐπὶ τῆς γάλα ἐχούσης εὐθὺς γινώσκομεν, ὅτι τετοκυῖά ἐστιν.

Now the dialecticians say that a sign is a proposition which forms the pre-antecedent in a sound conditional, and which reveals the consequent. Of signs some are indicative, some commemorative. A commemorative sign is a sign which, having been observed together with its significatum, leads us, as soon as the sign becomes apparent, to a knowledge also of its significatum, as is the case with smoke; for if we see it, we immediately know that it has originated from fire. — An indicative sign is a sign which has not been observed before together with its significatum, yet on the appearance of which we come to the knowledge of its significatum, for example, we immediately know in the case of a woman having milk that she has given birth.

(Diels, Doxogr. Gr. 605, 10–18)

First a note on the text. I have followed Diels except for changing Diels' *prokathēgoumenon* into *kathēgoumenon*, a change proposed by M. Burnyeat as a more likely correction of the *kai hegoumenon* found in the manuscripts.[39] The similarity of what is reported here by Pseudo-Galen to the material expounded in Sextus will need no argument. Yet we should notice that the proposed reading *kathegoumenon* puts this text closer to the *M* version of the theory of signs than to the one in *PH*.

It would be rash to assume right from the start that the 'dialecticians' mentioned in this passage are members of the Dialectical school. They are usually equated with Stoic logicians.[40] Hence in my translation I have not allowed them to enter the scene with a capital D. Yet I shall argue that we are justified in changing the small letter into a capital one.

Notice first that the author of this treatise seems to know of the existence of the Dialectical school. In chapter IV, where he explains the denominations of different philosophical sects, the Dialectical school is mentioned twice in Kühn's edition.[41] Diels, however, has put the first mention in brackets and has omitted the second altogether along with the clause in which it occurs in Kühn's edition.[42] The

---

[39] Burnyeat, n 1 above, 222 n 70.

[40] Thus Diels, *Doxogr. Gr.*, 246, Burnyeat, above n 1, 212 n 47. The text is not included in *SVF*.

[41] Cf. *Galeni Opera*, ed C. G. Kühn, vol xix (Leipzig, 1830), 230.

[42] After the text as given in Diels, *Doxogr. Gr.*, 602, 5, Kühn's edition offers the following bit of text: *hē d'apo merous philosophias ho malist' epitēdeusan, hōs dialektikē*. It is not clear whether this text is in a manuscript or whether it is due to a conjecture by

Dialectical school is not mentioned in chapter VII (*On Sects*) but this is perhaps not very telling, for the division there is made on the basis of the tripartition into dogmatic, sceptic, and eristic philosophers (cf. Diels, *Dox.* 604, 5–8), and the author of the *Historia philosopha* provides each subdivision only with some prominent representatives. Thus, we find that other candidates who get mentioned in chapter IV are omitted here as well, for example the Cynics and the Peripatetics. Notice, however, that among the philosophers representing the Eristics Clinomachus, the founder of the Dialectical school (cf. D.L. I. 19), is also mentioned.

Yet even if the unknown author of the *Historia* (or his source) knows about the Dialectical school, this will not suffice to warrant the inference that the dialecticians in chapter IX are members of this school. They may be Stoic logicians all the same. So further argument will be needed to establish the conclusion I am heading for. For this further argument I shall take it for granted that besides the Stoics and the Dialecticians (now with a capital D) there are no other contenders to the doctrine expounded in this chapter of the *Historia*. It belongs either to the Stoics or to the Dialecticians. Hence, if this theory can be shown not to belong to the Stoics we are obliged to hand it over to the Dialecticians. I shall thus argue using Chrysippus' fifth *anapodeikton*, better known as the *modus tollendo ponens*. Let me try to establish the *proslēpsis* of this argument.

Let us notice as a first point that the terminology in this chapter of the *Historia* shows no sign of Stoic influence: *gnōsis* (605, 14 and 16) and *gignōskein* (605, 15 and 17) are the terms used to denote the intellectual achievements brought about by the use of a sign. *Katalēpsis*, the term used to characterize the cognition of the significatum in the Stoic context of *M* VIII. 253, does not occur, and neither does the verb *katalambanein*. No reference is made to the division of things non-evident which we have found established by means of the Stoic concept of *katalēpsis/katalambanesthai* in *PH* II 97–9 as well as in *M* VIII. 145–50. So nothing compels us to regard the doctrine reported here as being of Stoic origin.

The second point to be made is stronger: this doctrine cannot be Stoic for the account of the indicative sign as well as the example

Kühn; Diels does not mention it in his *apparatus criticus*. Yet, as is shown by Diels' *apparatus criticus*, the *dialektikē* (sc. *hairesis*) gets a mention in the best manuscript (i.e. the Laurentius A, cf. Diels, *Doxogr. Gr.*, *Prolegomena* 241).

offered for it are in open conflict with the account we find in Sextus. To see this let us go back to the explanation of the indicative sign in *M* VIII. 154. There we were told that the indicative sign

does not admit of concomitant observation with its significatum—for the naturally non-evident object is in principle imperceptible and therefore cannot be observed together with one of the things apparent. . . .

Now the example illustrating the indicative sign in the *Historia*—'If this woman has milk, she has given birth *(tetokuia estin)*'—simply does not comply with this requirement in *M*. Parturition is not something naturally non-evident. And there is nothing that would, by logical or physical necessity, preclude its being observed together with lactation.[43] Moreover, the account of the indicative sign in the *Historia*, in accordance with the example offered and in opposition to the explanation of this type of sign in the *M* version, does not require that the significatum *cannot be observed* together with the sign but merely that the sign

has not been observed before together with its significatum *(mē proteron sumparatērēthen tōi sēmeiotōi)*.

This weaker requirement does not restrict the significata of indicative signs to the class of things unobservable by nature, that is, to the naturally non-evident things. So, parturition may well come in as a significatum of an indicative sign.[44] To come to a preliminary

---

[43] This has been noticed by Philippson, above n 1, 60. Philippson erroneously takes the consequent in the Stoic example *ei gala echei hautē, kekuēken hautē* to be about parturition, not about conception.

[44] It might still be objected that the milk example is, after all, ill-chosen, for the doctor who tells you that lactation is a sign of preceding parturition may well have observed lactation together with childbirth on previous occasions. Yet this objection is based on a mistaken assumption, i.e. on the assumption that the example belongs to the doctor's consultation room. It does not. It has its place in a forensic context. This will become clear immediately when we turn to the first text where the milk example is used, i.e. Plato's *Menexenus (Mx)* 237e, a passage strangely neglected in recent discussions of the theory of signs. There Socrates says the following: 'Every creature that brings forth possesses a suitable supply of nourishment for its offspring; and by this test it is manifest also whether a woman be truly a mother or no, but brings in another's child as her own, if she possesses no founts of nourishment for her child' (*Mx.* 237e2–5; I have used Bury's translation, restituting the *all' hupoballomenē*, e4, which Bury, following a proposal by Hartmann, has omitted in his translation). The question whether a woman is merely pretending to have given birth to a child or not, does not occur in a medical but in a legal context. This is corroborated by the use made of the 'milk test' in the New Comedy: in Menander's *Samia*, suckling a baby *(titthion didonai)* is taken to be a confirmation of someone's being a mother of the child in question, cf. *Menandri Apis et Samia*, ed C. Austin (Berlin, 1969), *Samia* v. 276 (where the assumption turns out to be erroneous),

conclusion: the theory of signs, as reported in Pseudo-Galen, is, in one important respect, incompatible with the theory of signs as expounded in *M*.

What about the source exploited by Sextus in *PH* II. 97–101? At first sight, it seems to be compatible with the account found in the *Historia*; for the indicative sign is explained here as

> that which, not having been observed together with its significatum in a clear manner, signifies that of which it is a sign by its own nature and construction.
>
> *PH* II. 101

This definition does not contradict the account of the indicative sign as stated in the *Historia*. Yet, what makes the report found in *PH* also incompatible with chapter IX of the *Historia* (and what makes *PH* itself inconsistent in a way) is the fact that, in the immediately preceding paragraphs, the class of things naturally non-evident has been allotted to the indicative sign, the class of things occasionally non-evident to the commemorative sign (cf. *PH* II. 99). This is to say that, in *PH* as well as in *M*, the indicative sign can get its significata only from the class of things naturally non-evident. That, however, is incompatible with the account as well as the example of the indicative sign in Pseudo-Galen.

We may further notice that the example furnishing an instance of the indicative sign in *PH* is the same as the one used for this purpose in *M*: the bodily movements as a sign of the soul (cf. *PH* II. 101 and *M* VIII. 155). Yet *M* states explicitly that the soul is one of the things naturally non-evident. Finally, in its account of the indicative sign itself, *PH* sticks to the requirement found in *M* that this sign 'signifies that of which it is a sign by its own nature and construction' (*ek tēs idias phuseōs kai kataskeuēs*) (*PH* II. 101, cf. *M* VIII. 155). Hence, even if the source used in *PH* differs from the one underlying the *M* version as far as part of its account of the indicative sign is concerned, *PH* agrees with *M* (in opposition to the *Historia*) in the instance chosen for this type of sign,

---

536, 540. (I am indebted to Egert Pöhlmann, Erlangen, for drawing my attention to these passages in Menander.) It should be noticed that the example as adduced in the *Menexenus* concerning a particular child would only allow an inference from *not* having milk to *not* having given birth to *this* child. Yet if this qualification is dropped, the argument might easily be turned around so as to grant the inference from lactation to childbirth, as we find it used in Aristotle's *Rhetoric* (I. 2. 1357b14–16): 'She has given birth because she has milk.' A further point to be noticed in the *Mx.* example is that it is based on a general teleological premiss and, hence, does not presuppose any previous observation of a concomitant occurrence of lactation and childbirth. This feature may have facilitated the use of this example as an instance of an indicative sign.

in part of the account of the indicative sign and also in the allotment of the class of naturally non-evident things to this sign. Thus, on the whole, what we find in *PH* about the indicative sign is much closer to the report in *M* than to the one in the *Historia.*

In order to prove the non-Stoic character of what Pseudo-Galen tells us about signs, I have so far taken into consideration the indicative sign only. Yet its semantical sibling may also deserve some attention in this context. It should be obvious that the different accounts of the indicative sign found in Sextus, on the one hand, and in Pseudo-Galen, on the other, are bound to have consequences for the construal of the commemorative sign. If the significata of the indicative sign are restricted to the class of things naturally non-evident, then whenever a sign is related to a significatum open to perception at least in principle, this sign must be a commemorative sign, unless the disjunction indicative/commemorative is no longer exhaustive. So, when I infer from a sign some phenomenon which I never observed before—I may carry out for the first time a specific experiment and, from analogous cases, correctly infer its result—this is bound to be a commemorative sign. This, in turn, means that *using a commemorative sign is no longer connected to remembering the significatum.* Given the connotation of *hupomnēstikon* as well as 'commemorative', this seems to be a rather unwelcome consequence.

By the same token it should be clear that the distinction of occasionally and naturally non-evident things is of no use in the distinction of the two sorts of sign as defined in Pseudo-Galen's report. For chapter IX of the *Historia* restricts the significata of commemorative signs to phenomena whose (type-)occurrence has been observed before and which, therefore, can correctly be said to be remembered. The commemorative sign, according to the exposition in Pseudo-Galen, *essentially involves a use of our memory.* Consequently the significata of indicative signs as defined in the *Historia* include more than things naturally non-evident. Thus the absence of the distinction of occasionally and naturally non-evident things in Pseudo-Galen is not merely accidental but, for systematic reasons, this distinction cannot occupy a place in the *Historia* exposition. The *fundamentum divisionis* employed in Pseudo-Galen's source for the division of signs into commemorative and indicative ones is not the accessibility of things (*pragmata*) to mental or perceptual apprehension (*katalēpsis*).

From the observations just made we may derive a further conclusion. Since talk of a 'commemorative' sign is appropriate in cases where we actually remember the significatum of a sign and is rather misleading in other cases, we may conclude that the source used in Pseudo-Galen's exposition chronologically precedes the Stoic sources of Sextus' reports. For the use of a technical term in a literal sense may reasonably be supposed to precede the use of that term in a somewhat inappropriate way. Since, as I have argued above (cf. 95 f, 100 f), the (ultimate) source used in the M version is earlier than the one underlying *PH*, we may now rank our three versions of the theory of signs according to the age of their respective sources: *Historia, M, PH*.

Let us come back to the issue of the Stoic vs. non-Stoic character of the theory of signs as reported in the *Historia*. The material found in Sextus and the report by Pseudo-Galen agree in their definition of the sign and in the nomenclature of the two classes of sign. Yet closer scrutiny of the respective accounts of the indicative and the commemorative sign as well as of the example offered for the indicative sign has unearthed a fundamental incompatibility between the Sextonian and the Pseudo-Galenian versions respectively. This incompatibility is most conspicuous with respect to the undeniably Stoic ingredients in the reports offered by Sextus, that is, in the subdivisions of non-evident things and the use made of this classification in demarcating the two classes of signs from each other. In agreement with this we have noted the absence of any specifically Stoic terminology in chapter IX of the *Historia*.

Hence, I conclude that the theory of signs as reported by Pseudo-Galen is not of Stoic origin and, having thus established the minor premiss in my *modus tollendo ponens* argument, I further conclude that we are justified to crown the dialecticians in the *Historia* with a capital D. Since there is evidence to attribute a treatise *On Signs* to Philo, the Dialectician, and since the definition of sign as explained in Sextus, works with the Philonian interpretation of the conditional, I think it is fair to assume that the material found in Pseudo-Galen ultimately goes back to Philo *On Signs*.

VII

I am now in a position to put the pieces of this jigsaw puzzle together and shall try to tell a coherent story, where what is provable may to some degree be completed with what is probable.

Philo, it seems, is the first on the stage. He states the definition of sign that was to become canonical in the subsequent discussion, probably using his truth-functional propositional logic in explaining this definition. Although Philo was not the first to attribute a propositional character to signs—in this respect he was preceded by Aristotle (cf. *APr* II. 27. 70a6–7: *sēmeion de bouletai einai protasis ktl.*)—he seems to have been the first to make it a requirement of sign that a sign *reveals* some fact that is not evident. This feature is implied in the milk example as used in the *Menexenus* (237e) or else in Aristotle's *Rhetoric* (II. 2. 1357b14–16), but it is Philo who brings it into the open by making it part of the definition of sign. It is this move which promotes the notion of sign to its prominent place in epistemology.[45]

Moreover, Philo introduces a division distinguishing between two classes of signs. The first group includes those signs for the use of which you have to rely on your memory, the other one contains those signs for the use of which you have to rely on your reasoning faculty alone. This distinction is based on the *nature of the link* connecting sign and significatum: associative in the case of the commemorative, logical in the case of the indicative sign. Philo, after all, was a logician. Notice that according to this distinction it is by no means excluded that a sign may be a commemorative sign for one person and an indicative sign for another. The milk sign, Philo's example of an indicative sign, may be a commemorative sign for the midwife. Yet this only testifies to the soundness of this distinction. It may indeed depend on the background of information available to the user of a sign whether a sign is indicative or commemorative.

Next to appear is Zeno. I take it that the material reported in *M* (VIII. 141–55, 245–56) ultimately goes back to Zeno's treatise *On Signs*. In *M* VIII. 245–56, we see him labouring the new propositional logic he has learned from Philo. Being a bold Stoic and a poor logician,

---

[45] Notice that Aristotle, in his analysis of sign in *APr* II. 27, does not pay heed to this feature of sign; cf. 70a7–9: 'That which coexists with something else, or before or after whose happening something else has happened, is a sign of that something's having happened or being' (Tredennick's translation). Aristotle's use of the milk sign as a sign of pregnancy (70a13–14) seems to confirm this observation, for lactation occurs only in the last months of pregnancy. In the history of the use of this example, its use as a sign of a present state is rather an exception, perhaps due to a wish on the part of Aristotle to bring the milk example into line with his other two examples which are also signs of concomitant significata. Notice that there is one unknown factor in the history of the theory of signs between Aristotle and the Stoics, i.e. Theophrastus' treatise *peri Sēmeiōn* (cf. D.L.V. 45).

at least if we are to believe Cicero (cf. *de Finibus* (*de Fin*) IV. 9), he thinks he should replace the example of the *TT* case in Philo's truth table for the conditional by an example helpful to make a bit of propaganda for his Stoic Weltanschauung (cf. *M* VIII. 246), instead of sticking to an example that comes out trivially true on the occasion or in general.

Yet when Zeno attends Philo's logic lectures he is already in possession of his epistemological concept of apprehension (*katalēpsis*). He makes use of this concept to divide up the *terra incognita* of things non-evident (cf. *M* VIII. 145–50). Things excluded from apprehension altogether (VIII. 147, 149) go into the class of things altogether non-evident. Things excluded in principle from being perceived but not from being apprehended make up the class of things naturally non-evident (cf. *M* VIII. 146; cf. also *PH* II. 98). Finally, things excluded only occasionally from perception constitute the class of things occasionally non-evident (cf. *M* VIII. 145). Only members of the latter two classes can be revealed by a sign (cf. *M* VIII. 149–50). That much can easily be granted. Yet Zeno now intends to build the distinction between the indicative and the commemorative sign on this demarcation among things non-evident:

As, then, there are two distinct classes of things which require sign, sign also has revealed itself as twofold—the 'commemorative', which appears to be chiefly of use in the case of things occasionally non-evident, and the 'indicative' which is deemed proper for adoption in the case of things naturally non-evident.

(*M* VIII. 151)

To assess the merits or mistakes implied in this idea of Zeno's let us examine the alterations he is compelled to introduce into his Philonian material. To make the indicative sign fit his division of things non-evident, that is, to make it match the class of things naturally non-evident, he has to strengthen the Philonian requirement so as to *exclude the possibility* of the significatum's being observed together with its sign (VIII. 154). Although he sticks to Philo's terminology (cf. his talk of *sumparatērēsis M* VIII. 143, 152), the underlying idea has radically changed. Whereas Philo wants to classify signs according to the *nature of the relation* holding between sign and significatum, Zeno means to divide signs with respect to one of the *fundamenta relationis*, that is, the significatum. If we are justified to infer from the Dialectical example of the indicative sign—lactation as a sign of preceding parturition—that, on the Dialectical account, a phenomenon indicating some significatum is not allotted once and for all to one of the two classes of signs but, in certain cases, may count either as an indicative sign or as a commemorative sign (or even as no sign at all) depending on the background of a person's information, then we may say that the change in the *fundamentum divisionis* of the two sorts of signs which has been effected by the Stoics constitutes a momentous turn in the history of epistemology. For this change eliminates from the theory of signs the regard to the differences in background knowledge which may exist between different persons. There is at least evidence to the effect that Zeno's construal of the indicative sign is meant to exclude the possibility of something's being an indicative sign for one person and no sign for another.[46] For he adds to his account of the indicative sign the requirement that

entirely from its own nature and construction, all but uttering its voice aloud, it is said to signify that whereof it is indicative.

(*M* VIII. 154)

A sign uttering its voice aloud will speak to everyone. It is not possible for such a sign to be heard by one person and not by another.[47]

Philo's example of an indicative sign—lactation indicating child-birth—is no longer of any use as an illustration of this type of sign as understood by Zeno. So it is replaced by the bodily motions indicating the soul which is, as Zeno takes care to point out, 'one of the things naturally non-evident' (*M* VIII. 155). Yet even more telling is the alteration we find applied to the milk sign itself when it turns up in the material preserved in Sextus. It is not used in *M* VIII. 141–55, but it comes up in the other 'Zenonian' passage (*M* VIII.245–56), and in this (*M* VIII. 252) as well as in its other two occurrences in Sextus (i.e. *M* VIII. 423; *PH* II. 106) the predicate in the consequent invariably is *kekuēken*, 'she has conceived'. Conception has replaced parturition, an event naturally non-evident has been put in for an observable event.

---

[46] As a bodily symptom may be a sign for the physician and no sign for a medical layman, cf. S.E., *M* VIII. 204.

[47] The vivid metaphor meant to underscore this feature of the indicative sign smacks very much of the man who used to illustrate his concept of apprehension by using his hand and fingers (cf. Cicero, *Acad.* II. 145). Notice also that Zeno seems to have used *kataskeuē* as a technical term in his account of duty (*kathēkon*, cf. D.L. VII. 108). For the coupling of the two terms *phusis* and *kataskeuē* see *SVF* III frs. 366 and 368.

Thus altered the example now fits the Stoic account of an indicative sign.[48]

I have started my discussion of the Stoic material with what Zeno has to say about the indicative sign since here the contrast to the Dialectical material is most conspicuous and, hence, also most helpful to evaluate the changes introduced by Zeno. Notice that, as a consequence of his restricting the indicative signs to signs connected to naturally non-evident significata, Zeno is confronted with a dilemma. If he wants his classification of signs to be exhaustive, he is forced to enlarge the class of commemorative signs so as to include all signs with significata that are open to perception in principle, even if (a type-occurrence of) the significatum has never been perceived before. Philo's example of an indicative sign (lactation indicating childbirth) on this account would be a commemorative sign even to any medical layman/laywoman. If, however, he intends to include in his class of commemorative signs those signs only which presuppose previous perception of analogous cases, then his classification is no longer exhaustive. Philo's example of an indicative sign would no longer have a proper place in one of Zeno's two classes of signs.

It is not really clear for which horn of the dilemma Zeno wants to opt. He uses the defining formula stated in the *Historia* (*sumparatērēthen tōi sēmeiōtōi*, M VIII. 152; cf. Diels, *Doxogr. Gr.* 605, 12–13), but he drops the *hoper* which, in Pseudo-Galen, precedes this formula. Thus one might be inclined to think that he means to turn the *definiens* of the *Historia* account into a description of what seems to be the most prominent case of a commemorative sign on this explanation. Yet he explicitly claims that his two subsequent examples of a commemorative sign—the scar indicating a previous wound, the puncture of the heart foretelling death—can be dealt with on the same account (VIII. 153), whatever that may mean in the second case.[49] This seems to indicate that he sticks to Philo's definition of a commemorative sign. That,

---

[48] It is noticeable that the use of the milk sign as a sign of *conception* seems to be restricted to the passages in Sextus. Whenever the milk sign occurs in later authors its significatum is childbirth. See, e.g., Philoponus, *In Aristotelis Analytica Priora commentaria*, ed M. Wallies (Berlin, 1905), 35 l 23; *In Aristotelis Analytica Posteriora commentaria*, ed M. Wallies (Berlin, 1909), 21 l 12.

[49] Zeno, in replacing *gnōsis* by *hupomnēsis* and in talking of 'recalling' (cf. *ananeoumetha*, VIII. 152, 153) makes his account suffer from the type-token ambiguity. We do not, on seeing smoke, *recollect* the unseen fire for we have never seen this (token-occurrence of) fire before. We recollect that on previous occasions we always saw smoke produced by fire and from this we *infer* that the smoke we now see must also be generated from fire.

in turn, amounts to saying that his classification is not exhaustive after all.

We need not decide this issue in a definite way. Seeing the dilemma resulting from Zeno's change in the definition of the indicative sign should be sufficient to make us realize that Zeno's attempt to classify signs according to the epistemological status of the significata is no improvement over what I have argued to be Philo's theory of signs. When Cicero tells us (cf. *de Fin.* IV. 9) that Zeno's work in logic partly was no improvement over that of his predecessors, here, I take it, we have come across a case in point.

What about the *PH* version of the theory of signs? The part of my story relating to this material will not be quite as straightforward as the story about Zeno in *M*. We have seen that the material in *PH* is later than the source used in *M* and that it is also superior to *M*. Its Stoic credentials are beyond doubt, and we have found reason to attribute it to the early Stoics. I suspect that the Stoic logician used in this passage by Sextus or by his source is either Cleanthes or his pupil Sphaerus. Both have written on topics of logic (cf. D.L. VII. 175 and 178 respectively), although there is no extant evidence that either of them has written a treatise *On Signs*. Cleanthes, we are told, joined the discussion about Diodorus' master argument (cf. Epictetus II. 2 and 9). If he did so, he must have been one of the leading logicians of his time. So he may well qualify as a candidate for the source exploited in *PH*.[50]

Let us examine as to how the author of this source (Cleanthes or Sphaerus) deals with the classification of signs into indicative and commemorative ones, since on this issue we find Zeno departing from Philo. As in *M*, the classification of signs is preceded by the division of things into evident and non-evident ones and the further sub-division of the latter class. *PH* agrees with *M* also in establishing a connection between the class of things occasionally non-evident and the commemorative sign on the one hand, between the class of naturally non-evident things and the indicative sign on the other (cf. *PH* II. 99).

The definition of the commemorative sign (*PH* II. 100) uses *verbatim* the formula from *M* VIII. 152 together with the example of smoke and fire, omitting *M*'s comments on this example. That our

---

[50] M. Frede (above n 11, 23) argues that Cleanthes deserves a better treatment as a logician in comparison to Zeno than he is usually accorded.

author is indeed working from Zeno's *On Signs* (the source used in *M*) is confirmed by his definition of the indicative sign as stated at *PH* II. 101: it retains Zeno's formulation (cf. *M* VIII. 154) that the indicative sign signifies that of which it is a sign 'from its own nature and construction'; it also brings in M's example of an indicative sign, that is, bodily movements indicating the soul, again omitting *M*'s comments on this example.

Yet our author diverges from *M*'s, that is Zeno's account of the indicative sign in an important respect. The indicative sign is no longer said to be that sign which *does not admit of being observed together* with its significatum, due to the non-observability of the latter (cf. *M* VIII. 154), but the sign which *has not been observed together* with its significatum. Hence, the author of the definition of the indicative sign at *PH* II. 101 retracts the change introduced into the Philonian account by Zeno. We are back to the Dialecticians.

The advantage of this move is obvious: the definitions of the two types of sign now again yield an exhaustive classification of signs—notice the parallel construction: *ho sumparatērethen tōi sēmeiōtōi* (comm.), *ho mē sumparatērethen tōi sēmeiōtōi* (indic.). However, the price which our author has to pay for thus mending Zeno's classification seems to be rather high. For we are now left with two accounts of the distinction indicative/commemorative sign: the one at *PH* II. 100–1 and the preceding one at *PH* II. 99 which is based on the division of things naturally and occasionally non-evident. Either of these two accounts yields an exhaustive classification of signs, but they do not tie in with each other. Take Philo's example of the indicative sign—lactation indicating precedent childbirth. This would be a commemorative sign on the basis of the account at *PH* II. 99, for the significatum is not one of the things naturally non-evident. On the basis of the account at *PH* II. 100–1, this would be an indicative sign for any person that never witnessed parturition, since in that case the sign and its significatum cannot have been observed together at any earlier time.

One might argue that the material used by Sextus in *PH* II. 97–9, on the one hand, and the material used in *PH* II. 100–1, on the other, come from different Stoic sources. Sextus' text at *PH* II. 97–101 does not seem to reflect a continuous argument as does the parallel passage in *M* VIII. 245–53. Yet the Stoic author responsible for the definitions preserved at *PH* II. 100–1 must still have worked from the material used in *M* (i.e. from Zeno's account) and, hence, would have deliberately ignored the use of the distinction of things naturally and things occasionally non-evident in his predecessor. So this suggestion does not look satisfactory either. Thus, we had better stick to the idea of a single Stoic source underlying the material in P*PH* II. 97–101, and we may say that Cleanthes(?) here has mended the mess left by his master as best he could.[51]

Chrysippus is the last on the stage. He is a brilliant logician and a loyal Stoic. As a loyal Stoic, he directs his fire not against his Stoic predecessors, but against Philo, choosing Philo's *On Signs* as the target of attack. As a logician, he may have swiftly discovered the many shortcomings of the theory of signs: first of all, he may have realized that treating signs as antecedent propositions in certain conditionals amounts to confusing implicational and inferential consequence.[52] Secondly, even if this mistake is corrected and signs are allowed the status of a premiss in an argument, they are still taken to the propositions, although asserted ones. Yet construing a sign as a proposition again amounts to confusing a functional aspect of an object or an event with what can be truly said about this object or this event. Furthermore, even if we were at all justified in treating signs as well as significata as propositions, this would exclude a large number of cases from being counted as signs, that is, all signs telling us what to do instead of informing us about what is the case. A military signal or the red traffic light do not reveal some hidden fact but are rather like commands. The interest Chrysippus takes in sentences of a non-propositional character (cf. D.L. VII. 191) may lend some probability to the idea that he has seen this affinity between commands or imperatives and a class of signs.

Yet with this we come close to the realm of speculation. We do not know what arguments Chrysippus may have used against Philo. Nor do we know whether he intended to replace the theory of signs of his Dialectical and Stoic predecessors with an improved theory of his own.

---

[51] One thing, however, should be obvious: the suspicion raised by several authors (for references see above n 15) that Sextus introduces the distinction commemorative/indicative (sign) into Stoic material which is free from it, seems to be unfounded. Yet by now it should also be clear how this impression could arise: because the Stoics themselves tried to bring a distinction which originally was not theirs into line with their own epistemology. This may also help to explain why the subsequent medical literature, as pointed out by Glidden (above n 1, 229), does not base this distinction on that of different kinds of things non-evident. The doctors got it directly from the Dialecticians.

[52] It is worth noting that the Stoics in Philodemus' *de Signis* seem to use 'Since *p*, *q*' as the canonic formula of a sign inference, a formula for which Crinis (cf. D.L. VII. 71) has offered the analysis that it is true iff (1) 'if *p*, *q*' and (2) '*p*' are both true. On this point cf. Burnyeat, above n 1, 218 with n 60 on Crinis.

As for Chrysippus, we eventually have to concede: *ignoramus et ignorabimus.*[53]

Universität Erlangen

[53] This essay corresponds to part of a forthcoming monograph on 'Dialektiker und frühe Stoiker bei Sextus Empiricus'. A first version of this paper was read in March 1985 to an audience at Princeton University, and a German version at the Universität Würzburg in January 1986. I have profited from discussions on both occasions. I am grateful to Julia Annas and Jacques Brunschwig for useful suggestions on the first version. Special thanks go to David Sedley and Myles Burnyeat for their written comments which proved most helpful in rewriting this essay. Finally, I gratefully acknowledge the help of Ann Grösch in eradicating mistakes and inelegancies from my English.

EPICURUS ON FRIENDSHIP AND ALTRUISM*[1]

P. MITSIS

I

DISCUSSIONS of altruistic friendship figure prominently in Epicurean ethical theory. At first glance, this is rather surprising. Given the strength of Epicurus' commitments to hedonism and egoism, we might expect the Epicurean to be a kind of Hobbesian egoist. Lucretius, for instance, adopts a harsh, almost neurotically bitter view of man's social condition. The world of *de Rerum Natura* V is populated by solitary and brutish individuals who, acting from purely selfish motives, inevitably collide and inflict mutual harm. Under the best of circumstances, it can be hoped that agents, schooled by their suffering, will grudgingly restrain their immediate appetites and realize the advantages of avoiding a self-destructive competition for goods and power. Indeed, it is only when individual interests have reached such an equilibrium that any semblance of stability or civil life can emerge. Thus, one readily understands why it might be in the interest of rational agents to agree to a kind of wary co-operation; but it is extremely difficult to see why anyone in such a setting should be altruistic and care for others apart from their merely instrumental value.

Epicurus' ethical theory commonly is taken to be narrowly egoistic[2]

---

* © P. Mitsis 1987
[1] Earlier versions of this paper were presented in a seminar at Harvard and at the annual meeting of the American Philological Association in San Francisco. I am grateful for the friendly criticism and advice I received on both occasions. I would like to thank David Glidden, Gordon Kirkwood, Matt Neuburg, Daphne O'Regan, Piero Pucci, and Chris Shields for their many valuable comments on earlier drafts. Also, I am very greatly indebted to Elizabeth Asmis, Terry Irwin, David Konstan, John Rist, Jennifer Whiting, and, most recently, Julia Annas and Tony Long for extremely helpful and detailed criticism of my overall argument.
[2] A common verdict of the doxography (and most modern scholarship) is voiced by Lactantius: 'dicit Epicurus neminem esse qui alterum diligat nisi sua causa' (*Institutiones Divinae* (*Inst.*) III. 17. 42).

and many of his maxims on friendship reveal a correspondingly prudent and careful attention to self-interest. His emphasis on the security and utility afforded by friends, his continual effort to link friendship and pleasure, his description of friendship as a means to relieve anxiety—all give strong indications of a somewhat timid, but none the less inflexible egoism. Clearly, if personal pleasure is the ultimate goal of the Epicurean's actions, his hedonic calculations can include others only as a means to his own selfish gratification. Altruistic friendship requires, at the very least, an interest in others for their own sake.[3] Thus, given its general structure and principles, Epicurus' ethical theory would seem unable to allow for the kinds of motivation and concern for others' interests we are inclined to think necessary for altruistic friendship.

It would be reasonable to suppose that, within such an ethical framework, Epicurus might endorse what Aristotle calls friendships of advantage or pleasure. Moreover, it is quite easy to imagine him, with characteristic vehemence and disdain, deriding altruistic friendship either as a misguided illusion or the result of hedonic miscalculations. Yet rather unexpectedly, he commends altruistic friendship so zealously that at times he seems to be almost a kind of pagan high priest of *agapē*.[4] In Diogenes Laertius, for example, we find that the Epicurean wise man sometimes will die for a friend, 'καὶ ὑπὲρ φίλου ποτὲ τεθνήξεσθαι' (D.L. X. 121b). Elsewhere, it is reported that the *sapiens* will endure the greatest pains for his friends, 'ὑπὲρ τῶν φίλων τάς μεγίστας ἀλγηδόνας ἀναδέχεσθαι' (Plutarch, *Adversus Colotem* VIII. 1111b). Initially, it is tempting to explain away these passages as merely apparent cases of altruism. After all, Epicurus parts company with egoists such as Hobbes who, when reckoning with death, rank self-preservation even above pleasure as the ultimate goal of conduct. For Epicurus, death is nothing to us; nor should it be of concern to us since it in no way is able to affect our pleasures (*Kuriai Doxai* (*K.D.*) 19). Therefore, on such a view, dying might easily be preferable to the anxious, vulnerable, and hence painful life one might face without friends. Instead of being the ultimate sign of altruism, sacrificing

---

[3] '. . . aut quis (potest) amicus esse cuiquam quem non ipsum amet propter ipsum?', Cicero, *de Finibus* (*de Fin.*) II. 78; cf. Aristotle *Rhetorica* 1380b36ff, *Nicomachean Ethics* (*EN*) 1156b7 ff, 1156b31 and the classic discussion of Gregory Vlastos, 'The Individual as an Object of Love in Plato', in *Platonic Studies* (Princeton, 1973), 3 ff.

[4] Cf. Norman De Witt, *Epicurus and his Philiosophy* (Minneapolis, 1954), 31 ff for the rather odd notion of altruistic hedonism and a view of Epicureanism as a kind of *praeparatio evangelica*.

oneself for a friend might be an acceptable egoistic strategy for avoiding pain.[5] Similarly, although he has more reason to fear pain than death, the Epicurean can expect to enhance his prospects for *asphaleia* and its consequent pleasures by enduring even very great pains for the sake of friendship.

Other evidence, however, resists translation into an egoistic calculus. At *de Finibus* I. 68, we find the requirement that a wise man feel exactly the same towards his friends as he does towards himself.[6] At *Gnomologium Vaticanum* 23, Epicurus insists that all friendship is choiceworthy for itself, '*πᾶσα φιλία δι᾽ ἑαυτὴν αἱρετή*', apart from its instrumental benefits.[7] These passages strongly suggest an unselfish

---

[5] Epicurus grants, for example, that the *sapiens* should commit suicide if his overall prospects for pain outweigh his prospects for pleasure. Given the Epicurean view of death, an egoistic justification of self-sacrifice might be possible along the lines I have suggested. But it is important to note that Epicurus himself nowhere formulates such a defence; nor does the Epicurean, Torquatus, who thinks that dying for a friend is the clearest indication of genuine altruism. At the beginning of his exposition of Epicurean friendship (*de Fin.* I. 65), Torquatus likens Epicurus to mythical figures willing to die for their friends. Similarly, Cicero contrasts this type of 'Pyladic friendship' (cf. *Laelius* (*Lael.* 24) with ordinary friendship (*de Fin.* II. 80). The evidence is too scanty to determine whether Epicurus thinks that dying for a friend ever can be consistent with egoism. But Cicero suggests that Epicureans are defending Pyladic friendships (II. 84) which are not justifiable only on the basis of self-interest. Thus, although dying for a friend can perhaps be given an egoistic justification by bringing together various elements in Epicurus' thought, we should be wary of artificially removing altruistic elements from Diogenes Laertius (D.L.) X. 121b.

[6] 'Quocirca eodem modo sapiens erit affectus erga amicum quo in se ipsum, quosque labores propter suam volumptatem susciperet eosdem suscipiet propter amici voluptatem.' Cf. *Gnomologum Vaticanum* (*S.V.*) 56.

[7] Cf. *K.D.* 27, *de Fin.* I. 65, II. 83. *S.V.* 23 is a brief but fundamental text: '*πᾶσα φιλία δι᾽ ἑαυτὴν αἱρετή· ἀρχὴν εἴληφεν ἀπὸ τῆς ὠφελείας.*' *αἱρετή* is Usener's correction; Jean Bollack ('Les maximes de l'amitié', in *Actes du Congrès G. Budé 1968* (Paris, 1969), 221 ff) retains the manuscript reading, *ἀρετή*. Rist (*Epicurus: An Introduction* (Cambridge, 1972), 131) finds it strange to speak of friendship as an *aretē* (but cf. Aristotle, *EN* 1155a2). The real difficulty for Bollack's view is that it is hard to see what it means for friendship to be a virtue *di' heautēn*. Rist, reading *hairetē*, tries to soften the contradiction by drawing a parallel to Stoic usage and suggesting that '*hairetē*' is equivalent to the Stoic '*proegmenon*': 'When Epicurus says that friendship is to be chosen for itself, perhaps he merely means not that it is ultimately valuable, but that it leads directly and without intermediaries to the acquistion of pleasure' (132); cf. also Reimar Müller, *Die Epicureische Gesellschaftstheorie* (Berlin, 1972), 118 ff. This is an interesting suggestion given the Stoics' and Epicureans' many mutual borrowings of terminology. However, it is unclear on Rist's view why the virtues (especially prudence) would not be *hairetai* as well, since they lead directly (and with even fewer intermediaries) to the acquisition of pleasure; cf. *Epistola ad Menoeceum* (*Ad Men.*) 132 and A. W. H. Adkins, *From the Many to the One* (Ithaca, 1970), 259. Rist's suggestion further neglects how in this particular context we can attribute an instrumental sense to *di' heautēn*, since it clearly is being contrasted with *apo tēs ōpheleias*. For an opposing view,

picture of friendship and seem to enjoin the positive, altruistic concern
for others' interests rejected by the Hobbesian. Surely though, any
recommendation of unselfish friendship sharply conflicts with Epicurus'
much repeated claim that only one's own pleasure is the *telos* of action
and desirable for itself. Herein, then, lies the dilemma of Epicurean
friendship.

Unhappy with these inconsistencies, scholars have attempted to
explain the divergent elements in Epicurus' account of *philia* by means of
either associationist or Hobbesian arguments. Associationism acknowledges the possibility of altruism, but attempts, none the less, to set
altruistic action on a firmly egoistic foundation. Like Mill's miser, who
begins by valuing money for its use, then comes to regard it as an end
in itself, individuals initially form friendships for mutual advantage, but
in time come to value friends for their own sake, regardless of any
instrumental benefit. Altruism, on this view, is entrusted by Epicurus
to the effortless custody of habit; it is aroused by degrees and it results
unreflectively, and somewhat mechanically, from habit and continual
association. In contrast, on the Hobbesian construal of Epicurus'
theory, altruism merely is disguised egoism, an unintended result of
hedonic miscalculation, or, perhaps, just simply irrational. If it is
reasonable only to pursue pleasure, and pleasure necessarily is an
egoistic state, all actions, no matter how seemingly altruistic, are either
self-regarding or irrational. Therefore, if Epicurus recommends
friendship, it is argued, it must be as an egoistic ploy for maximizing
personal pleasure.

Curiously, these recent characterizations of Epicurus' theory bear a
striking correspondence, at least according to Cicero, not to Epicurus'
own doctrine, but to theories formulated by his *diadochoi*. At *de Finibus*
I. 65 ff, Torquatus outlines three distinct theories of friendship held
by Epicureans.[8] He briefly discusses associationism (I. 69) and
friendships based on self-seeking, Hobbesian contracts (I. 70).

---

cf. Long's recent defence of the manuscript reading ('Pleasure and Social Utility—The
Virtues of Being Epicurean', in *Aspects de la philosophie hellénistique*, *Ent. Fond. Hardt* 32
(Vand.-Geneve, 1986), 305). Elsewhere, in the handful of surviving occurrences of
'*hairetos*' and '*hairesis*', Epicurus, unlike the Stoics and Aristotle, is quite fastidious
about its non-instrumental sense (cf. *ad Men.* 129, *S.V.*16).

[8] A fourth, discussed at *de Fin*. II. 80 ff, suggests that Epicurus is a strict egoist in
theory, but a disinterested friend in practice ('facere melius quam dicere'). This view
grows out of the testimony for Epicurus' lofty practice of friendship and the belief that he
is committed to a strictly egoistic theory. I argue that there is also within Epicurus'
theoretical framework a commitment to altruism, thereby removing the asymmetry
between his theory and his practice of friendship.

Arguing that these were later developments in Epicureanism, not attributable to Epicurus himself[9], he presses another view of friendship (I. 66 ff) which he takes to be Epicurus' own. From Torquatus we learn that Epicurus requires the wise man to love (I. 67) and feel towards (I. 68) his friends exactly as he loves and feels towards himself. Thus, Torquatus' description of these altruistic elements in Epicurean friendship appears to fit coherently with Epicurus' own contention that friendship is choiceworthy in itself, *di' heautēn hairetē* (*S.V.* 23), since by showing disinterested concern for friends, one treats friendship as a non-instrumental end. Taken together, these passages suggest a set of requirements consonant with the demands of altruistic friendship. Even though Cicero clearly is at great pains to emphasize the essential links that Epicurus sees between friendship and pleasure (I. 68), it is difficult to ascribe to Epicurus a consistent Hobbesian egoism, since the Hobbesian cannot advocate that anyone, let alone a wise man, regard a friend as another self. Cicero's testimony, in conjunction with *S.V.* 23, should give us some grounds, then, for questioning recent attributions or either associationist or strictly self-seeking friendship to Epicurus. Moreover, the *de Finibus* provides an extremely plausible theoretical and historical backdrop against which to examine and articulate Epicurus' own sometimes disconnected pronouncements.

An answer to the questions raised by friendship and altruism is important for the general interpretation of Epicurus' ethics. Efforts at minimizing the conflicts in his discussion of friendship have been motivated partly, no doubt, by a desire to preserve the 'elegant simplicity'[10] of his ethics and of his modes of ethical enquiry.[11] By

[9] '. . . numquam dictum ab ipso illo' (*de Fin.* II. 82).

[10] A. A. Long, *Hellenistic Philosophy* (London, 1974), 72.

[11] Since the time of Guyau, Epicurus' ethical theory and methods of ethics have been equated with hedonist theories in the British empiricist tradition. Even Epicurus' most sympathetic critics have viewed him as a proto-Benthamite, methodically applying his felicific calculus to all human action. Although these critics mean to differentiate Epicurus' doctrine from less refined sorts of hedonism, they regularly attribute to him a mode of ethical enquiry which is insensitive to common beliefs; they argue that Epicurus rather obsessively attempts to reduce all conduct to fit his hedonist theory by riding roughshod over many central ethical beliefs and intuitions. In this view, Epicurus' hedonism is consistent, but it buys consistency at too high a price: it neglects a large body of evidence and therefore, must necessarily fail to capture many important intuitions about morality. Such a view, however, may need modification. At least in his account of friendship, Epicurus seems quite willing to concede the common belief that friendship requires valuing others for their own sake, even though this creates difficulties for his hedonism. This concession to ordinary beliefs and intuitions may force him into inconsistencies, but it shows that he has at least some sensitivity and respect for the *endoxa*.

taking these inconsistencies seriously, however, we can ascribe to Epicurus a considerably more complex, though perhaps less tidy, theory of altruism and of motivation in general.

In many respects, Epicurus' predicament over the relation of pleasure and altruism closely resembles Mill's well-known difficulties in formulating his principle of utility. In attempting to modify the hedonist doctrines of his contemporaries, Mill criticizes orthodox Benthamites for having an excessively narrow conception of human nature and motivation. Accordingly, he complains that missing from Bentham's 'Table of the Springs of Action' are other pursuits and ideal ends which are valuable for their own sakes. These include the desire for self-perfection and for virtue; the love of beauty, of order, and of action; and even the 'love of loving' ('Bentham' in *Dissertations and Discussions*). In Chapter 4 of *Utilitarianism*, Mill further explains:

> The principle of utility does not mean that any given pleasure, as music, for instance, or any given exemption from pain, as for example health, is to be looked upon as means to a collective something termed happiness, and to be desired on that account. They are desired and desirable in and for themselves; besides being means, they are a part of the end.

In order to give a broader and more plausible conception of happiness than Bentham, Mill feels constrained to countenance intrinsic ends and sources of value other than pleasure. Strictly speaking, though, this conflicts with the demands of his hedonism by admitting into his theory, as Sidgwick notes, 'non-hedonistic grounds of preference'.[12]

Epicurus' thoughts on friendship are the expression of an ethical impulse and a philosophical motivation akin to Mill's. In asserting that friendship is *di' heautēn hairetē*, Epicurus recognizes a value and an end other than pleasure. However reluctant, this acknowledgement is not just a casual or momentary lapse into benevolence; nor is it merely an isolated feature of his ethical thinking which should be explained away in light of his other views. In Epicureanism, rarely is there smoke without fire. By attending carefully to the conflicting signals in his theory of friendship, we can isolate something of the specific manner in which ethical questions presented themselves to Epicurus and, indeed, to other Hellenistic moral philosophers. Moreover, by examining the nexus of issues which includes altruism and friendship, we can bring into sharper relief Epicurus' most characteristic ethical aims and goals, not all of which are smoothly compatible.

[12] Henry Sidgwick, *The Methods of Ethics*, 5th edn (London, 1893), 95, 148.

II

At this point, it will be helpful to examine the two accounts of friendship developed by Epicurus' *diadochoi*. Each isolates and further elaborates an important strand of Epicurus' thought on altruism, but not without violating other central features of his theory. One group, whose views Torquatus finds a bit faint-hearted, maintains that an awareness of the intrinsic value of friendship may blossom (*efflorescere*, I. 69) from an initial pre-occupation with one's own interest.[13] A proponent of this type of associationist theory might appeal to psychological or to historical criteria to explain the possibility and the origins of altruism. Torquatus' discussion lends itself more readily to psychological interpretation, but scholars have found for the theory the requisite historical framework as well. In Lucretius' discussion of the formation of mankind's first communities, there occurs a passage which, on some accounts, gives historical justification for the Epicurean's pursuit of friendship:

tunc et amicitiem coeperunt iungere aventes
finitimi inter se nec laedere nec violari,
et pueros commendarunt muliebreque saeclum,
vocibus et gestu cum balbe significarent
imbecillorum esse aequum misererier omnis.
nec tamen omnimodis poterant concordia gigni,
sed bona magnaque pars servabat foedera caste;
aut genus humanum iam tum foret omne peremptum
nec potuisset adhuc perducere saecla propago.

(de Rerum Natura (RN) V. 1019–27)

Farrington, for example, finds in this passage a historical warrant for the Epicureans' rejection of civil society and their espousal of simple communities based on friendship. On his view, friendship is an

---

[13] '. . . cum autem usus progrediens familiaritatem effecerit, tum amorem efflorescere tantum ut, etiamsi nulla sit utilitas ex amicitia, tamen ipsi amici propter se ipsos amentur' (*de Fin*. I. 69). J. M. Guyau, *La Morale d'Épicure* (Paris, 1886), 136 ff has been the most influential proponent of this view (reluctantly and inconsistently followed by C. B. Bailey, *The Greek Atomists and Epicurus* (Oxford, 1928), 520). In 'Vita Prior in Lucretius', *Hermathena*, LXXXI (1953), 59–62 and 'Lucretius and Manilius on Friendship', *Hermathena*, LXXXIII (1954), 10–16, Benjamin Farrington describes the historical genesis of altruism; Hermann Usener, *Kleine Schriften* (Leipzig, 1912), 234 ff and David Konstan, *Some Aspects of Epicurean Psychology* (Leiden, 1973), 42 ff describe the psychology of forming altruistic attachments.

attempt to recapture a golden age of innocent reciprocities prior to the evils of civil society. Unfortunately, although this passage has been the source of many fertile misunderstandings, it provides evidence for neither the history nor the anthropology of friendship.[14] Clearly, Lucretius is only describing the foundation of justice, the basis of which is a contract for avoiding mutual harm (*nec laedere nec violari*, *K.D.* 31–3). To the extent that these primitive *foedera* (V. 1025) only guarantee mutual non-interference, they do not reflect the mature vision of friendship practiced by the sage.[15] Nevertheless, even though surviving Epicurean texts furnish no clear historical justification of friendship, it is easy to see how such a defence might be formulated on the basis of associationism.

In a similar fashion, the associationist can invoke psychological criteria to explain the growth of altruistic attachments. To a certain extent, these later Epicureans anticipate a kind of Freudian mechanics of desire which takes as its initial premiss the psychological and rational priority of egoism. Initially, individuals are endowed with feelings of narcissistic self-love; but as self-love becomes differentiated and more limited, they form external attachments to others.[16] They may come to love friends even without expecting any personal

---

[14] Lucretius' use of 'amicitia' at *RN* V. 1019 has been the source of considerable misunderstanding. Konstan, above n 13, 43 correctly claims that in this context 'amicities' cannot mean friendship (*pace* Rist, 'Epicurus on Friendship', *Classical Philology*, LXXV (1980), 123). Relying on Lilly Ross Taylor and Syme, he argues that 'amicities' refers to political alliances, as it regularly does in the literature of the Republic. Such linguistic considerations alone, however, cannot support his position, since 'amicitia' covers a wider range of relationships (cf. P. A. Brunt, 'Amicitia in the Late Roman Republic', in R. Seager (ed), *The Crisis of the Roman Republic* (Cambridge, 1969).

[15] Long (above n 7, 310) argues that Lucretius is describing the imagined origins of friendships at *RN* 1019. I find at least four serious difficulties for his account: (*a*) Even at this stage, the content of these 'friendships' would be exceptionally impoverished. It seems highly implausible to suggest that friendship ever consists in nothing more than friends leaving each other alone (*nec laedere nec violari*). (*b*) The expression *nec laedere nec violari* clearly translates the Epicurean formula for justice *mē blaptein mē blaptesthai* (*K.D.* 33) and uses terminology familiar from Roman legal texts and inscriptions. (*c*) The appeal to a prior standard of fairness (*aequum*) in 1023 has no place in Epicurean discussions of friendship, nor does *concordia* (1024) with its implications of widespread societal harmony. (*d*) The process by which these relations are formed is neither strictly rational (thus the appeal to sentiment and pity in 1023) nor are its results (*nec potuisset adhuc perducere saecla propago*) included among the usual aims of Epicurean friendship.

[16] Aristotle's account at *EN* 1166a1–2 can be fruitfully compared (cf. Charles Kahn, 'Altruism in Aristotle', *Mind*, LXXXIX (1981), 20 ff). Cf. Thomas Nagel, *The Possibility of Altruism* (Oxford, 1970), 19 ff on the general problem of normative inferences from facts about our psychologies.

pleasure.[17] Unfortunately, evidence for the actual mechanism of this process is not forthcoming in surviving Epicurean texts and the *vox Ciceroniana*, '*efflorescere*', is too vague to allow any very precise formulations. But associationism is a plausible move for these later Epicureans to make in defending the possibility of friendships which are *di' heautas hairetai*. Given the Epicurean emphasis on self-evident truths based on perception, a defence of altruism grounded in empirically verifiable psychological facts is not surprising. By a somewhat similar move, Epicurus, in maintaining the self-evident truth of hedonism, merely notes some facts about our psychologies which he takes to be readily apparent to perception. Thus, an unkind critic might suggest that these later Epicureans are merely indulging a similar dogmatic impulse.

Yet despite the rational status of his first principles, Epicurus is quite clear about particular desires, like altruism, and their justification. These later Epicureans neglect their master's continual warnings that all particular first-order desires and impulses must be evaluated carefully and prudently. The important question for Epicurus' ethics is neither the causal origin of a desire nor its empirical description as arising from association. On the contrary, he is concerned with the proper evaluation of each desire and its place in one's life. During the course of our psychological development we may acquire desires to benefit our friends at the expense of our own self-interest, or perhaps such desires grow and become more firmly rooted in each successive generation. We may, moreover, have good empirical evidence that altruistic sentiment has its origins in imitation, habit, learned psychic dispositions, institutions, etc. The central question for Epicurus, though, is whether it makes good hedonic sense to satisfy a desire (*S.V.* 71). Altruistic desires might be necessary, like desires for food, shelter, etc., or merely unnecessary and liable to interfere with one's peace of mind and tranquillity. If, as in the case of ambition of avarice, altruism is unnecessary and harmful, the *sapiens* should eliminate it from his life in accordance with the dictates of the hedonist calculus. Even if indulging in altruism were a psychological necessity, the *sapiens* would

---

[17] *Pace* Rist, above n 14, 124, who argues that in this passage 'utilitas' means 'particular advantages' but not 'pleasure'. For Rist the associationists sever friendship from advantage (I. 69), but not from pleasure. Cicero, however, mirroring Epicurus, moves freely between 'voluptas' and 'utilitas' in his discussion of self-interested action (cf. I. 33–4, and Reid, ad loc.); and it seems clear enough that, for these Epicureans, friends must be willing to value others apart from any hedonic benefit ('etiam omissa spe voluptatis', II. 82).

want to reduce his concern for others to a minimum, if such concern diminishes his *eudaimonia*. Therefore, if an Epicurean wants to justify the pursuit of friendship, he is constrained to show how it can contribute to an agent's overall interest.[18] This demand precludes some standard defences of altruism based either on sentiment or on an agent's present aims and goals[19]; but it is hard to see how these later Epicureans might otherwise hope to justify their theory.

Two further difficulties naturally arise in this context and Cicero quickly notices them. First, he registers the Kantian complaint that sentiment provides too idiosyncratic and contingent a basis for altruism. He argues that an Epicurean's altruistic feelings might soon fade in a friendship devoid of advantage. Possibly, later Epicureans thought that altruistic emotions are able to be distinguished from more contingent and transitory emotions such as passionate love. Thus, they might have hoped that altruistic emotions, by being ingrained and habituated through association, could become stable enough to provide a foundation for more steady attachments.[20] Such a development would be intriguing and important in Epicurean thinking about the passions; but it clearly would be a deviation from Epicurus' own conception.

Second, it is possible to dispute the associationists' description of the growth of altruistic desires. Cicero argues that, rather than merely being the result of habit, altruism requires the prior recognition of non-hedonic value. For this reason, the associationist misconstrues both the psychology and the mechanisms of altruistic friendship, since from a desire for pleasure and advantage only expedient friendships will arise (II. 82). It is not that one comes to associate altruism and pleasure by experiencing the pleasures of altruism. Nor can we explain the value of friendship merely in terms of the feelings associated with it. Rather, as Aristotle and the Stoics argue, one will find altruism

---

[18] πρὸς πάσας τὰς ἐπιθυμίας προσακτέον τὸ ἐπερώτημα τοῦτο· τί μοι γενήσεται ἂν τελεσθῇ τὸ κατὰ τὴν ἐπιθυμίαν ἐπιζητούμενον, καὶ τί ἐὰν μὴ τελεσθῇ; (*S.V.* 71); cf. *S.V.* 46; *ad Men.* 132a, 'the pleasant life is produced by sober reasoning searching out the motives for all choice and avoidance'.

[19] Derek Parfit gives an account of the present-aims theory and its justification of altruism in *Reasons and Persons* (Oxford,1984), 127 ff.

[20] Cf. L. Blum, *Friendship, Altruism, and Morality* (London 1980), for a defence of friendship based on stable altruistic emotions. Three basic objections to the emotions which Bernard Williams describes in Kant find sympathetic anticipation in Epicurus: the emotions are too capricious; they are passively experienced; proneness to experiencing them is fortuitously distributed (cf. Williams, 'Morality and the Emotions', in *Morality and Moral Reasoning*, ed John Casey (London, 1970). Moreover, for the Epicurean, it may be that no kind of social emotion is natural (Epictetus, *Discourses* 1.23.3 In. 1.21).

pleasant to the extent that one already independently values its pursuit.

In any case, as Cicero notices (II. 82), associationism admits too much. It recognizes pursuits which have a value independent of their capacity for producing pleasure. Nor is it enough to argue that altruism arises from habit and association. Merely describing the genesis or explaining the acquisition of a desire gives no reason for further cultivating it.[21] Therefore, the associationism of later Epicureans violates Epicurus' basic demand that we foster our desires reflectively and voluntarily; and we can safely assume that this is a development in Epicureanism that he himself would reject.

The contractual account of friendship[22] bears witness to a contrary attitude in later Epicureanism. Torquatus' statement of its precepts is extremely compressed:

Sunt autem qui dicant foedus esse quoddam sapientium ut ne minus amicos quam se ipsos diligant.

(I. 70)

First, it is important to notice that for Epicurus, unlike for Locke or for Rousseau, the idea of contracting, by itself, can carry no independent weight. To the Epicurean, the procedural fairness of a contract's formation is altogether irrelevant in deciding whether or not one should adhere to it. In his account of justice, Epicurus argues that a contract has *tēn tou dikaiou phusin* only if it continues to reflect agents' mutual advantage (*K.D.* 37–8). To a certain extent, then, Cicero is justified in his charge that an Epicurean has few reasons to honour, and no reason to value, an unprofitable commitment. For Epicurus, a

---

[21] Epicurus fears the loss of rational control in passionate love (*S.V.* 18 and Plutarch., *Amat.* 767c where Epicureans are called *anerastoi*). Similarly, he allows little weight to custom, to habit, or to convention since he wants our happiness to be securely in our own hands. Cf. Guyau, above n 13, 136, for an account which makes friendship involuntary, instinctual, and mechanical rather than reflective. For a discussion of these issues see J. Narveson, *Morality and Utility* (Baltimore, 1967), 60 ff. Also noteworthy in this context is Cicero's use of *amare* and *diligere*, since he uses *amare* only in connection with associationism.

[22] *De Fin.* II. 83 suggests that Epicurus did not hold a contractual theory and there is no hint of such a view in any of the fragments. *S.V.* 39 describes the mutual obligations of friendship, without, however, giving a contractual justification of those obligations (Lucretius' expression 'vincula amicitiai' (III. 83) shows a similar avoidance of the technical vocabulary of contracts). Of the theories which appear in the *de Fin.*, only the contract explicitly captures Aristotle's demand for the reciprocity of friendship. The associationist, by failing to take sufficient notice of self-interest, may form friendships unwisely or too readily (cf. *S.V.* 28 for Epicurus' strictures against this). Perhaps by means of the contract some later Epicureans attempted to give more formal recognition to the type of sentiment expressed at *S.V.* 39; or perhaps the ambiguities of 'amicitia' facilitated a later conflation of Epicurus' theories of justice and friendship.

contract must explain why a particular kind of behaviour is conducive to an agent's overall interest. Consequently, some have supposed that arguments analogous to those for contractual justice can be employed to preserve the egoism of contractual friendship. Just as the sage contracts with society as a whole to refrain from mutual harm, he might form compacts with friends for mutual help.

The arguments, though, are disanalogous in one crucial respect. A sage can form a contract to refrain from mutual harm with no regard for another's sake. If friendship included merely a contract for mutual positive help, it perhaps could be given a similar egoistic foundation.[23] But the requirements of the pact described by Cicero are noticeably stronger, since a wise man makes a contract to love another as much as himself. In effect, such a contract commits the sage to an inconsistent set of beliefs concerning his *telos*. He must treat both his own and his friend's pleasure as the goal of his actions. This condition is not so strong as the hedonist paradox which requires one to forget one's pleasure completely in order to maximize it; rather, it requires that the sage regard his own and his friend's good as equal parts of an end which he intrinsically desires. It might be argued that in so doing, he maximizes his pleasure. But as Bishop Butler (*Sermons* xii) argues, he no longer can treat his own pleasure as the only *telos*.[24]

Cicero (II. 83) exploits this feature of contractual friendship by arguing that if a sage succeeds in loving another as himself, he cannot regard his friend as a means to his own pleasure. Conversely, if he does view friends as a means to his own pleasure, he has not fulfilled the terms of the contract. If the sage values another only as a means, or if he has contracted for the sole purpose of mutual help, he will perhaps adhere to an unprofitable commitment. But, Cicero argues (II. 74), he cannot do so without inner frustration or even, perhaps, without longing for his friend's death to release him from an

---

[23] Rist, in spite of Cicero's testimony, attributes to Epicurus a theory of friendship which is contractual and strictly egoistic. He argues that self-sacrifice can be explained in terms of the sage's loyalty to his contractual partners (above n 7, 133; above n 14, 128). But this emphasis on *fides* is not Epicurean (*Lael.* 65); moreover, the contribution of loyalty to one's overall pleasure needs to be rationally explained and defended. Whether or not Rist is correct in arguing that a contract for mutual help can always be hedonically justified, the compacts formed by later Epicureans require more than mutual help; they require concern for another's sake.

[24] Guyau, above n 13, 139 ff, defending an associationist position, is similarly inconsistent. He claims that the sage learns through association to maximize his pleasure by valuing others for their own sake. Thus, what the associationist discovers through chance and habit, the contractualist attempts to turn into a reflective strategy.

unprofitable tie. In order not to consider such a friendship merely as an impediment to one's *ataraxia*, one must treat friendship as a non-instrumental end and value a friend's pleasure as much as one's own.

On the basis of Cicero's testimony, it is possible to form a fairly plausible picture of the genesis and the motivation of these later Epicurean theories. Almost by itself, the fact that Epicurus' followers give such diametrically opposed assessments of the nature and value of altruism suggests an initial obscurity in his own account.[25] Each of these theories defends and further elaborates commitments which are in an uneasy tension in Epicurus' thought. In accordance with *Gnomologium Vaticanum* 23 the associationist allows friendship to float loose as an independent criterion, but fails to give a motive for its continued pursuit. The Hobbesian attempts to subordinate friendship to personal gratification by means of a self-conscious technique, but fails to show why friendship is choiceworthy for itself. Both are plausible developments of an impulse that is more obscurely felt in Epicurus' theory. But Epicurus himself is decidedly more reticent about severing friendship from pleasure or subordinating friends to one's own interest.

III

In turning to Cicero's presentation of Epicurus' theory we are faced with an initial exegetical difficulty. Torquatus begins his exposition of Epicurus' own view of friendship by denying that friends should value each other's pleasure as much as their own (I. 66).[26] He then proceeds

---

[25] Cicero (I. 69) says that 'Epicurei timidiores' hold the associationist view. From this, Rist (above n 7, 131) concludes that Epicurus was a strict egoist and that later Epicureans elaborated altruistic doctrines in response to criticism from the Sceptics. Rist's historical account relies on disputable claims. He implies that Cicero calls the proponents of associationism 'timidiores' because they affirm altruism; but it is not their concern for altruism that is the source of their timidity. What distinguishes these Epicureans is their claim that altruism can be severed from self-interest, 'etiamsi nulla sit utilitas ex amicitia, tamen ipsi amici propter se ipsos amentur' (I. 69). An unwillingness to link altruism to an agent's pleasure is the source of their timidity. Given the general doctrinal conservatism of Epicureans, it is unlikely that, because of Academic criticism, a concern for altruism would have arisen in the face of a strictly egoistic formulation by Epicurus. It is more plausible to assume that these later theories were primarily attempts to explain and defend doctrines of the master which increasingly were seen to be problematic.

[26] Scholars have been troubled by this initial premiss. Rist (above n 7, 129), following Madvig, finds the development of the argument problematic. He denies that this premiss

somewhat paratactically to the claim that the *sapiens* will feel exactly toward his friends as he does toward himself and will exert himself as vigorously for his friend's pleasure as for his own (I. 68). This move is not precisely explained and one might suspect Cicero of offering up a pot pourri of Epicurean doctrine or perhaps of giving a wry caricature of Romans who do not quite see the full implications of espousing Epicureanism. Closer examination, however, shows that Cicero rather neatly captures the unresolved philosophical tensions which surface in Epicurus' own writings.

Given his general theoretical commitments, there are two ways that Epicurus can move from his initial egoistic premiss to an affirmation of altruistic friendship. The general strategy of the first is already familiar. Pleasure is our sole aim in life and friendship is an especially productive means of attaining it. A necessary condition for maintaining reliable friendships, however, is that we treat friends as we treat ourselves. Therefore, in order to gain the maximum hedonic benefits from friends, we must treat them altruistically. As in the contractual theory, there is an attempt to preserve important and generally accepted requirements of friendship along with egoism. But this attempted reconcilliation of egoism and friendship suffers from the same inconsistency and psychological implausibility[27] as the contractual theory. In order to regard his friend's pleasure as his own, the sage must hold beliefs which are inconsistent for a hedonist: he must regard

---

accurately reflects Epicurus' own view. But it surely is consonant with Epicurus' widespread commitments to egoism and hedonism; moreover, Cicero clearly presents it as part of one united position. Evidence from Plutarch (*contr. Ep. Beat.* XV. 1097a) is sometimes adduced in this context: 'τοῦ εὖ πάσχειν τὸ εὖ ποιεῖν οὐ μόνον κάλλιον ἀλλὰ καὶ ἥδιον εἶναι'. But the use of this passage in discussions of friendship is misleading. Bailey, above n 13, 520 correctly argues that it is without parallel and not supported by argument elsewhere. *S.V.* 44 suggests that if by chance a wise man gets many possessions he can distribute them to win the gratitude of his neighbours. It is more pleasurable to give to one's neighbours because the sage needs nothing from them, except to be left alone (cf. *de Fin.* I. 52 for benevolence not associated with friendship). Although this passage may explain other sorts of benevolence, it is not compatible with the requirements of friendship; one must treat a friend's pleasure as one's own (I. 68). Nor is it clear how this would be a threat to altruism if it merely shows that we get more satisfaction by doing something for others (cf. W. Frankena, *Ethics* (Englewood Cliffs, 1963), 20). In order for the pleasure of giving to be strictly egoistic, we need the further claim that one's sole aim in giving is one's own pleasure (cf. *EN* 1120a6 ff).

[27] It is in one's interest not actually to value another as oneself but to seem to do so (*de Fin.* II. 78). Given Epicurus' emphasis on inner states of character, as opposed to rule-directed behaviour, such an egoistic strategy would threaten to engender constant inner frustration.

both his own and his friend's pleasure as the final goal of his actions. This first option, then, collapses into a less formal version of the contractual theory. For that reason it fails as an interpretation of Epicurus, since we know that he does not hold a contractual theory. Moreover, because it treats friendship only as a means to a further end, it does not explain why Epicurus would call friendship *di' heautēn hairetē*.

A second option brings us back to Mill and the claim that something can be valued as a means to an end as well as for itself, as part of an end. Perhaps Festugière intends to attribute to Epicurus a position akin to this when he asserts that Epicurean friendship is an 'end in itself, an integral part of wisdom, a way of life equivalent to happiness'.[28] Although Festugière does not explain how we are to understand these claims in a hedonist context, his conflation of pleasure and its sources is instructive. Such a reconciliation of altruistic action with egoism depends on a slide from 'sources of happiness or pleasure' to 'parts of happiness or pleasure'. An illegitimate move from 'pleasure-able pursuits' to 'pleasures' led Mill to the belief that things other than pleasure could be valued by a hedonist as parts of an end.[29] The confusion that Sidgwick diagnoses in Mill's discussion trades on an ambiguity which Greek[30] shares with English and is based on the idea that if something is pleasant, it is a pleasure. Therefore, if friendship is a pleasurable pursuit, and hence a pleasure, it can be regarded as *di' heautēn hairetē*, since pleasure clearly is choiceworthy for itself. Epicurus' hedonism is especially vulnerable to this kind of conflation because, like Mill, he consistently fails to separate pleasure from the pursuits which give rise to it. There are many indications of this in his accounts of pleasure; but perhaps the most important is that he does

[28] A.-J. Festugière, *Épicure et ses Dieux* (Paris, 1946), 37.

[29] H. Sidgwick, above n 12, 93 for Mill. See the discussions of T. H. Irwin, *Plato's Moral Theory* (Oxford, 1977), 255, 341 and B. J. Diggs, 'Rules and Utilitarianism', *American Philosophical Quarterly*, I (1964), 44. Malte Hossenfelder ('Epicurus—hedonist malgré lui', in *The Norms of Nature*, ed M. Schofield and G. Striker (Cambridge, 1986), 249 ff) senses a tension between Epicurus' particular choice of pleasure as the end and his general eudaimonist project which attempts to show that happiness consists in 'reaching all of the goals' that agents have chosen for themselves. An important source of this tension for the hedonist lies in the ambiguity of 'reaching all of one's goals', which may suggest (wrongly) that one's particular aims, activities, and goals can be included as intrinsically valuable components of one's final good. See below n 33.

[30] Cf. C. C. W. Taylor, *Plato, Protagoras* (Oxford,1977), 168; T. H. Irwin, *Plato, Gorgias* (Oxford, 1979), 200; J. Gosling, *Pleasure and Desire* (Oxford, 1969), 8 ff.

not attempt to systematically isolate and describe a special, uniform quality of feeling; rather, he ranks various pleasurable activities on the basis of their immunity from chance interference and frustration.[31]

A comparison with Aristotle might help to clarify both the temptations and the difficulties which such a conception of the good presents for Epicurean hedonism. Epicurus regularly argues that without a reference to an agent's interest, we cannot understand an action (*de Fin.* I. 32). But a reference to an agent's interest is not necessarily incompatible with altruism. We might claim, for instance, that our ultimate interest, or happiness, consists of various parts or ingredients. Clearly, some of these may be non-solipsistic. If my happiness is composed of various activities desired for themselves, I might value friendship as an intrinsic element or ingredient of my happiness. My friends' interests, therefore, can be treated as part of a way of life that I value for its own sake. Such a view is available to Epicurus from Aristotle, who makes friendship a component of happiness. Friendship retains, for Aristotle, an egoistic reference to an agent's ultimate interest or *eudaimonia*. In itself, however, this does not preclude altruism, since he conceives of happiness as consisting of parts, some of which are altruistic. Analogously, by confusing pleasure and its sources Epicurus can treat happiness as if it consists of parts[32] and therefore allow non-instrumental concern for another's sake.

At I. 69, Torquatus closely links friendship to an agent's pleasure. Inasmuch as Epicurus regularly argues that pleasure is a necessary and sufficient condition for happiness, a severe difficulty remains for him. If happiness is a pleasurable solipsistic state to which all other actions contribute instrumentally, it cannot include non-solipsistic components. Thus, a component conception of happiness might explain, though it does not justify, an Epicurean regarding his own and his friend's good as equal parts of an end. But, however accommodating to altruism, a composite view of the good conflicts with the rigid instrumentalism of

---

[31] In defending qualitative differences between sensual and more lofty pleasures, Mill must rely on non-hedonistic grounds of preference. Similarly, Epicurus relies on a non-hedonic criterion when defending his view of pleasure against the sensualists (*ad Men.* 130 ff): he prefers pleasures which are completely up to us (*par' hēmas*) and not subject to chance.

[32] For example, *K.D.* 28 (*S.V.* 13) may reflect a component view (*tou holou biou*) and the influence of Aristotle (cf. *de Fin.* II. 19 for component conceptions of the final good and Epicurean attitudes towards them). Epicurus' formulation (treating another as oneself) makes both a component conception and a slide from pleasure to its sources attractive.

the rest of Epicurus' doctrines. Thus, like Mill, Epicurus claims that something can be valued both as a means to an end and also for itself, as a part of an end; but it is not clear how a hedonist can defend this.[33]

Before proceeding, it might be worth noting briefly the relative weight given to the interests of others in Epicurus' formulation. Torquatus mentions two conditions:

(*a*) I treat my friend's pleasure as my own.
(*b*) I treat my friend exactly as myself.

We may wonder what relation he sees between these two claims. Perhaps we move from hedonic benevolence (*a*) to a wider conception (*b*). But (*a*) needs to be limited by (*b*), since (*a*) alone might generate a problem: if I can view my friend's pleasure as my own, why can I not view my pain as *his* own? If it is rational for me sometimes to choose a pain of mine for the sake of a future pleasure, would it not be rational to choose a pain for my friend in order to procure my future pleasure? For Cicero, though, even (*b*) is inadequate. He complains (*Lael.* 56 ff) that the mere symmetry of treatment in Epicurean friendship is insufficient for altruism ('Quam multa enim, quae nostra causa numquam faceremus, facimus causa amicorum!'). Some recent theorists, such as Nagel, in defending altruism on the basis of objective reasons, might find Cicero's motives for giving greater weight to a friend's interests overly paternalistic or, perhaps, even egoistic. But Cicero clearly is drawing on a common and important intuition about the requirements of altruism. As Aristotle's discussion of friendship shows, these considerations generate interesting puzzles about the

---

[33] Long, above n 7, 305–6, disagrees and suggests that eudaimonism can allow for something to be both instrumentally and intrinsically good. This is true, I think, of eudaimonist theories such as Plato's and Aristotle's which take happiness to consist of ingredients and activities which are not strictly reducible to pleasurable states of consciousness. For a eudaimonist theorist who embraces hedonism, however, it is, as Sidgwick remarks, 'mere looseness of phraseology' to treat activities such as friendship as intrinsically valuable components of happiness or pleasure. It is perhaps worth quoting Sidgwick in full on this point: 'It is more remarkable to find J. S. Mill (*Utilitarianism*, ch iv.) declaring that "money"—no less than "power" or "fame"—comes by association of ideas to be "a part of happiness", an "ingredient in the individual's conception of happiness". But this seems to be mere looseness of phraseology, venial in a treatise aiming at a popular style; since Mill has expressly said that "by happiness is intended pleasure and the absence of pain", and he cannot mean that money is either the one or the other. In fact he uses in the same passage—as an alternative phrase for "parts of happiness"— the phrase "sources of happiness" and "sources of pleasure": and his real meaning is more precisely expressed by these latter terms' (*The Methods of Ethics*, 93 n 1). I wish to thank Terry Irwin for bringing this passage to my attention.

possibility of friendships between unequals, the sage's attitudes to unvirtuous or unwise friends, etc.; but perhaps a more pressing question is why an Epicurean should engage even in limited forms of altruism.

IV[34]

From Seneca (*Epistulae Morales* (*Ep. Mor.*) 9.1) we learn that against Stilbo and the Academics, Epicurus argued that the wise man[35] will seek friends even though he is self-sufficient. Similarly, the Epicurean gods form friendships, although they need nothing and harbour no traces of insufficiency.[36] In Greek ethics there is a long tradition of attempting to account for this seemingly paradoxical relation between friendship and self-sufficiency. For Epicurus, though, the problem arises in an especially acute form because his commitment to the self-sufficiency of the *sapiens* is further entangled with a belief that the happiness of a sage is entirely invulnerable to the incursions of fortune. In order to understand his reasons for defending the pursuit of

---

[34] This section is greatly indebted to an unpublished paper by Terry Irwin, 'The Good Will in Greek Ethics', and to discussions with Jennifer Whiting. Difficulties for an adaptive conception of happiness are taken up by Irwin in 'Socrates the Epicurean?', *Illinois Classical Studies*, forthcoming.

[35] Unfortunately, it is not altogether clear whether Epicurus limits altruistic friendships to the wise. At D.L. X. 9, we find the claim that Epicurus numbered his friends (presumably not all wise) by cities (cf. *de Fin*. I. 65 'amicorum greges') and this has led some to argue that a spirit of universal friendship developed in Epicureanism (cf. André Tuilier, *La Notion de philia dans ses rapports avec certains fondements sociaux de l'épicurisme ACGB*, (Paris, 1969) 319 ff) who claims that Epicureans, under the influence of Alexander's political syncretism, moved away from Aristotle's more exclusive and *polis*-bound conception of friendship. But *S.V.* 78 claims that the *gennaios* will be most concerned about wisdom and friendship; *K.D.*, 27 and *de Fin*. I. 65 suggest that wisdom alone is productive of friendship. Torquatus mentions the *sapiens* in only two accounts of friendship, I. 68 (which suggests a wise man will treat his friend exactly as himself, but does not claim that his friend must be wise) and I. 70 (which restricts contracts to the wise). Thus, there is a marked tendency in Torquatus' account to limit Epicurean friendships exclusively to the wise. It would be useful to know the extent to which this reflects a distinction made by Epicurus, and whether the bond between wise men is different from that of ordinary friends (II. 84). One senses Aristotle's discussion lurking in the background; but in Epicurus' ethics there are strong reasons for making the *sapiens* the sole possessor of knowledge, hence of *eudaimonia* and friendship.

[36] Michael Slote, *Goods and Virtues* (Oxford, 1983), 133 ff, questions the coherence of such a view for reasons which have much in common with associationism. He wonders how a self-sufficient being can come to value friendship without having first experienced the dependency of a prolonged childhood.

friendship, it will be useful to begin by examining some general features of his ethical theory.

Epicurus thinks that *eudaimonia* consists, at the very least, in the satisfaction of all of an agent's aims or desires. Some of these are first-order desires (for food, shelter, etc.) while others are second-order desires focused on these first-order desires. We may have to restrict the scope or strength of our first-order desires to ensure that they are all satisfied. If we fail to eliminate unsatisfied desires, however, we will be frustrated and unhappy. Moreover, Epicurus thinks that all of our particular desires are extremely flexible, inasmuch as he insists that we can adjust their strength to any situation by means of reason (*K.D.* 26). The *Epistola ad Menoeceum* constantly reiterates his belief that the pleasant life is achieved through reason 'which makes every choice and rejection tend toward one's final good'. Reason, therefore, is the most reliable means to the good life. 'Reason has controlled the wise man's greatest and most important affairs, controls them throughout his life, and will continue to control them' (*K.D.* 16). In order to see the strength of Epicurus' rationalism, one need only compare the sanguine call to happiness which introduces the *ad Menoeceum* (οὔτε γὰρ ἄωρος οὐδείς ἐστιν οὔτε πάρωρος πρὸς τὸ κατὰ ψυχὴν ὑγιαίνον) with Aristotle's more pessimistic attitude in the *Nicomachean Ethics*. The whole missionary appeal of Epicurus' philosophy, his exhortation to mend evil habits, his belief in a good life available to everyone based on the rational selection of pleasures and the knowledge of the nature of things—all these reflect an optimistic, rationalist account of human action. At *Gnomologium Vaticanum* 16, he even affirms the Socratic paradox by suggesting that no desire is too difficult to master. For Epicurus, then, all of our desires and wants can be modified by reason and focused on our final good.

We may reasonably question his Socratic[37] denial of incontinence,

---

[37] *S.V.* 17, 21, 46. Cf. Giovanni Reale, *Storia della filosofia antica* (Milan, 1979), vol iii, 169 ff, for some general connections between Socrates and Epicurus. The only exception to this rationalism is a somewhat dubious report by Plutarch (*de Tranquillitate Animi* 466a) which suggests that Epicurus thought that one may be better off giving in to thoroughly entrenched desires for political gain. This completely neglects Epicurean claims about the natural limits of desires and probably has been conflated with Stoic *persona* doctrines. Epicurus' emphasis on the memorization of the *stoicheiomata* of his thought (cf. Diskin Clay's discussion, *Lucretius and Epicurus* (Ithaca, 1983), 56 ff) has implied to some a strong Epicurean concern with moulding and habituating (unconscious) desires. But this process is more rational and less hypnotic than it sometimes is taken to be by those attempting to reconstruct Epicurus' doctrines on the basis of social practices in Epicurean communities. One can readily explain repetition

occasional indifference, and his claim that we always can eliminate unsatisfiable desires. His motivation, however, is fairly straightforward and shows the essential link between his rationalist moral psychology and his conception of happiness. At *ad Menoeceum* 131, Epicurus argues that those with extremely flexible desires will be unafraid of chance, *pros tēn tuchēn aphobous*. This is a reaction to Aristotelian and, perhaps, Platonic[38] conceptions of *eudaimonia* which make even the most competent deliberators vulnerable to chance. By including external goods as necessary ingredients in happiness and maintaining that happiness must meet exacting objective standards, Aristotle suggests that there are certain conditions in which *eudaimonia* is impossible.[39] Epicurus strongly disagrees, contending that no real harm can come to wise men (cf. *de Fin.* I. 62–3) since their happiness cannot be diminished by chance (*S.V.* 47; Porphyrius, *ad Marcellam* 30).[40]

There is, perhaps, an initial plausibility in Epicurus' conception of *eudaimonia*. If I am hungry and there happens to be no cheese, but a ready supply of bread, it seems reasonable for me to adjust to my situation and eat bread. All things being equal, I will be happier than individuals with inflexible desires for cheese who refuse or are unable to redirect their desires. Those with inflexible desires incur more frustration, are more vulnerable to chance features of the world, and will perhaps begin taking dangerous risks to gain their satisfactions.

and memorization as parts of Epicurus' materialist view of memory. Repeated exposure to doctrine will fix memory traces more securely in one's mind. This is strictly a rational process which does not involved training one's desires (cf. *RN* III. 514 ff). More importantly, if our desires required long and careful training and were not susceptible of rapid modification, we would become vulnerable to chance.

[38] Cf. J. Annas, *An Introduction to Plato's Republic* (Oxford, 1981), 316–17.

[39] For an opposing view see John Cooper, *Reason and Human Good in Aristotle* (Cambridge, 1975), 123 ff (but cf. *EN* 1095b32–1096a2).

[40] Long (above n 7, 306) thinks that we should not overestimate the Epicurean sage's invulnerability to fortune and argues that the 'Epicurean wise man should not be equated with his Stoic counterpart'. However, at *de Fin.* I. 62 Torquatus makes this equation explicit and claims that the Epicurean wise man is always happy ('sapiens semper beatus'). Furthermore, although the *sapiens* may in a trivial way be interfered with by chance, his happiness is invulnerable. In the same passage which Long cites to show the vulnerability of the sage (*ad Men.* 135), we find the claim that Epicurean doctrine makes it possible for us to live as gods among men. Cf. also *Tusculanae Disputationes* V. 9. 27, where Cicero attributes to Metrodorus a version of Epicurus' proud boast at *S.V.* 47: 'Occupavi te, inquit, Fortuna, atque cepi omnisque aditus tuos inclusi, ut ad me adaspirare non posses.' Cf. Diskin Clay, 'Individual and Community in the First generation of the Epicurean School', in ΣΥΖΕΤΕΣΙΣ. *Studi sull' Epicureismo greco e romano offerti a Marcello Gigante. Biblioteca della Parola del Passato 16* (Naples, 1983), 260 ff for a judicious account of the relation between these two passages. Cf. Diogenes of Oenanda, fr 41.

Epicurus' view of flexible desires has the merits of making happiness up to us, *par' hēmas*. If I am unable to adjust and redirect my desires, I give up control over my life and my happiness in important ways.

Flexibility is a plausible criterion to build into an account of happiness. Without limits, however, this demand for the flexibility of desires can become pernicious and destructive. Epicurus' view becomes far less attractive if it only gives reasons for restricting and eliminating desires. At *ad Menoeceum* 128 ff, Epicurus vacillates between two very different conceptions of desires and their satisfaction. He is crucially obscure about whether he requires for happiness a broad range of desires or just the fewest possible desires.[41] This is partially polemical. Epicurus thinks that most people have too many demanding desires which force them into competition and continual frustration. But more importantly, his equivocation reflects a concern to make *eudaimonia* entirely up to us. Epicurus cannot require that we cultivate and always satisfy a broad range of desires without making us vulnerable to possible frustration and unhappiness. Thus, given his determination to ensure that we can achieve happiness in any situation, he allows the scope of happiness to expand and contract to fit individual circumstances.

Adapting ourselves to every situation, however, might not lead to anything we would be inclined to call happiness. For instance, Epicurus claims that even on the rack the *sapiens* will be happy. If wise men can adjust their desires so thoroughly that they can find happiness on the rack, we may wonder if Epicurus really is giving us a recipe for happiness. Adjusting our desires to some conditions will not necessarily secure happiness. Under extreme conditions (concentration camps, torture, etc.), those who still can envisage and desire a better state of affairs are better off. Epicurus might claim, of course, that those with less flexible desires, even in extreme conditions, are just compounding their misery with more frustration. But at this point, it is no longer clear why frustration and unsatisfied desires are to be avoided. Some discontent with camp-life would be a hopeful sign, as would

---

[41] This helps to explain the very different conceptions of Epicurus as quietist, ascetic, vitalist, sensualist, etc., which appear in the doxography. We might think of *ataraxia* as a desireless state in the sense of a total removal of desires. (For the difficulties in this view, Martha Nussbaum, 'This story isn't true: Poetry, Goodness, and Understanding in Plato's Phaedrus', in *Plato on Beauty, Wisdom, and the Arts*, ed Moravscik and Temko (Totowa, 1981). But it is also possible to regard *ataraxia* as a state in which one's desires are continually satisfied. Presumably we do not have friends to totally remove a desire for friendship.

unsatisfied desires to be out of the camp. Those in a concentration camp who still can recognize that their desires are being frustrated and that their lives are being diminished are considerably closer to happiness than those who, recalling past pleasures, feel completely content with camp life. To see the real force of Epicurus' claim here, it should be remembered that he not only argues that one can be happy on the rack, he also is committed to the claim that one can be just as happy on as off the rack. In effect, Epicurus can give no rational criteria derived from our own happiness for use to prefer being out of a concentration camp or released from torture. Thus, in order to give a more plausible characterization of *eudaimonia*, Epicurus needs to set limits to the flexibility of our desires.[42] But in so doing, he would have to qualify his claim that happiness is entirely *par' hēmas* and modify his subjective conception of *eudaimonia* based on the mere satisfaction of desires.

Part of the initial plausibility of Epicurus' model of happiness stems from an unclarity about the relation of desires and their objects. The objects of some desires are easily interchangeable. If I am hungry, for instance, it would be irrational to hold out very long for a particular type of food when other foods are readily available. The objects of other desires, however, more clearly reflect an agent's long term deliberations, values, and goals[43]; hence they are not so easily substituted. Thus, since friends are not substituted very readily nor are relations with them entirely *par' hēmas*, it is difficult to see how altruistic friendships[44] can conform to Epicurus' view of flexible and easily eliminable desires.

These general considerations are important for his account of *philia*. Epicurus urges us in the strongest possible terms to develop friendships. But what if someone decides to exclude all concern for

---

[42] It might seem that in order to practice the virtues the Epicurean needs at least some minimal constraints on the flexibility of desire. However, Epicurus attempts to revise ordinary conceptions of the virtues, including justice, to fit his conception of happiness. The aim of all the virtues is to control desires rationally and thus ensure their satisfaction. This task need not be entirely negative: 'temperantiamque expetendam non quia voluptates fugiat sed quia maiores consequatur' (*de Fin.* I. 48). Nevertheless, the virtues are parasitic: they control our desires and adjust their strength; but they cannot ensure that the range of our desires in certain situations will not collapse to a level unacceptable for happiness.

[43] Cf. Michael Slote, above n 36, 44 ff, for further difficulties in regarding goods such as friendship as ends of action for which we can reasonably plan.

[44] As Aristotle notices (*EN* 1156a19–20), friendships based on pleasure or advantage are more easily broken off or formed to fit circumstances.

others and cultivate a very narrow range of desires which are easily satisfiable? Or what if someone rather monomaniacally decides to focus on just one easily satisfiable pursuit? Can he show that such people are any worse off without friends? At times, Epicurus gives an expansive view of the sage's happiness, and many of his remarks anticipate Butler's admonition that a selfish and narrow character is not promising for attaining happiness. For example, at *ad Menoeceum* 135, he recommends that Menoeceus practice his doctrines with another who is *homoion seautōi*. Similarly, he insists that it is more important to find someone to eat with than to find something to eat (Usener 542). Presumably, he does not mean merely feeding in the same place, as cattle (Aristotle, *EN* 1170b13–15). Rather, like Aristotle, he implies that being fed is less important than actively taking part in a shared pursuit.

These features of Epicurus' account suggest motivations akin to Aristotle's[45] for his espousal of altruistic, as opposed to strictly exploitative, friendships. Given his conception of the final good, however, it is difficult to see how he can successfuly introduce such non-instrumental considerations into his account of *eudaimonia*. Joint activities are not entirely under our own rational control. Moreover, as Cicero objects (II. 83–4), these elements of friendship cannot be justified strictly on the basis of their hedonic worth, since the value of shared pursuits cannot be reduced completely into terms of pleasantly invulnerable psychological states. But there is still a deeper difficulty for Epicurus' account of friendship. Given his view of the sage, it becomes difficult to see how he can give even a purely instrumental defence of friendship's contribution to the pleasant life. For instance, Epicurus claims that for the sake of friendship we should run risks 'δεῖ δὲ καὶ παρακινδυνεῦσαι χάριν φιλίας' (*S.V.* 28). It is unclear, however, that he can justify any risk-taking given his model of pleasure and

---

[45] Zeller ascribes such sentiments to Epicurus' 'effeminacy' and the need for Epicurean friends to ground the truth of their convictions in mutual approval (*Die Philosophie der Griechen*, v. iii (Leipzig, 1903), 467). A kinder construal is possible by pointing to Aristotle's emphasis on shared activities and the corresponding gains in self-knowledge which depend on the knowledge of one's friends (*EN* IX. ix), cf. John Cooper, 'Aristotle on Friendship', in *Essays on Aristotle's Ethics*, ed A. Rorty (Berkeley, 1980). Philodemus (*de Dis* 3, fr 84, col 13, 36–9, 36 Diels) finds conversations and mutual contemplation to be central elements in divine friendship. Cicero describes this aspect of Epicurean friendship at II. 85 ('at quicum ioca, seria, ut dicitur, quicum arcana, quicum occulta omnia'). Interestingly, in contrast to associationism, on this account altruism becomes psychologically prior to self-esteem (cf. Julia Annas, 'Plato and Aristotle on Altruism', *Mind*, LXXXVI (1977), 532 ff).

rational agency. If opportunities for making friends are abundant, perhaps the desire for friendship can be easily satisfied and will involve no trouble. Friendship, however, is among the external goods; τῶν ἐκτὸς ἀγαθῶν (*EN* 1169b10–11), which Aristotle suggests will make one more vulnerable to chance. For Epicurus this feature of friendship is problematic and presents an awkward dilemma. If friendships are crucial for happiness, he must admit that the sage can be vulnerable. By developing friendships we become more vulnerable to chance, pain, and betrayal.[46] Even if Epicurus denies that friendship makes one vulnerable in this sense, he must admit, however, that without friends a sage's happiness will be somehow incomplete.[47] Epicurus does not think that a sage's happiness can be augmented or diminished and he carefully avoids distinguishing gradations in the happiness of sages in the manner of Antiochus (*de Fin.* V. 84). The strength of his claim, however, successfully undermines any justification for forming friendships. Instrumental appeals for developing friendships lose their force if the sage's happiness is completely invulnerable.

If friendship is necessary for happiness, happiness can no longer be entirely *par' hēmas*, nor can we always avoid the frustration of our desires. Epicurus, then, must either modify his account of *eudaimonia* and rational agency or weaken his commitment to friendship. By doing neither he is forced into an inconsistency. He defends the pursuit of *ataraxia* based on his model of happiness as the satisfaction of desire. But in trying to add friendship as an additional requirement for happiness, he undermines his account of *ataraxia*. Accordingly, Epicurus needs an independent evaluative criterion for justifying the possible frustration and loss of rational control involved in friendship. He must appeal, moreover, to sources of value in activities which are independent of their ability to easily satisfy desire. This need for an

---

[46] Friendship is a source of security, but a riskier source than justice, since if a sage suffers injustice it will not upset his whole life. Epicurus by no means downplays the role which *asphaleia* plays in friendship, but when he counsels Menoeceus to practice Epicureanism with a friend, he echoes Aristotle's emphasis on the importance of shared activities. This emphasis on *asphaleia* is not necessarily inconsistent with the claim that friendship is valuable for itself. There is no reason why something valuable for itself cannot be valued for other benefits as well. But if friendship were merely a matter of security, it would be safer for the sage to cultivate justice. In distinguishing the pleasures of altruistic friendships and ordinary friendships of advantage, Epicurus would need either to (*a*) rely on 'a non-hedonistic ground of preference' of the sort he elsewhere denies or (*b*) show how the desire for altruistic friendship is more easily satisfied and requires fewer risks than ordinary friendships. Neither alternative is very promising.

[47] Philodemus recognizes, for instance, that the gods' happiness would be less complete without friendship (*de Dis* 3, fr 84, col 1, 2–4).

independent criterion explains, perhaps, why Epicurus is led to call friendship *di' heautēn hairetē.*

Rist[48] claims that although the gods are self-sufficient and enjoy the purest katastematic states, they form friendships for the sake of kinetic pleasure. Would a similar argument be available to justify human friendship? If I can enjoy complete katastematic pleasure without friends, do I have reasons for cultivating friends for the sake of richer kinetic experience? Such a defence is unlikely inasmuch as Epicurus neither gives a rational method for ranking kinetic pleasures nor claims that we have any rational concern for kinetic pleasures, since they are not *par' hēmas.* If I can enjoy the highest katastematic state on bread and water, and the kinetic pleasures of cheese merely vary[49] but do not increase my satisfaction, I have no reason for wanting anything but bread and water if they are more readily available. If different kinetic pleasures cannot increase my happiness, I may perhaps try cheese on a whim, if it involves no risks. But for the sake of kinetic pleasures, Epicurus can justify no risk-taking whatsoever. Nor, since they are mere variations, would it matter much if I make mistakes in my evaluations of them. As we have seen, however, Epicurus thinks that friendships involve risks and must be carefully evaluated. Similarly, at *ad Menoeceum* 130 ff, he claims that those who least need luxuries are best able to enjoy them; he does not claim that the wise man gets more pleasure from luxuries. The sage, then, has no reason to prefer one kinetic pleasure to another. If friendship is merely a kinetic pleasure, the sage has no grounds for valuing his friends any more than a nice salad or a fine wine.

Epicurus, of course, has no systematic programme for eliminating all desires. In fact he encourages us, if the opportunity presents itself,

---

[48] Rist, above n 7, 154. The relevant passage in Philodemus is *de Dis* 3, fr 84, col. 1, 2–9, 15–16 Diels.

[49] Here I follow the Diano/Rist account of the relation between kinetic and katastematic pleasures. Corresponding problems in justifying friendship on the basis of kinetic pleasure would be generated by other accounts as well. For instance, Giannantoni ('Il piacere cinetico nell'etica epicurea', *Elenchos*, V (1984), 25 ff) argues that kinetic pleasures arise only from the satisfaction of unnecessary desires; but then the pleasures of friendship, if they were kinetic, would be unnecessary. Similarly, Merlan's view that kinetic pleasures are merely momentary (*Studies in Epicurus and Aristotle* (Wiesbaden, 1960)), would give no justification for cultivating lasting, stable relations. Gosling and Taylor (*The Greeks on Pleasure* (Oxford, 1982), 345 ff) think that kinetic pleasures fall into the same class as katastematic pleasures. Such an account might avoid problems of incommensurability; but it still would not show why the particular pleasures of friendship should be cultivated, if they are vulnerable to chance and future frustration (cf. 371).

'to indulge harmless desires. Lucretius, in the proem to *de Rerum Natura* VI, even suggests that the growth of such desires was crucial for the development of a society which made Epicurean philosophy possible. But the Epicurean cannot assign such pleasures any value, since to do so would threaten the sage's complete happiness. By distinguishing kinetic and katastematic pleasures in this way, Epicurus creates a difficulty familiar from Stoic and Kantian ethics, the problem of comparing incommensurables. If katastematic and kinetic pleasures are incommensurable, there can be no way of rationally comparing them, since they are not on a uniform scale of value. Hence the preference for the right katastematic state cannot be a rational one. Although Epicurus is only too ready to admit this, at the same time, however, he can no longer rationally defend his attitude toward kinetic pleasures. Therefore, an attempt to base friendship on kinetic pleasure not only trivializes friendship, but it also precludes the possibility of recommending friendship on the basis of reason. As we have seen, for Epicurus, altruism requires a rational defence.

At *ad Menoeceum* 127–8, Epicurus claims that of the necessary desires, some are necessary for happiness, others for the repose of the body, and others for life itself. Unfortunately, we do not know which desires Epicurus thinks are necessary for happiness. If he argues that the satisfaction of a broad range of desires is necessary for happiness, it would have important implications for his ethical theory. It would allow him to build in certain limits to the flexibility of our desires. For instance, I may want many friends, but if I were in a situation which offered few opportunities for friendship, I could have a few friends and still be happy. But I could not be happy without any friends at all, since my desires are flexible only within certain limits. If Epicurus maintains that friendship is a necessary desire, however, his dilemma returns in another form. By including desires for an external good like friendship among those necessary for happiness[50], he would make the sage vulnerable to chance and frustration. Again, Epicurus would have to revise his conception of happiness by subordinating satisfaction and rational control to other values.

---

[50] Epicurus might limit the flexibility of desires by describing an underlying structure of desires whose mutual dependence makes their satisfaction interentailing. If I have a set of desires (a, b, c, d) which I try to restrict by satisfying only a and b, I will not realize that the satisfaction of a and b depends on the satisfaction of c and d as well. But this attempt would also fall prey to the same objection; it would make me vulnerable to chance and frustration if, say, c and d could not be satisfied.

V

We have seen the various tensions in Epicurus' ethical thinking which force him into inconsistencies. This is partly of historical interest, inasmuch as it shows a hedonist's attempt to return to Socratic conceptions of rational agency and control over individual happiness. Epicurus attempts to make happiness invulnerable to chance. At the same time, though, he is attracted to an Aristotelian conception of *eudaimonia* which includes *philia* as an essential ingredient of happiness. His position is philosophically instructive as well. Like Mill, Epicurus thinks that we can value something for its own sake apart from its instrumental contribution to our satisfaction. This is inconsistent with the claims of his hedonism. But it shows that any hedonist who wants to give a plausible account of happiness must appeal to intrinsically desirable sources of value and concede that the achievement of happiness is not entirely in our own hands.

In Epicurus' analysis of friendship, we find the realization that, to a certain extent, we must relinquish control over our happiness if we are to find it worth possessing. This discovery creates an observable tension in his thought about the ultimate good. Indeed, in the context of the central pre-occupations of Hellenistic moral thinking such a discovery is almost paradoxical. Epicurus' solution to the problem of friendship represents, as does the parallel Stoic discussion of preferred indifferents, a distinctive attempt to account for important elements of our ethical beliefs and practices while making *eudaimonia* an invulnerable psychic state. Moreover, like the Stoics, Epicurus adopts a Socratic moral psychology and shows little reluctance in abandoning the complexities of Platonic and Aristotelian views of moral motivation. But, interestingly, he reveals some dissatisfaction with a strictly subjective conception of happiness and appears reticent about giving up all of the benefits of an Aristotelian account of the final good. In many ways, his attempt to reconcile the demands of a strictly rationalistic moral psychology with a more expansive conception of happiness is paradigmatic of the kinds of problems bequeathed to Hellenistic moral philosophers by their predecessors. Moreover, Epicurus' account of *philia* shows the limits which moral psychologies can place on conceptions of happiness and exemplifies the difficulties which beset Hellenistic philosophers in fitting their moral psychologies to plausible accounts of happiness.

Cornell University

PLOTINUS ON THE GENESIS OF THOUGHT AND EXISTENCE*

A. C. LLOYD

THERE are accounts of the genesis of thought and existence, that is to say more than allusions and incidental information, in say, eight or nine tracts. They cover the whole of Plotinus' writing career, though with a gap in the middle; they do not in my opinion indicate any significant changes of mind on his part. What may at first sight be disconcerting is that some of the stages or events are stated in more than one order. But this, which might have been thought important in the description of the process, is balanced by two further facts. Plotinus does not for the most part present the set of events *as* an order, that is, with temporal terms like 'then,' 'next', 'after', so much as *in* an order, which of course anyone using language must do. Secondly he tells the reader more than once that events which he places in an order—and not merely because he must, but because on each occasion he presents them for a purpose—are really simultaneous. But there must be some marks of order since they are presented as a process from the One. Neoplatonic metaphysics has definite indications of stages in such a process. These are the familiar criteria of increased complexity (i.e. diminished unity), diminished reality (copies in place of the original), and so on. They demarcate, as we shall see, certain stages, even if logical, not temporal, in the genesis of thought and existence in the *Enneads*.

While aware that the reader may be familiar with them I propose to start by surveying a number of texts without deference to such familiarity. (There are commentaries on only a handful of tracts, and some philological discussion will be necessary.) The two stages of the genesis which will emerge are also the ones which have been noticed by most writers on Plotinus' metaphysics. But a treatment of the topic

* © A. C. Lloyd 1987

as a whole may be useful.[1] Scholars have done much admirable work on the historical antecedents of Plotinus' doctrines. But, save one 'model' in Aristotle, these are not my concern. After the attempt to see what (as one might say) is going on in the genesis the questions I should like answered are what light the genesis throws on Plotinus' concepts of thought and of existence, and whether it contributes anything to the placing of them in a modern context.

In Porphyry's chronological order passages which describe the whole or major parts of the genesis can be found in V. 9. [5]. 8, V. 4. [7], V. 1. [10]. 5–7, V. 2. [11]. 1, V. 6. [24]. 5, III. 8. [30]. 11, VI. 7. [39]. 15–18 and 40, V. 3. [49]. 11.

Most of these descriptions represent existence as a later stage than thought, even though not a temporally later stage, and even though their identity is an integral part of Neoplatonism. And it will make the material more manageable if we first have more to say about the relation of thought to the One and later about the relation of existence to thought. The sometimes awkward suggestion of Plotinus' procedure that thought is prior to existence may be felt to follow from the concepts which he applies to the procession of the One, looking, seeing, contemplating. But this explanation puts the cart before the horse. He has other concepts at his disposal which are objective and not anthropomorphic and which are no less adequate for describing the initial impulse. He has the concept of *energeia* and the concepts of limit and the unlimited or the indefinite dyad. But when he uses the concepts of looking and seeing he does so because it is the genesis of the subjective, or thinking, not the objective, or being, which he is concerned to explain. So it is more a case of the author's concern determining the concepts and the priority; we shall see examples of this later. The reason for his concern is a continual polemic which Plotinus maintains against the proposition that the One possesses thought even of itself. The path from Middle Platonism had to be taken in two steps. It was not enough to show that *Nous* was not the highest god: philosophers had to be restrained from simply adding the divine activity of *Nous* to the One.

The earliest description of the genesis of thought and implicitly of

---

[1] A. H. Armstrong, *The architecture of the intelligible universe in the philosophy of Plotinus* (Cambridge, 1940; repr. Amsterdam, 1967), chs iv and v are concerned with the topic; there is less on it in J. Trouillard's suggestive *La procession plotinienne* (Paris, 1955). I have not been able to see J. R. Bussanich, *The relation of the One and Intellect in Plotinus* (Diss. Stanford, 1982).

existence is the little tract V. 4. [7]. It is exceptional in allowing some
kind of thinking to the One, even though a 'different kind' from that of
Intellect (4. 2. 19–20). No doubt this is only partly to be accounted for
by the exceptional purpose of the tract, which is to take only the first
step from Middle Platonism and Stoicism by showing that there is a
'principle' beyond Intellect. But there is nothing in the stages
attributed to the genesis of Intellect which significantly contradicts
anything we find in the other passages. Whatever is first in the
hierarchy or procession, it argues (1. 6 ff), must be simple. In chapter 2
three questions are answered. The first is raised at line 3: why should
this first 'generator' not be (the hypostatized) Intellect. The answer is
that Intellect, because it is both thinking and the object of thinking, is
not simple. For its 'thinking is one which sees its object, is turned
towards it ['reverts' to it] and is completed by it, for it was indefinite
like sight [i.e. the faculty or capacity of seeing] but is made definite by
the object of thought'. Here it is easy to recognize (as of course writers
on Plotinus have recognized) the application of Aristotle's account of
the actualizing of thought by a *noēton* in line with the actualizing of
sight by a visible object.

It is not however a statement about thought in general. That is ruled out by the
grammar of ll 4–7. They contain a succession of participles with no main verb
because they are in apposition to the *noēsis* of the preceding question and so
equivalent to 'I mean the thought which . . .' ('intelligentia, inquam, spectans . . . ,'
Ficino). The sentence is most naturally understood as restricting the topic to
the hypostasis.

At l 5 it is tempting to distinguish the referents of the demonstrative
pronouns by supposing that Plotinus is distinguishing the One and the One as
noēton. He did so distinguish them, I shall argue later: but he is not doing so
here, for in ll 12 ff *noēton* must refer to the One. Nevertheless one might
speculate that he had not yet worked out the distinction in this very early tract,
and that this has something to do with the exceptional attribution of thought
and life and self-consciousness to the One. It is at least remarkable that in later
accounts they are *not* attributed to the One and they *are* attributed to the One
as *noēton* which is between it and Intellect. But it is true that V. 1 [10] which
seems to include the distinction comes only three places later in Porphyry's
list, and any lack of it here is as likely to be due to the abbreviation of a
standard account.

The question how Intellect comes from the One (ll 12 ff) is the
second of the questions to be answered by the chapter. The One,
which is the object of the generated thought—all this being conveyed

by *to noēton* at line 13—remains what it is. It contains and co-exists with everything and is identical with some kind of self-thinking (to adopt a convenient term). This object of thought, which is still apparently the One, generates. (Until it generates we may call it the potential object of thought, although Plotinus does not call it that, and we must return to the matter.) Plotinus had already given the reason for this in chapter 1 (27–33) and he will now repeat it. It is the application of another general thesis, based on a model taken this time from Aristotelian physics. Every entity, once it reaches its perfection, or actualization, generates something additional. Fire, as we can observe, produces heat in something else, drugs have their specific effects on a patient. What the One generates is 'thinking', but an indefinite thinking like sight in the Aristotelian psychological model. Like Aristotle Plotinus considers the sight which anyone possesses who is not seeing anything, but who is not blind, as indefinite or indeterminate seeing because its objects are any possible objects of seeing.

But when it has been made definite—'as it were perfected', corresponding to Aristotle's 'actualized'—by its object, the One, it is the hypostasis of thought, or Intellect. Lastly this Intellect is an object of thought for itself. (For, although this is not explicit here, self-thinking is the highest and therefore the original form of thinking.) It replaces as it were, the One as a second and secondary *noēton* (ll 10–12).[2]

The remainder of chapter 2 spells out the Plotinian version of Aristotle's physical model (ll 27–33), to which we shall return. This version attributes an activity, exemplified by the heat of a fire or of the sun, *of* the essence/substance and an activity *from* the essence, exemplified by the transference of heat to something else or by the rays of the sun. The first activity is what 'remains' when something is 'generated' by the second activity.

The treatise V. 1. [10], *On the three principal hypostases* which was probably close in time to the one we have been examining, repeats it to a notable degree. But in chapters 5–7 it enlarges on Intellect's procession from the One. The Plotinian version of Aristotle's physical model is again spelt out and (in 3. 7–12 and 6. 30–9) applied also to the generation of Soul by Intellect. But its non-Aristotelian feature is insisted on: the product of the 'activity from' a cause is only an image of the cause. Plotinus also emphasizes that activity from the One

---

[2] ἄλλο τῷ μετ᾽ αὐτὸ νοητόν l 10: instrumental dative, sc. εἶναι.

cannot be a case of change or movement (6. 15–27). We learn rather more about Intellect as Existence. Soul looks towards Intellect in order to be Soul—this is of course the regular function of reversion in the triad which is never prominent in the *Enneads*. And Intellect looks towards the One so as to be Intellect.[3] But (to go back to the end of ch 5) 'it is determined [literally, 'formed'] in one way by the One, in another by itself, like sight actually exercised'. And here, combined with the *Republic*'s simile of sight and knowledge, we have more of the psychological model from Aristotle. For as well as being actualized by its object sight can, indeed must also be described according to the *de Anima* as actualizing itself; for it is not passive alteration but 'a progress to itself' (417b6), although as in Plotinus the impetus has to come from something else.

There are some problems of text or translation which I think published comments have not exhausted. V. 1. 6. 17–18 says that if anything comes into existence μετ' αὐτό (indisputably the One) it must have done so ἐπιστραφέντος ἀεὶ ἐκείνου πρὸς αὐτό. The question is whether this means that the One reverted to itself or that what came after it reverted to the One. (Everyone would agree that eternal reversion of Intellect to itself is not one of the possibilities here.) Arguments from the grammar have been propounded in favour of both interpretations: but in view of Plotinus' flexibility in grammar none of them carries much weight. They can be found in Atkinson's excellent discussion of the passage.[4] What must be borne in mind is that it is the conclusion of an argument to the effect that the One must be immobile. Harder and Hadot have thought that the reversion of Intellect would be irrelevant to this.[5] This is surely mistaken? If Intellect is being referred to the genitive absolute will have an instrumental force—what comes into existence is doing so by its own reverting, with the implication that it is not by the One's movement. (So even on this hypothesis we have a positive reason for the genitive instead of the nominative which some scholars have thought it demanded.) For the same reason if the self-reversion of the One is being referred to there is no need for the instrumental force: the One's movement is excluded by the fact that it is turned to itself, not to the something else which movement requires (l 16). A valid objection made by Hadot to identifying the subject of reverting as what comes after the One is that before it can revert this would have already to have come into existence. But we saw in V. 4 how there

[3] In this passage (6. 45–8) Plotinus uses the Stoic term λόγος, sc. προφορικός in place of πρόοδος, for he has said in 3. 7–9 that they are equivalent.

[4] M. Atkinson, *Plotinus: Ennead V. 1, a commentary with translation* (Oxford, 1983), 135–40.

[5] R. Harder, *Plotins Schriften, Deutsche Übersetzung*, Bd 1 (Leipzig, 1930), 501; P. Hadot, Review of Henry-Schwyzer II, *Revue de l'histoire des religions*, LXIV (1963), 92–6.

was an indeterminate thinking generated before actual Intellect and that actual Intellect came to exist precisely by the reversion of that thinking. So it is reasonable to infer that what comes after the One in the present account is not Intellect itself but the indeterminate thinking.

Atkinson finds it surprising that the reversion should have been mentioned when the preceding generation has not: but we saw that it has at least been alluded to at the end of ch 5. Nevertheless there does seem to be a fresh start with the repetition at the beginning of ch 6 of the question: How did Intellect come from the One? For while the question, How does it see? may suggest the second, actualization stage of its genesis, this is immediately followed by the 'general' (ὅλως) question, How did it come to exist so as to see?, and taken at its face value this must be about the previous, generation stage. And there is a cogent logical argument which I should add to support the many scholars who have followed Ficino in thinking that the One is turning to itself. If we suppose that Plotinus means only to describe the actualization we are left with the objection that whatever is said about that will be insufficient to imply the immobility of the One, for it will not have covered the original act of generation. On balance I conclude that the passage is about the generation of Intellect without distinction of indeterminate and determinate stages, so that the debated participial expression at V. 1. 6. 18 means that the One is turned towards itself. It is certainly better not to translate it 'reverts', for that suggests its correlation with remaining and proceeding and would be unsuitable in the context. In fact it takes the place of the 'remaining' attributed to the One in V. 4. 2. 19 ff but is not, *pace* Harder, identical with it. Some scholars find it hard to swallow Plotinus' saying that the One is eternally—better perhaps, uninterruptedly (ἀεί)—turned towards itself. The passage which should have been quoted but has been surprisingly passed over in this controversy is VI. 8. [39]. 16. 11–29.[6] Except for the omission of οἷον the present one says no more than what is said there.

V. 1. 7. 5–6, τῇ ἐπιστροφῇ πρὸς αὐτὸ ἑώρα is usually treated on all fours with the clause we have been considering in the previous chapter. But I agree with Igal (loc cit, 139 ff) that the context is different, and that there is less in it to stop one from taking the subject to be Intellect which is in is indeterminate stage but whose reversion to the One makes it Intellect proper. Indeed Plotinus' next sentence says, 'this seeing is Intellect'; and if the subject of ἑώρα were the One this would imply that the One's own seeing was Intellect—which is not Plotinus' view. 'Seeing', we must already have realized, is a kind of code word for the actuality of the pre-intellectual Intellect. Various objections to this reading of 7. 5–6 are adequately disposed of by Atkinson (op cit, 157–60). At l 2, where ἐκεῖνο is predicate, πως means in effect 'in the way in which a copy *is* what it is of'.

---

[6] The reference is given as a parallel, though unluckily misprinted, by J. Igal, 'La genesis de la inteligencia en un pasaje de las Eneadas de Plotino (V. 1. 7. 4–35)', *Emerita*, XXXIX (1971), 133 n 2.

Chapter 7 goes on to explain how Intellect's reversion to the One is not just the genesis of (actual) thought but of existence or substance. I shall defer this subject until later and notice for the present only the demarcation of the agency of the One and the agency of Intellect. The One, Plotinus says, is the power (*dynamis*) of all things. But thinking sees them by splitting off, so to speak, from this power; it would not otherwise have been Intellect (ll 9–11). For Intellect has in its own right first a consciousness of the power, which is its own power although derived from the One, to generate existence/substance; so that of itself it delimits its own being; but secondly it has a consciousness of the fact that existence/substance is, so to speak, a part of what belongs to the One and therefore *from* the One. Life, thinking and everything come from the One because it was not constrained by any shape or form. For the same reason the One is not among the contents of Intellect: but these are all substances because each of them is delimited, that is, has a kind of shape or form.

At 7. 13 δύναται οὐσίαν is exponential of τῆς δυνάμεως and so does not need to mean 'makes', *pace* Rist, but 'has the power to make'—a not unattractive Plotinianism to my mind.[7] At l 12 *what* it is which has the consciousnes of this power (i.e. the subject of ἔχει) is controversial. I have taken it to be Intellect. For (i) if it were the One the ἐπεί which governs the clause would be wrong because the clause would not be explaining the relative independence of Intellect that is being attributed to it; and if what was to be explained was rather the power of the One, whatever Intellect is conscious of would not be a good explanation of that; (ii) Intellect is credited with consciousness (*synaesthesis*) elsewhere in the *Enneads* and in the same context (VI. 7. 19–20, 7. 35. 1–2). It will follow from (i) that what has the power to make substance (i.e. the subject of δύναται, l 13) is also Intellect. Furthermore Intellect's own power to make/be substance is, as we shall see, Plotinus' universal doctrine. This power is the same as the power of seeing its own contents mentioned at VI. 7. 35. 20–1. To return to the ἔχει, would it remove reason (i) for taking its subject to be Intellect if we took its subject to be the One but still took the subject of δύναται to be Intellect? No: for that would give the One's consciousness of Intellect's power as an explanation of Intellect's independence, and it is not that but Intellect's power which explains it.

Other points are discussed by Igal (loc cit, 149–55) and Atkinson who also reach this conclusion and by T. A. Slezák, *Platon und Aristoteles in der Nuslehre Plotins* (Basel-Stuttgart, 1979), who does not.

I think that ll 13–14 are wrongly punctuated by Henry-Schwyzer. αὐτὸς γοῦν . . . δυνάμει is better taken as a parenthesis, so that καὶ ὅτι . . . is the

[7] J. M. Rist, *Plotinus: the road to reality* (Cambridge, 1967), 45–7, discusses V. 1. 7.

second conjunct governed by ἔχει συναίσθησιν. I think that the standard punctuation has led Armstrong (Loeb Classical Library) to mistranslate l 15, where ἡ οὐσία is not 'its' substance: it is certainly the οὐσίαν of l 13.

Even with other solutions to the philological questions it would be clear that Plotinus wants to present the genesis of thought in two stages. He does not depart from this. Indeed the last of the passages that I listed, V. 3. [49]. 11, belongs to a tract composed at the end of his career and contains most of the features that we have seen and none that we have not. This tract, *On the cognitive hypostases and that which is beyond*, covers the same grounds at V. 1 and has the same end in view. It is focused rather more on the return of Soul and Intellect than on their genesis; and chapter 11 may appear to infer stages of the genesis from experiences of the return. But in fact it is a deduction from what had been shown in the chapter before, that in contrast to the One thought is necessarily multiple. The abstract nature of the argument is clear from the allusion in that chapter to the first of the two stages. Unless the object of thought is multiple, Plotinus had concluded, there is not thought but contact, 'which is a pre-thinking before thought has arisen' (V. 3. 10. 40–4).[8] The grounds for the 'multiplicity' can be left for the present.

He continues (11. 1 ff) by saying that this multiple *Nous* tries to grasp the One in its simplicity but emerges always with something else, which is no longer simple, in its grasp. So its original impulse was not as *Nous*, or thinking, but as sight which did not yet see; and it emerged possessing what this sight had itself multiplied. It started with an unlimited desire for something it could in some manner imagine: but what it now possesses is an impression of what it saw, otherwise what it saw could not have come into existence within it. When this impression became multiple instead of single, or simple, *Nous* saw what it saw as something it knew (i.e. as an object of knowledge), and then the unseeing sight became a seeing sight. At this point it is Intellect (as we can call it) which thinks and Existence; before that it was not thinking because it had no object of thought.

Some readers may think that the two stages are less separated or even less distinct, but they will not question that they are there.

---

[8]   46–50 reinforce the point; for οὐδὲ δεήσεται cannot have a completely new subject and the lines must be about that which thinks. The additional (εἶτα) argument is that < if this were a single thing > it would not need to think because it would already possess its essence. This is to accept Sleeman's τοῦ for νοῦ at 48; the corruption can be explained by the scribe's having taken the two sentences (as Armstrong takes them) to refer to the One.

Certainly the obscurity of *what Nous* saw needs to be removed. First of all, that it is 'other', that is, not identical with the One, has now come into the foreground. But the reader has on his hands at least two 'others' or images of the One, none of which at first sight is merely Intellect itself, but each rather something necessary for Intellect to emerge. That this is true of the first other is clear from V. 2. [11]. 1, written immediately after V. 1. 5–7, which we have already dissected. Here the external activity (the *energeia* from the essence: cf. l 17) of the One generates something other than itself; and this other turns into existence by being at rest in relation to the One, 'in order to see it', while by turning (or reverting) to the One and seeing it it becomes thought/Intellect. As for the 'other' which is the subject of both transformations we have no reason not to identify it with the first stage of the genesis of Intellect, namely the pre-thinking which he also calls indefinite thinking. As for the object of its sight, it is the One, for the text cannot, I think, be read in any other way. (It does not affect it whether we translate 'in order to see it' or 'in order to see'.) Nor need this contradict what we have just been told in V. 3. 11, where it failed only to 'hold' or 'possess' it; indeed it tried to hold it only because it had seen it.

V. 6. [24]. 5, however, while otherwise following V. 2. 1, introduces a further element. This is an image of the One possessed by the indefinite thinking. The thesis of the tract is again the absence of thought, and hence independence from Intellect, on the part of the One. The One here is most often called the Good because Plotinus wants to talk about desire for it (compare I. 6. 1. 7 ad in). This will be mentioned (as we have seen) in the later V. 3. 11 and it is expounded again in VI. 8. [39]. 13. 11–46, but it is in any case implicit in the reversion common to all the previous accounts. Here the movement towards the Good from desire of the Good brings thought into existence 'because the seeing faculty's desire is seeing'. I think that the desire attributed in V. 3. 11 to the first stage of *Nous* is 'unlimited' or 'indefinite' for the same reason that the 'sight which is not yet seeing' is indefinite.

This is on the assumption which is preferable to that of most translators, that at V. 3. 11. 7 ἀορίστως modifies ἐπεθύμησεν not ἔχουσα.

Here in V. 6. 5. 10 the sentence ἔφεσις γὰρ ὄψεως ὅρασις is puzzling. Bréhier's alteration of ὅρασις to ὅρασιν would be a solution, 'generated' being readily supplied from the previous sentence. But preserving the text I have proposed to take ὄψεως as a possessive genitive. ὄψις will be the faculty, as in Plato, *Republic* 507–8, and equivalent to the ὄψις 'not yet seeing' of V. 3. 11. 5, which at l 12 is identified or at least associated with desire. There is some exaggeration in identifying the seeing with desire but not the dubious sense of identifying it with the desire for seeing: what is desired is a visible object. Plotinus, by the way, has no fixed terminology for distinguishing the faculty and the activity: ὄψις and ὅρασις can be used synonymously, so that what either signifies can be potential or actual (III. 8. 11 ad in, V. 1. 5 ad fin, V. 3. 10. 13, VI 7. 35. 14 and 15).

One might have expected him to distinguish the desire for the Good from the fulfilment of the desire, and thus the movement towards the Good and the sight of it. Perhaps he is constrained not to because the fulfilment would be possession or union and not the subject–object duality of thought which the 'sight' implies here. III. 8. [30]. 23–4 speaks of Intellect uninterruptedly desiring the Good and uninterruptedly attaining it: but as lines 18–19 indicate this is no more than its full possession of the form of the Good. Plotinus is of course following the letter of *Republic* VI. 507–9, but in a different spirit because *his* form is not the Good. The fact provides a warning against reading him too simply which will have to be borne in mind while we read of any relation of Intellect to the One in its genesis. The relation may be an indirect one owing to the Neoplatonic principle that anything 'received' is altered by its recipient.

Indeed the duality of thought is tied to the fact that the One is present to Intellect from the very first stage, but as an image. For we find this image playing two parts. In V. 6. [24]. 5, in III. 8. [30]. 11 and in VI. 8. [39]. 13 it is the attribute of goodness, which makes Pre-intellect (as we may call the first 'other' or product of the One) desire to possess the One/Good as object, that is, to revert to it. In V. 3. [49]. 11 on the other hand, it corresponds to the object of thought in the psychological model from Aristotle. In this role it appears first as 'some kind of presentation' or 'object of imagination':[9] but in seeing the One Intellect (as it now is) finds that the 'impression' (l 8) it now has of what it sees is something complex, or multiple. As I understand it the vaguely single, or simple 'presentation' has turned into a definitely complex 'impression'. Corresponding to actual sight the final state is thought—which at this level will be indistinguishable from knowledge—because its object is an object of knowledge (c. V. 3. 11, VI. 7. 16). This object is not of course directly the One, for the One cannot be

---

[9] φάντασμά τι, l 17; οἷον φαντασίαν, V. 6. 5. 15. The same term is used for its *first role* in VI. 8. 13. 46.

known, but an image of it which is necessarily imperfect since knowing or thinking it entails its not being *one* at all.

V. 3. 11. 9–10: another subject of debate. But I think that it can safely be simplified. In l 9 οὗτος is almost certainly ὁ τύπος (so Henry–Schwyzer and Armstrong). For (i) Pre-intellect, the subject of the previous sentences has been referred to as ὄψις and mentioned only in the feminine; (ii) its multiplication would lack here any explanation, while the multiplication of the impression by Pre-intellect/Intellect is what the previous sentences have been about. However, the subject of εἶδεν in l 10 must be νοῦς, covering Pre-intellect and Intellect. Of course it is Plotinian theory that the object of knowledge is one and the same as the knowing subject: but this theory is totally off the point here. Finally that the reader should understand that εἶδεν has a different subject from that of ἐγένετο is more important than deciding whether this requires reading οὕτως for the second οὗτος (l 10) or even emending γνοὺς to γνοῦσα (Harder); if οὗτος is left it will be picking up the νοῦς of l 1 which is the subject of the chapter up to l 5.

There are then three distinct things or states in the whole process which are called traces or images of the One/Good. There is first the 'other' which is the indefinite state of Intellect and called an image at V. 1. 6. 33. It in turn contains or possesses according to V. 6. 5 and V. 3. 11 an image of the Good; and this is replaced by a third, this time complex image or impression according to V. 3. 11 and VI. 7. 15–16. Why such a thicket for Plotinus' readers to enter? To justify it they must remind themselves that images are the correlates of participation, which is always incomplete but purports to explain the possession of attributes. It is primarily as an attribute of Pre-intellect that Plotinus sees the form of the Good in *Republic* 508e–509d becoming the motive force for turning it into actual Intellect, that is, knowledge. But images and traces are more directly things than they are attributes; and this encourages Plotinus to call anything which possesses an attribute of something else an image of it. He explains the law that participation in a cause by an effect or product is always partial and mixed by saying that what is received is necessarily altered by the recipient.[10] We must also remember that at this level of reality subject and attribute are

[10] cf. V. 3. 11. 8–9, VI. 4. 11. 1–9, VI. 7. 18. 11–12. Armstrong claimed (op cit, 60) that a developed form of 'reception according to the capacity of the recipient' appears 'as an alternative to emanation in . . . the relation of *Nous* to the One'. I cannot myself see that he shows this and believe that the 'alternatives' are really two sides of one medal. D. J. O'Meara, *Structures hiérarchiques dans la pensée de Plotin* (Leiden, 1975), and J. S. Lee, 'The doctrine of reception according to the capacity of the recipient in *Ennead* VI. 4–5', *Dionysius*, III (1979), 79–97, are more concerned with the application to matter and the sensible world.

abstractions. So the life and power which are received by Pre-intellect come to be treated in VI. 7. 15 as Pre-intellect under other names. This makes the process less complex, but Plotinus does not always persist in it. Nor does he make clear here what he wants to bring into the foreground, a distinction between the creative activity of the One and a creative, or self-creative, activity of Intellect.

This distinction he makes in VI. 7 [39]. 15 by saying that when Intellect looked at the Good it could not have been thinking of nothing, nor could it have been thinking of what the Good contained, otherwise it would not itself have been producing its own product. So what it received was the power to produce and to be filled with its products. He goes on to identify power in general with life and the power '*of* all that is' with the vision of the Good (17. 32–3). When it looked at the Good it was not thinking nor even seeing but '*living*, turned towards it' (16. 14–15). Thus the power of all that is can be equated with the power to produce, which is itself equivalent to Intellect's latent possession of an existent plurality. Plotinus is uncertain whether Existence is the internal or external energeia of Intellect, officially calling it internal, that is, the activity of the essence, but sometimes external. It should be the former since it is not manifested in something else. But perhaps he sometimes thinks of it as generated by Pre-intellect in Intellect. He is anxious to dissociate it from the direct agency of the One.

This anxiety is expressed when he tells us to distinguish among the gifts of the Good (*a*) what is bestowed *for* the first *energeia*, (*b*) what is bestowed *on* it, and (*c*) further gifts (18. 12–13). As in the parallel passage of V. 3. [49]. 15 the first *energeia* is Intellect (whose *einai* is *energeia*, V. 3. 7. 18). And the immediately succeeding sentences leave it beyond doubt that (*a*) is true Life, or Pre-intellect, (*b*) is the goodness appropriate to true Intellect, that is, Intellect as a simultaneous whole, and in effect whatever makes it Intellect, and (c) is the goodness appropriate to it as a divided plurality, and in effect the forms.[11]

So 'bestowed for' (that is, as a necessary condition), 'power to produce', 'the first other': all three refer to the first of the two stages in the genesis.

'Bestowed on', 'producing' on the part of Pre-intellect/Intellect, the second 'other', the image: these three refer to the second stage. The additional image of the Good that has been mentioned is a modification of the first made by Intellect's multipying it (7. 15. 20–2).

---

[11] For this distinction between (*b*) and (*c*) cf. 7. 17. 21 ff. One could take it to include, or alternatively to comprise only, souls: the choice is unimportant.

We recognize too in the first stage the external activity of the cause or generator, in this case the Good/One, which produces a latent and indefinite manifestation of the new entity.[12] And to continue our stock-taking I propose to look at its dependence on assumptions which belong to the causal model from Aristotle's physics. This dependence was well grasped by C. Rutter; Armstrong and others have seen a Stoic source, particularly the material emanation from the sun of the 'ruling principle' in man.[13] But I think that texts of the *Enneads* and Plotinus' use in our context of a number of Aristotelian technical terms show that he found the chief abstract properties of his 'emanation' foreshadowed and even authenticated by an accepted model in Aristotle. It follows, in my view, that the examples of heat and the like are examples and not merely metaphors and analogies which is how they are usually described. But there will still be a 'transposition' from the physical to the non-physical. It follows too that however little the model or its transposition are valid, it is not right to state that Plotinus does not appeal to theory to expound the genesis.[14]

The causal model from the *de Anima* is recognized by almost all readers. Both Aristotelian models were incorporated, if only allusively, in the text from which we started (V. 4. 2). The physical model helped to explain the first stage of the genesis and the psychological model the second stage. The two explanations however overlap simply because the basic structure of the second model is Aristotle's application to psychology of his physical model.

As is well known *Physics* VIII. 4 proposes to start from the ambiguous reference of 'potential and actual': (i) the learner potentially knows before he has been taught, (ii) he is then in another way potentially knowing when he is not exercising the knowledge he has learnt. In (i) the potential (the scholastic *potentia prima*) becomes actual (*actus prior* = *potentia secunda*) whenever agent and patient are compresent. But in (ii) the potential (*potentia secunda*) is always and necessarily actual (*actus secundus*) unles something prevents it. Aristotle takes this as applicable to the case of an activity which affects

---

[12] The identification with the 'activity from', which we saw in V. [4]. 7. 2, will be explicit also in VI. 7. [38]. 21. 5, although Plotinus is more careful at this period to avoid mentioning an *ousia* of the One. See in general VI. 8. [39]. 11 and 13. In VI. 8. 20 he called the One an activity without subject or *ousia*.

[13] C. Rutter, 'La doctrine des deux actes dans la philosophie de Plotin', *Rev. philos.* CXLVI (1956), 100–6. Armstrong, in A. H. Armstrong (ed), *Cambridge history of later Greek and early medieval philosophy* (Cambridge, 1967), 240.

[14] As M. I. Parente states in her interesting *Introduzione a Plotino* (Roma-Bari, 1984), 100.

something else. Something cold which has been sufficiently heated is already fire (its *actus prior*) and has also the *potentia secunda* of heating or burning other things: but it is a contradiction of the nature of fire *not* to heat or burn things (*actus secundus*), just as something light goes upwards, unless it is stopped, since that is what it is to be light.

Physics III. 3 had claimed that the actualized movement or process in an agent was the same 'in subject/substrate' as the one it caused in the patient but that they differed in 'being/essence'; in other words they are numerically the same event but conceptually different. If *A* exercises his ability to teach and *B* his ability to learn there is one fact expressed by '*A* teaches *B*' and '*B* learns from *A*', but there are two descriptions of it since 'teaching' does not have the same meaning as 'learning'. The partial identity is expressed by Aristotle in a terse formula: the agent's activity 'is not cut off [separated]—it is *of* something *in* something else' (202b7–8).

Turn now to Plotinus. The 'external activity' that follows from something's 'repletion' or perfection is his version of the transmitted change/motion which is the *actus secundus* of any actualized *potentia prima*. In VI. 3. [44]. 23 he broadly reproduces the doctrine of *Physics* III. 3 and mentions that it applies as much to 'generation' (of substances) as to qualitative change. The *necessity* of emanation can be seen as the absence of need (according to Aristotle) for an additional cause of this second actualization.[15] Where his version departs from Aristotle is over the inferiority, the lower degree of reality, of the effect or product to that of the cause or agent. But he does not admit this as a departure: he simply writes as though the partial identity constituted by 'same in substrate but different in essence' is the partial identity of his own pair, original and image (V. 3. [12]. 49. 44–5; VI. 4. [22]. 9. 37–42). Hence too the correlation of the agent's motion with the patient's is readily transposed into the 'remaining' which is correlative with the 'procession'. Plotinus regularly borrows the metaphor from the formula of the *Physics*: the product is not cut off from its origin—in V. 3. 12. 44 'neither cut off nor identical'—and commonly in connection with remaining.[16] His readers will already have noticed how often in describing the production of thought he is undisturbed by

---

[15] Emanation necessary e.g. for hypostases VI. 6 ad in (Intellect), IV. 8. 3 ad fin (Soul), II. 9. 7. (Nature).

[16] Of the light of the sun ~ external activity of the Good (I. 7. 1. 27, V. 3. 12. 44); of Being and its 'powers' (VI. 4. 3. 9, 9. 16); of Nature as an image (VI. 2. 22. 34). Plotinus quoted the term (which Plato had not used in this way) in his résumé of the *Physics* chapter (VI. 3. 23. 19).

crediting the One with properties and activities which strictly belong only to lower hypostases; he *intends* it to fit into a pattern which will be repeated lower in the scale; and he tries, often successfully not to say everything at once.

Physics VIII. 4 did not say that all the agency was on the part of the *actus prior*, the heat that burns or the knowledge that elicits learning, although it is the cause proper. For we can ask what actualized the burning or the teaching (the *actus secundus*). VII. 3 says categorically that what is potentially knowing comes to know not through a change in itself but through the presence of something else, a particular or a universal—the text is uncertain—which it recognizes. The same is true of the original acquisition of knowledge, the concept formation, which is called the soul's coming to rest after turbulence. But let me interpose here that the distinction between this intellect *in habitu* and the exercise of it was not supposed by Plotinus to explain the same fact as his own distinction between pre-intellect and intellect, and to look for a correspondence there is unrewarding. It is well known that Aristotle repeats the *Physics'* position in the *de Anima* with regard to perception and thought: their respective objects act on them to make them perceive or think (429b29). This position which, though of course part of his physics, I referred to as the psychological model from Aristotle, is applied by Plotinus to the second stage in the genesis, the reversion to the One that turns the pre-thinking into thought and existence. The physical model for the transmission of the *actus secundus* was supposed to account for the emanation of Pre-intellect. And the reader may be puzzled by being asked to see in the second of Plotinus' stages a model which in an Aristotelian physical process belonged to an earlier stage than the transmission of the *actus secundus*; for it explained how the *actus secundus* itself arose from the prior potentiality. But Plotinus is not explaining a physical process in which a series of potentialities would be successively actualized. The first act in his series is on the part of the One, and this can only be an 'activity from' which has no prior potentiality but which nevertheless corresponds to the *actus secundus* and is therefore to be described by the physical model. On the other hand what this activity produces is without equivocation a potentiality, for it requires 'perfecting'; and if there is an Aristotelian model it will naturally be the one from his psychology which explains how a prior potentiality is perfected or actualized. Before this point Plotinus has no room for it.

It is evident however that he combines the simile of the sun as the

Idea of the Good from *Republic* VI. 507–9. Perhaps the key passage for the combination is 508d4–6 (tr. Lindsay): 'Now consider the soul in this same manner. When it is stayed upon that on which truth and being are shining, it understands and knows and is seen to have reason [*nous*].' Now one detail of it now another is echoed. Plato's anology of light, which in Plotinus is often the *energeia* between a cause and its product, helps him to assimilate the psychological model on account of the part played by the medium, particularly light and air in Aristotle's theory of perception; and in this respect he presses the symmetry between perception and thought farther than Aristotle had done. But it is important to realize that his own theory of perception, which did involve action at a distance, has no role in his account of the genesis of thought.

As for the reversion stage the law of actualization by the object absorbs the function assigned to the Idea of the Good for the obvious reason that Plotinus has made the Good the object of Pre-intellect's vision. *Ennead* III. 8. [30]. 11 is an important example of the combination: but it suggests problems which may have occurred to some readers. The ultimate aim is once again to show that the Good is above thought, but the cause of it. Intellect or thought, he begins, is a kind of sight—a seeing sight, which is an activitated capacity. What was one before it saw has become two and the two have become one. (Plotinus means that as the mere faculty it had no object, for the duality he has in mind is that of seeing and the visible object. But the pair has at the same time 'become one' because, as in Aristotle, its members are identical in subject/substrate, as of course are thinking and its thoughts.) This activation comes from the object which is seen, while the sight which belongs to thinking is activated or 'completed' by the Good. When this happens thought/Intellect receives from the Good a form which makes it good and to which it constantly inclines; it thus contains desire.

The problems are these. First the chapter is silent about the indefinite image already possessed by Intellect/Pre-intellect. Moreover the form of the Good which it does describe corresponds dubiously to the indefinite form when it has been (as in VI. 7. 15) multiplied by Intellect. We can leave the matter at that. Or we can put the weight on the purpose of the chapter, which is to distinguish the Good from what is good, namely Intellect. To make this distinction it appeals to the famous description of the form of the Good as that which imparts the powers of knowing and of being known; and under this dominant influence Plotinus may have chosen to ignore, or just ignored, the details of his regular account of the genesis.

There is a passage which has never, I think, been properly explained or even examined in print, but whose explanation depends on recognizing details of Aristotle's psychological model. It is in VI. 7. [38]. 40, and it is one of the few abstract or generalized descriptions of the genesis of existence/being, and intended as such. Nor is it surprising that it should use Aristotle since it is directed against the Aristotelians. I shall refer to *ousia* for the present as 'being' so as to be able to talk as Plotinus does of its coming into existnce. Those who have been in contact with the Good, he begins, know that there is no thought there: but we must add argument to experience.[17] Argument tells us 'that all thinking is from something and of something. The thinking that is attached to that which it is from has as its subject that which the thinking is of, but it occurs as a kind of addition to that which it is of—it is the subject's actuality and completes what the subject was potentially, without itself producing anything, for it belongs to the subject only as its perfection. On the other hand the thinking that is accompanied by being and that caused being to exist could not have been contained in that which the thinking came from, for if it had been it would not have produced anything.' In fact, Plotinus proceeds (ll 13 ff) on familiar lines, being a productive power its activity (*energeia*) is the being which accompanies it and in all but concept is identical with it. It is the first *energeia*. Had this activity been *of* the Good instead of from it that is all it would have been and it would not have had an existence of its own. These last lines will be incomprehensible if the passage is inadvertently taken to be about the two stages which we have so far found described.

Plotinus appears to have started his abstract argument here by distinguishing the source of thought from the possessor of it, or thinker. I have translated the Greek literally, but so far as the Greek goes he could be distinguishing the source from the object of thought (the word I have translated 'subject' being equally capable, as in English, of meaning 'subject matter' or 'object'). For the moment I shall try to show how the first construction makes good sense.

Plotinus divides thinking into two kinds which are really levels or

---

[17] ll 1–4 refer to the appeal to experience, 'mixed necessity' (4–5) to the mixture of this with logical demonstration, 'understanding' (5) to logical demonstration, which is what follows for the rest of the chapter and is picked up again in ch. 42 ('led by reasoning', l 2).

moments of thought, (*A*) thinking as it attached to the Good, or in fact from the Good, and (*B*) thinking as it is attached to being, or in fact responsible for its existence. If we interpret (in the mathematician's sense of 'interpret') the description of (*A*) in non-abstract terms it can be seen to be isomorphic with the description Aristotle gives of seeing, hearing, or any perception:

> Seeing (1) has as its subject a seer (2);
> but (1) is really an addition to (2),
> because it is the actuality of (2)'s capacity to see,
> not the agent of its seeing
> [the agent is the object of sight].

> Thinking (1) belongs to Pre-Intellect (2),
> but as an addition to (2)
> because it is the perfection of (2)'s potentiality
> without having generated anything
> [what generated thinking was the One as seen by (2)].

The explanation in the last line does not occur in the present passage, but it does so incidentally at the end of the chapter, in an argument against the prime mover (ll 43–54). A self-thinking principle, the argument runs, is either the completion of some other subject (as it is in Plotinus) or an element in a compound existence (as it is for Aristotelians according to Plotinus); either case entails something prior to it, and when it is thinking itself 'it is as it were discovering what it possessed as a result of contemplating something else'. There we have an abstract version of the familiar genesis of Pre-intellect.

Committing Plotinus to saying that thinking belongs to Pre-intellect is of course inaccurate: but we are having to describe a dynamic situation in static terms. If we had him saying that it belonged to Intellect it would be inaccurate to call it an addition to Intellect. Once Pre-intellect has been perfected it is (*B*), the thinking as it is attached to being. (*A*) and (*B*) do not make a division which corresponds to the usual two stages of the genesis. They are two levels or aspects of thought within the second, or reversion stage. But they presuppose the first stage, the creation of an 'other', which we shall later identify as Pre-intellect in a different guise, but which functions like the object of perception in Aristotle's psychology. And since those two levels or aspects are roughly the only two which could be seized on in Plotinus by opponents who were bent on a last ditch defence of thought on the part of the Good they serve the aim of the chapter.

For the upshot of the argument with respect to (*A*) is that thinking is not caused by a prior perceiving. Nor is this beating a man of straw, for every student knew Aristotle's law that there must be a cause which is actually what the effect is potentially. By apparently breaking that law the psychological model has furnished Plotinus with an *ad hominem* argument against it. Earlier in VI. 7 he had enunciated his own law that a giver does not have to possess what it gives (17. 3–4) and then enunciated the Aristotelian law. He did not put them in conflict but used an argument (7. 6–13) which aimed at showing that the Aristotelian law was inapplicable to the present case, but which was somewhat sophistical—or perhaps we should say dialectical and provisional.

With respect to (*B*) he can go farther: the thinking which is inseparable from being *cannot* have belonged to the first principle, or the first principle would not have produced it.

l. 6, συνοῦσα: used by Plotinus as a semi-technical term for something's internal activity (e.g. V. 4. 2. 23 ff; VI. 3. 10 ff), but obviously not here, otherwise the Good would be thinking. For its equivalence to 'not separated' which does hold for the external activity cf. V. 6. 1. 4–5.

8, ἐπικείμενον-ὑποκείμενον: in V. 1. 3–13 ~ external-internal activity and certainly means attribute-subject. I prefer 'addition' here, where Plotinus is eschewing too well defined uses in much of his terminology. (It is, incidentally, anachronistic to attribute, in those terms, the 'subject-object' antithesis of logic or grammar to perception and knowledge before quite modern times, as Hicks, *Aristotle De anima*, 435 points out.) Whether ὑποκείμενον means 'subject' or 'object' is naturally the same question as whether the καὶ τινός of the previous line is possessive or objective. In l 47 it seems to have the same ambiguity, for its reference at least includes the *noēton* which is created by the One and will be both subject and object. But it may there mean neither, but just 'object' in the general sense of 'thing', while its being an object of thought is left to the next sentence. Anyway for the meaning, 'subject i.e. possessor' at l 8 cf. III. 8. 8. 5 (the subject of contemplation, i.e. contemplator); and more generally thinking is distinguished from its possessor at V. 6. 6. 10. Among translators Cilento adopts this version, McKenna–Page and Theiler–Beutler the alternative; Ficino preserves the ambiguity.

The alternative sense would, I think, depend on its echoing a use in *de An.* III. 2 (mentioned by T.–B.) where at 425b14 τῆς ὄψεως καὶ τοῦ ὑποκειμένου χρώματος means '. . . the colour which is its subject matter', and similarly τοῦ ὑποκειμένου αἰσθητοῦ at 426b8. This is not too great a demand if, as I presume in any case, that chapter is presupposed here by

Plotinus. Or one might of course argue that a usage which was possible for Aristotle was independently possible for Plotinus.

With this sense the translation I have given will still hold if 'subject' is simply changed to 'object' or 'subject matter'. But the *interpretation* of (*A*) will come out as follows:

Seeing (1) has as its object colour (2);
but (1) is really an addition to (2)
because it is the actuality of (2)'s visibility,
not the agent of (1)
[the agent is (2) itself]

Pre-intellect's thinking (1) has as its object (2) the *noēton* produced the One;
but (1) is rather an addition to (2)
because it is the perfection of (2)'s capacity to be an object of thought
and has not generated anything
[what generated (1) was (2) as seen by (1)]

Instead of the more obvious identification of seeing and thinking with the actualization of the faculties of the seer and thinker we have them identified with the actualization of the capacities or dispositions of the objects. This is equally consistent with Aristotle. It follows from his physical model which makes the *energeia* of the agent identical at least 'in subject' with that of the patient; it is expressly applied to perception in *de Anima* III. 2 where actual sound is identified, save in essence/concept, with actual hearing (425b26 ff), and it is later applied to thought. Even with respect to (*A*) the upshot for the aim of the chapter will be the same, and nothing else is changed. Is one version better than the other? I do not myself see any point which is weighty enough to tip the balance between them.

So Plotinus is committed to the thesis that perception and thought are activated by their objects. Thought activated is the thought which is attached to, in fact partially identical with, being/existence; existence is simply its internal activity (VI. 7. 40. 15). But as we have seen in VI. 5 and VI. 7. 15 it is Intellect not the One which is to be credited with generating this existence although the power to do so was a gift of the One. In modern accounts of Plotinus, however, the object of Pre-intellect's thinking is usually represented as being the One, to which—as indeed we were told in V. 4 and V. 1. 5–7—it 'reverts' and by which or by the vision of which it is 'perfected'. And on the face of it this now presents a contradiction. For if it follows that the One, not Intellect, activates thought it follows that the One, not Intellect, generates existence; for this activation consists in so delimiting it that it becomes eo ipso Existence, precisely as the dyad when delimited by the One becomes *eo ipso* (ἤδη) number as *ousia* (V. 1. 5. 5–9). This problem is not solved by treating the genesis as no more than a theodicy in which the First Principle issued a fiat to Intellect, 'Go forth and multiply'. Even the One cannot enable something else to do what has already been done.

Should we therefore go back on the assumption that Plotinus accepted Aristotle's thesis of the object as agent? No. He does so explicitly in III. 8. [30]. 11. 6–8; and it is the keystone of his assimilation of *Republic* VI. 507–9. Could we divide Intellect from its *energeia* and credit the One with the first and Intellect with the second? This might be possible if existence were its external *energeia*, but it is the *actus primus*. Should we say instead that the One was object of Pre-intellect's vision, perhaps even only what it desired to see, whereas what it thought or knew was Existence? This would be a better suggestion, but inadequate as it stands since seeing is what Plotinus aparently called this thinking. Similarly Igal (if I do not misrepresent him) has the One acting as object of vision only as 'potency of all things' while the subject, the inchoate intellect extracts the forms from it (loc cit, 152): but again that does not seem to me to leave a comprehensible notion of an object of vision. Certainly Plotinus states that Intellect does the multiplying. But we have to resist the temptation to suppose that what it multiplies is the *totum simul* (πάντα ὁμοῦ) which is often described in the *Enneads*. For this *is*, already, *ousia*; and when thinking is occasionally said to separate the forms in it it is our thinking, not that of Intellect.

What we have to understand, I think, must be stated in two steps. First it is not the One which actualizes the sight (or capacity to think) of Pre-intellect, but *the One as seen (or thought)* by Pre-intellect. The two are not the same *simpliciter*: but Plotinus can call the One as seen the One because for him it is and is not the One in exactly the way that for him the good we desire is and is not the good. There is a good sense in which Aristotle meant by his 'object' which is agent the object as perceived. Otherwise their actualities would not be identical as events. It is not the vibration of the gong which he believed to be the same as the hearing of it, but its sound. (Similarly it is visible colour which is the object of sight, so that light is an additional agent, and Plotinus can use the fact to assimilate Plato's account of the Good as agent of knowledge and existence.) Certainly this may be said to leave us with correlates rather than causes and effects: but if Aristotle left room for additional efficient causes of perception and thought they are not relevant in a non-physical world to which the model is applied.

Secondly Intellect can be said to produce Existence. For it is the One as object of thought, not the One *simpliciter* which acts on Intellect/Pre-intellect and makes it Existence: but equally it is Intellect/Pre-intellect which makes the One an object of thought. This last proposition is in fact what VI. 7. 40. 5–10 told us if we accept the second possible version of it, which made it about the *object* of thinking. Again the analogy in Aristotle holds. There is a good sense in which he believed that hearing makes the sound and thinking makes the thought. At least this is the prevalent interpretation, and doubtless Plotinus', according to which the vibration becomes a sound only when it is heard. At the same time there is also a sense in which the One is responsible for Existence, namely the sense in which the One as thought is still the One just as a sound is also a vibration. But the sense in which it is not the same is more pronounced for Plotinus on account of his non-Aristotelian law that receiving always entails alteration.

If the perfecting of Pre-intellect by the One and the multiplication of it by Intellect can be reconciled this looks to me the least inadequate way. I am not confident that they can: but I am not confident that Plotinus was clear about the matter either.

At no place, I believe, does he say in so many words that it is the One only as thought (of) which delimits Pre-intellect so as to make it Existence/Substance. But there are passages which must imply it. In III. 8. 8. 31–2 he says that even in its original contemplation Intellect is not contemplating it 'as one'. (Naturally he is referring to Pre-intellect, for he adds, 'otherwise Intellect would not come into existence' [or 'it would not become existence'].) And we have already seen the same doctrine in V. 3. 11 ad in and VI. 7. 15. In the former Intellect tried to grasp the One as simple but found itself with something else. VI. 7. 15 suggested also the connection with Existence: when Intellect received the power to produce the ideas the Good could only come to it (*ergo* to them) 'in the form in which it could receive it.[18] But it is rather more than the power which Intellect received, for having said that, he added

---

[18] There is no possibility of τὰ πολλά being subject of ἦλθε at l 13, for the point here is the distinction of good and the Good.

'From the One came for Intellect a many' (l 20). It is plausible to interpret the 'dual formation' of Intellect at V. 1. 5 *ad in* in the light of this ambiguity of 'the One as object of thought'. Expressions of the form 'qua so and so' conceal pitfalls.

Whatever his belief Plotinus does not seem to have made up his mind how to express it or at least to have thought it desirable to have a single way of doing so. Let us ignore the question of the creation of Existence and take mechanically the question what is said to perfect or to delimit Pre-intellect in the reversion stage. (Perfecting and delimiting are predicated together in V. 4. 2. 5–7.) We are told: the One/Good (V. 1. 7. 16, VI. 7. 17. 16, III. 8. 11. 8), desire of the Good (V. 6. 5. 10), thinking (VI. 7. 41. 19), Intellect (V. 1. 7. 13–14), Intellect and the One together (V. 1. 5. 17–18), the One as object of thought (?) (V. 4. 2. 5–7), primary Existence (V. 5. 5. 16). But it cannot be inferred that he was unclear in his own mind; for given the complexity of the belief I have attributed to him these answers are not inconsistent, but each will tell part of the truth. Nor can we dismiss the complexity of the belief on the grounds that the contradiction it was supposed to avoid arose only because we forgot that the 'genesis' is only, in Plotinus' own expression, 'an expository tale'—that all its imagined events are simultaneous. For to accept that, it need hardly be said, would be to prevent the genesis from being expository by allowing it not to make sense.

Let us summarize the position I am proposing in the wider setting of the two stages of the genesis. We have first (1) *the external activity of the One*, which is equivalent to the indefinite Pre-intellect, that is the potentiality or power of Intellect to think. This in turn is identical with the power to produce Existence. Then we have (2) *the internal activity of Intellect*, which is Existence; and this is equivalent to the actualizing and/or delimiting of Intellect/Pre-intellect by the One as *noēton*, for this *noēton* = *ousia*/Existence. (1) corresponds to what the One bestowed *for* the first *energeia*, that is, Intellect, and (2) to what it bestowed *on* it. And they correspond to the first and second stages respectively of the genesis.

Making the One a *noēton* is equivalent to making a 'one many', or multiplying the indefinite image Pre-intellect had of the One: this is the work of Pre-intellect, not the One. Or rather, we should probably regard the indefinite image as identical with Pre-intellect, so that stage (2) of the genesis is a case of self-determination. And more than that: in so far as it would also follow that the object—still the One as *noēton*—which actualizes Intellect is identical with intellect, stage (2) is a case of self-creation. 'It (*Nous*) began as one but did not remain as it began', Plotinus sums it up (III. 8. 8. 32).

We can now focus our attention on Existence. (I shall continue to use the term for Plotinus' οὐσία or τὸ ὄν; he is very conscious of both as nominal forms of εἶναι.) It will be best to look at its chief attributes in passages concerned with its genesis. It would be reasonable to expect the second stage to have furnished causes or counterparts of all these attributes: but whether it did is open to question. We should bear in mind too what is not quite the same question: how far does what we found in the accounts of the genesis correspond to what would be found at least in Plotinus' account of all thought and existence? A good deal of this question can be settled in what follows immediately.

First existent means delimited. This integral feature of the genesis was doubtless a traditional Pythagorean element of Platonism: but that does not make it self-explanatory. In V. 1. [10]. 7, V. 5. [32]. 5–6, and VI. 7. [38]. 32 it is treated as equivalent to the reception of form by the One as *noēton*. This is turn is justified by VI. 7. 32 in terms which are neither mythological nor necessarily metaphysical: what is must be a something. The form is 'a sort of the One' possessed by each of the things that exist (V. 5. 5. 10–11), which will then be 'kinds' or Ideas. It has developed out of the original image of the One, and it is the fundamental element which makes the genesis correspond to the analysis of all existing or thinking. For Plotinus is taking for granted the Aristotelian thesis of the convertibility of 'existent' and 'one', a thesis which he regarded as anticipated by Plato in the *Sophist* and in Parmenides' second hypothesis.

Secondly existent means complex. It is other than one, or simple. This multiplicity takes various forms. Duality is regularly ascribed to Intellect. Its thinking is self-thinking, so that whether we pick on Intellect or on Existence either is a case of subject and object and therefore a pair, which is the minimal case of multiplicity. If we take one member only, the object, we have a different case. At its most universal, it embraces Plato's five 'greatest kinds'; for although these coincide they are distinguishable as concepts, and in the second hypostasis that means ontologically distinct (VI. 2. 7 ad in). But they are abstract attributes of whatever exists, not classes of what exists. For the more obvious plurality of classes we have of course the picture, copied from the *Timaeus* but confirmed by experience, of Existence as a whole of parts which are concrete species. In its version of the 'dual formation' (V. 1.5 ad fin) *Ennead* VI. 7. 15. 20–2 said that from the Good came what was for Intellect a plurality because it could only sustain it piecemeal; and despite the more mystical imagery which follows, this refers to genera and species. In this tract Plotinus likes to call it the 'variegated' realm of Being/Existence—it is diversified by the presence of otherness—or the 'variety' of the Ideas. [19] In just the same way each part, that is Idea, is variegated by containing 'parts', that is participant species, which are specifically different.

Although from the side of what *is* Plotinus may not provide a conceptual argument for this diversity he does so from the side of the Intellect which is identical with it. Any act of thought, he claims, contains 'variation'; there would be nothing intellectual about a process, if it can be called that, which was logically simple or identical throughout like a contact (VI. 7. 39. 16–9). In other places he requires thought to be 'discursive' or to contain 'transition'; and when, as is sometimes the case, the terms do not refer to inference they mean, I believe, that thinking involves transition from one concept to another because to think (and even to think of) is to think something about something else. If then there are to be true thoughts there must be a corresponding diversity among their objects—pairs corresponding to the subjects and predicates of the thoughts. Whether or not it also follows, it was of course believed by Plotinus that the diversity was one which would be represented by classifying the objects under genera and species.

Nevertheless Plotinus insists frequently that pure or true Intellect thinks and knows the Ideas 'all together', simultaneously. Here its object clearly reflects the attribute of unity which, as we saw, it must possess because, in spite of being altered even by multiplication, it is still the One qua *noēton*. It must here be 'the all', which is the subject of the second tract *On the self-identity and ubiquity of Being as a whole* (VI. 5. [23]) and is on my interpretation the quasi-genus of Being (for Plotinus allows a standard one no more than Aristotle). I shall not pursue this here. It involves many problems, not least the problem how it can be an activity of Intellect when Plotinus has laid the requirement on thought that we have just mentioned of being a process or movement.

So far we have seen attributes of Existence which the genesis account expressly provides for. But there is one whose omission may

[19] VI. 7. 13. 2 and 37, 7. 14. 5, 7. 32. 3; cf. 7. 17. 13, 7. 39. 17–18.

be surprising, for it is not omitted from the genesis accounts of the Athenian Neoplatonists. This is otherness or difference whose part in existent things as objects of knowledge does not need explaining. Kipling, when he asked, 'What do they know of England who only England know?' had not read the *Sophist*. But this is an opportune moment to remind the reader that Plotinus' genesis accounts, while they repeat a theme with few variations, are abstracted from a fairly dense score. He has not chosen to foreshadow otherness but merely to present it as one of the greatest kinds which therefore embraces and is embraced by Existence. Perhaps he has chosen not to write like Proclus. For we saw that he was well aware that the Pre-intellect which possessed or was identical with an image of the One was an 'other'.

Almost invariably the first product of the One's generation was presented as Intellect or thought with or without a potential stage. Even assuming the notion of emanation—or what is better seen as the theory of external activity—we are entitled to ask, why thought? (Why not love or the Niagara Falls?) Certainly we can point to a tradition which gave supreme value to *Nous* and which could be taken for granted by Plotinus. But what are his *grounds*?

The tract called *How that which is after the First is from the First* contains an argument that the first principle must be above Intellect because it is logically simple (V. [7]. 4. 1, and III 8. 9. 40–54 for the rule), and what is generated by that which is above Intellect must be Intellect. The argument fails formally to prove that Intellect must be the first product. But the gap can be filled by a chapter of *Ennead* V. 1. [10] *On the three principal hypostases*. This recognizes that the first product must be not just the One's image (6. 33) but the next greatest thing to the One (6.40; cf. V. 4. 2. 1 ad fin); it then argues that this is Intellect, for everything else comes lower than Intellect—soul representing only a weak expression of thought.

There remains the material weakness. I do not mean the assumption of the hierarchy in which Soul for example is lower than Intellect and Nature lower than Soul: for the *Enneads* are full of arguments for that. What we lack is grounds for the premiss that Intellect or thought is highest in the scale of value, not relatively to the other hypostases but to everything except the One. Logically the requirement is equivalent to the exhaustiveness of the hypostases. An alternative argument for thought being the first product will work better by using logical priority instead of axiological. It is not as explicit as I shall make it, but the components are. In the opening chapter of the tract *On the genesis and order of what are after the One* Plotinus claims that the One is the principle, or origin of all things (V. 2. [11]. 1). 'All things' we know is equivalent to Existence/Being. But, he says, Intellect is what made Existence. In other words the One necessarily generates Existence but thought is the necessary intermediary. This is simply the tale told by the 'genesis account' and we are back with the task of finding an interpretation of that genesis which will give us some reason to believe it.

Plotinus would protest that the question why thought should be the first product is misleading, for except in concept universal thought is the same thing as everything. This identity (or qualified identity) of Intellect and Existence is obviously bound up with his doctrine that real thought is self-thought (see e.g. V. 3. 5). The 'light' which is the external activity of the One is simply 'Intellect and the whole intelligible essence' (V. 3. 12. 39–41), for light sees another light (V. 3. 8).[20] None the less he finds it hard to expound the relation to the One without making thought logically prior to existence. Perhaps he betrays this by a lack of logical symmetry which may even have passed unnoticed in a formula of V. 1, for he means the formula to explain one of the most emphatic statements of the logical simultaneity and identity of the pair. Intellect, he states, by thinking makes being exist, being by being thought makes Intellect think and exist (V. 1. 4. 27–8). In general, I estimate that among his *explicit* statements on the subject the greatest part make Intellect and its object simultaneous and of the remainder less make Intellect than its object prior. But of these two or three on each side are corrected by the assertion that the priority holds only for the order of exposition. If one wants to make philosophical sense of it the matter cannot be left at that. We can take for granted what Plotinus more than once insists on but which for this purpose is comparatively superficial, that the genesis account cannot be a literal one because the terms of it are not events but eternal states. The question is the order of their *logical* priority. Plotinus understands the technical, Aristotelian notion of logical simultaneity, which means mutual implication, and attributes it to thinking and the forms; he characeristically wraps it in his metaphysical version of the Aristotelian physical model: they are one and the same *energeia* (V. 9 [5]. 8). His implicit and excellent grounds are that thinking and its objects—again, 'contents' would be better—are correlative.

---

[20] Reading *voῦν* at V. 3. 12. 40, with H.–S.[2], though still implicit in the context with H.–S.[1] text.

In the beginning I said that most of the genesis accounts at first sight represented existence as a later stage. This was because the first thing generated was most easily understood as a Pre-intellect. But a deeper analysis shewed that this first product was the One qua object of thought or potential object of thought, with the consequence that, the thought being self-thought, the first product was at once Pre-intellect and Pre-existence. So too in the second stage of the genesis the delimiting of Pre-intellect which turned it into actual thought could be described equally as the work of the object (as in the Aristotelian psychological model) and as the work of Pre-intellect.

If Plotinus gives the impression of the genesis as an unfolding of thought from the One to the lower hypostases there is a ready explanation. Either he or his reader or both are intent on seeing it as the reverse image of the soul's ascent to the One, and secondly this ascent is seen subjectively as stages of consciousness. But there are two questions posed now by the steps of the soul's ascent as we find them in the *Enneads*. Do they match steps we have seen in the genesis of Existence? Is such a match *the meaning* of the genesis?

The first question need not detain us. Every reader of the *Enneads* knows that the dominant theme of them is the soul's return to its fatherland. And they leave no doubt that its route is to be that by which it left Intellect and by which Intellect as it were left the One. *Ennead* III. 8. 8 is a good witness to this, and as the following chapter puts it, Intellect must return to what is 'behind' it. Looked at statically what we called the two stages of the descent—the external activity of the One and the internal activity of Intellect—reflect respectively an imperfect image of the One and the same image perfected as Intellect/Existence. In the ascent the first corresponds to the position or condition which is described in VI. 7. 35 as the 'loving' instead of 'thinking' Intellect and elsewhere in various ways, such as 'just intellectual contact' with the One (V. 3. 17. 25). The second stage of the descent is of course the resting place which is reached when (as in V. 8. 16) the soul abandons its own intellect to become pure intellect. Conversely the concrete relapse of the visionary from possession by the One can be described in the same terms as the abstract procession of the One to the One-many (V. 5. 4. 10). But Plotinus does not undertake anything more detailed by way of matching steps or items within these stages. But perhaps one would expect him to only if one restricted the meaning of the genesis to such a match and so in effect read the genesis as a fable.

His avowed purpose in recounting it was usually to show that being and thought both owe their existence to the One. This of course is not philosophy but myth unless the tale can be justified independently. To be something other than myth and other than fable it will have to involve some sort of analysis of being and thought. This it does.

The first stage explains that the One projects itself as an object of thought (*noēton*). The second stage explains what it means to be an object of thought; and what it does mean coincides with what it means to exist. But we shall not after all find here wholly independent grounds for thought being the first product of the One. For that depends on the identity of object (*on*) and object of thought (*noēton*); and this has to be assumed for the first stage and only expanded and confirmed by coherence in the second stage.

What is the difference between an object and an object of thought? Different philosophers will give different answers. But to give an example one difference among others might be that an object—something that happens just to be there—can be logically independent of every other object, while an object of thought cannot be independent of every other object of thought. (This may recall the debate about 'internal relations' which was fought in the revolt against British idealism at the beginning of this century.) That would have been Plotinus' opinion. It was also his opinion that there were no objects which were not objects of thought, except the limiting case of the One—limiting case because *eo ipso* it is not an *on*. The One is of course simple. Towards the end of V. 3. 13 he insists (ll 19 ff) on the plurality of the contents of Existence and argues that if it were simple and were to say, 'I am existence' it would not be talking the truth because it would not be talking about itself or about Existence.[21] He then asks (l 30) whether, if Existence will be thought (of) only if it is a whole of parts, it does not follow that none of the parts will be thinkable. His reply is that it does follow if you want to think of them singly and in isolation from one another. So he draws the required conclusion (l 34) that the absolutely simple can neither think nor be thought (of).

This holism is not of course based directly on language like Quine's but is a network of knowledge. That it is Plotinus' reading of Platonic dialectic does not need to be spelt out: but the fact is relevant because dialectic is the stage and means by which the soul exchanges its so called discursive intellect for the pure intellect, or Existence (see *On dialectic, Enn.* I 3. 4). As a manifestation of plurality the holism must

---

[21] Some lack of distinction between sense and reference makes it hardly possible to translate this sentence satisfactorily.

not only be distinguished from the plurality of the greatest kinds but from the duality in Existence and in Intellect which consists merely in each containing the other as its correlate. As the multiplication undergone by the One as object of thought this duality is much more commonly what is intended in the genesis accounts than is the plurality of forms. It is made evident in self-thought; and it is not a distinction between an object and an object of thought but between an object and the thought of it—horse and the thought of horse, justice and the thought of justice (V. 6. 6. 24–6). But the members of each pair are abstractions, for they are identical in substance. (Plotinus uses the Aristotelian formula, οὐσία but no doubt conscious of it as a synonym for his own hypostatized 'Existence', ibid, 1. 4. 5.) I shall not say more about this well-known identity of object and thought.

An object of thought is an intentional object which must by definition be what it is thought to be. This is the meaning, allowance made for anachronism, of Plotinus' claim that Intellect has no place for error (VI. 2. 8. 2–3). But it is essential to keep in mind that it is only in 'intellectual' thought that the intentional object, or noēton, cannot be separated from the object of reference, the on. Suppose someone thinks that beauty consists in a harmony of colour and shapes: the beauty which he is 'thinking' fails to match the real beauty. Does not this imply that the existent object is prior to the act of thinking? Certainly, and Plotinus often says so. But it is precisely the fact which indicates that the act of thinking is in this case only an image of real thought, a case of confused or (Plato's word) dim thinking. The genesis analysed thought universally inasmuch as it analysed thought at its best in accordance with the widely accepted theory that to define 'x' is to define 'x at its best'.

The notion of an object of thought is, I am afraid, the limit of what I can find the genesis contributing to the analysis of thought universally. But to the extent that it is not question-begging as an analysis of existence the identification of the notion with the notion of an object must be counted as a contribution. And by enabling us to attribute a number of properties to the notion of an existent object it did not tell us what we did not know before from Plotinus, but it validated the hypothesis that it rested on analysis. It will already have become clear that we either should not or need not envisage stages at all, but rather elements or factors in thought as Existence. I should prefer to say, 'need not', because it seems possible to me that Plotinus thought that he was also describing, not to say engaging in a process of thought about his topic which would contain stages in a way more familiar to us in Hegel, even if the topic, contrary to Hegel, had no stages. Be that as it may, what is implied by envisaging elements rather than stages in the genesis is that even in discursive thought, which takes time, they would be present simultaneously. Thus it would be a universal element that thinking was directed towards the One, and this in less high flown terms might mean that it was essentially synthesis, all the way from putting together a subject and a predicate to finding a genus of species. In pure Intellect even the vision of the One is said by Plotinus to be simultaneous, and not to 'take turns with', thought—unless he means only the capability of the vision (VI. 7. 35. 27–30).

With one foot in consciousness, as it were, and one in objectivity (the *an sich?*) the One as object of thought may also suggest to the modern mind the intentional object of phenomenology. Take for instance Sartre's interpretation of the intentionality as the emptiness ('purity') of consciousness. For this implies that consciousness does not come into contact with or even 'possess' its objects: they compose it.[22] Of course the comparison with Plotinus does violence to history. But one can read an ancient philosopher for many purposes.

To return to the text of the *Enneads*, that first object of thought, which we called Pre-intellect, is referred to in VI. 7 as Life (7. 14–15; cf. 7. 21. 4–6 of the One's external activity, and V. 3. 1. 8–9); it had no thought but *lived* facing the One (7. 16. 14–15); and accordingly Intellect is called delimited Life (7. 17. 25–6). In this context it is, I believe, the concept which Plotinus used to signify the dual character of Pre-intellect as intentional object or *noēton*, or rather the neutral character between the two aspects of Existence which it will possess when it is 'perfected'.[23] To understand the concept it should not be separated from the use (which I believe it to have) to signify the common nature, to the extent that there is one, shared by the range of behaviour which Plotinus classes as thought. For at neither the higher end of this spectrum nor the lower is his 'thought' accompanied by even the possibility of consciousness of self. But the closer it is to either of the ends the more his 'life', of which thought is but an instance, corresponds to our concept of life, at least in the extended or metaphorical sense of activity. The fact that at the upper end the

[22] See e.g. the little essay, 'Une idée fondamentale de la phénoménologie de Husserl: l'intentionalité' (1939), in *Situations* I.

[23] The dual character of 'life' between being and thought was expounded in P. Hadot's admirable 'Etre, vie, pensée chez Plotin et avant Plotin', *Entretiens Hardt* v, (Vandoeuvres-Genève, 1960).

activity is changeless may lead us to think the concept is inapplicable there: but it should not in my view lead us to think that Plotinus did not count changeless activity as activity.[24] In pure Intellect we reach knowledge or 'contemplation' which is 'living contemplation' or true thought. While of course echoing the *Timaeus*, the chapter (III. 8. 8) in which we learn this has more than most to tell us about Plotinus' still too obscure notion of Life.[25]

It is not an hypostasis and it is not even a category of Being. On the contrary, like *logos* and perhaps beauty, it is one of the pervasive elements of the hierarchy which fall as it were between the interstices of hypostases and are no less interesting and essential to the understanding of Plotinus. I have suggested its function in the genesis of thought and existence. I am inclined to believe that its use by Plotinus depended in part on his mystical experience or imagination; that is, the meaning and associations he attached to it derived in part, and an integral part, from such experience or imagination as opposed to antecedent philosophical formulas. There is not much positive evidence for this beyond perhaps some descriptions of the 'living creature', which is all existence (especially in VI. 7. 12) and of the life of eternity (especially in II. 7. 3). But it can have an affective and, so to speak, displaced application. When Proust's narrator tries or rather leans to kiss Albertine, 'la vie', he says, 'n'était pas hors de moi, elle était en moi'.[26] This is not to question the influence of the antecedent formulas in the *Sophist*, *Timaeus*, and *Metaphysics* Λ, to name those most evident in the *Enneads*. But they are hardly more than formulas; and however persuasive one finds Hadot's case for their development by the later Academy they seem simply insufficient to explain Plotinus' concept. Concepts which were comparatively abstract and familiar in the Schools were employed by him almost paradoxically in the biography of the interior life: but he characteristically gave their expression an additional meaning borrowed from experience of the interior life. This looks likely to have been one of those.

Hove, Sussex

[24] Interesting remarks which are relevant to this can be found in A. H. Armstrong, 'Eternity, life and movement in Plotinus' accounts of *Nous*', in *Le néoplatonisme*, Colloques internationaux du Centre national de la recherche scientifique, Royaumont 9–13 juin 1969 (Paris, 1971).

[25] I regret that I have not seen J. Trouillard, 'Vie et pensée selon Plotin', in *La vie, la pensée*, Actes du congrès des sociétés de philosophie de langue francaise, Grenoble 1954 (Paris, 1954).

[26] *A la recherche du temps perdu* (Pléiade edn, Paris, 1954), i, 933.

'SEPARATION' IN PLATO*

GREGORY VLASTOS

I SHALL argue that in the Platonic corpus, and also in Aristotle's testimony about Plato, the same metaphysical claim may be expressed by either [P] or [Q]:

[P] The forms exist 'themselves by themselves'.
[Q] The forms exist 'separately'.

I Plato

In the debate in the *Parmenides* Socrates puts his own thesis on the mat through the following question:

T1 Don't you believe that there exists a certain form of similarity itself by itself?[1] (128e–129a)

Plainly, this is [P]. When Parmenides enters the debate he begins by asking:

T2[a] Have you yourself, as you say, distinguished[2] in this way, on one hand, separately certain forms, on the other, separately in turn, the things which participate in them? (130b2–3)
[b] And do you think that similarity itself exists separately[3] from the similarity we have ourselves and that so too do unity and plurality and all those things of which you heard just now from Zeno? (130b3–5)

---

* © Gregory Vlastos 1987
[1] I give the literal translation of Plato's αὐτὸ καθ' αὐτό phrase. I would not object to 'alone by itself' (so Allen) or 'just by itself' (so Cornford): I take these to be only verbally different from the literal one. I would object to 'in itself' ('*en soi*' Robin here and often elsewhere in his translation of Plato, and Diès throughout his translation of the *Parmenides*): this is best reserved for ἐν αὐτῷ which Plato never uses as a variant for καθ' αὐτό (I have previously protested this translation in a parallel context: Vlastos, 'Happiness and Virtue in Socrates' Moral Theory', *Proceedings of the Cambridge Philological Society* (1984), n 85).
[2] διῄρησαι.
[3] τί ... ἔιναι ... χωρίς.

A word about the translation at this point. Cornford renders T2[a], 'Have you yourself drawn this distinction you speak of and separated apart' etc. There is no Greek for 'separated' in his text; *chōrizein* does not occur here nor anywhere else in the debate nor is it ever applied to the forms by Plato anywhere in his corpus. The difference between *chōrizein* and the word Plato uses here, *diairein*, is important. A purely logical use of *diairein* is normal from the earliest occurrence of the verb in Greek prose: *diaireōn panta kata physin*, Heraclitus B1. Could one imagine this apostle of cosmic unity writing the same sentence with *chōrizōn* substituted for *diaireōn*? The use of *diairein* for making distinctions without the least implication, or so much as insinuation, that the things distinguished are severed in nature is by no means confined to the philosophers. There are good examples of it in Herodotus.[4] This is how Plato uses the word from his earliest[5] to his latest[6] works; it is the mainstay of his 'method of division'.[7] Not so *chōrizein*, whose primary sense is 'to separate in space, divide locally'.[8] Though, as is well known, *chōrizein* can also be used at times in a purely logical sense, it generally stands for something far stronger, else Plato would not have used it to express the harshest of the dualisms in the credo of his middle period—that view of the soul which makes it an immigrant from another world, attached precariously to a piece of matter in this one, from which death shall 'separate' it (*chōrisei*, Republic (*R.*) 609d7) to 'exist separately' (*chōris einai*, Phaedo (*Phd.*) 64c6–8, 67a1) until its next incarnation. Nor would Aristotle have picked *chōrizein*, *chōriston*, to spearhead his attack on what he takes to be Plato's cardinal error: the assignment of 'separate', independent existence to the *eidos*, which, general in its very nature, can only exist 'in' in the particular individuals or actions which instantiate it.[9]

Thus Cornford's tranlation would seriously mislead English readers

---

[4] LSJ cites 7, 16, and 7, 103, 1 for διαιρέω. = 'to define expressly'. For more examples see J. E. Powell, *Lexicon to Herodotus*, s.v., sense 3.

[5] *Protagoras* 358a: 'From Prodicus' verbal distinctions (διαίρεσιν τῶν ὀνομάτων) I abstain'; *Charmides* (*Ch.*) 163d5, περὶ ὀνομάτων διαιροῦντος.

[6] *Leges* 895e8, λόγῳ δίχα διαιρούμενον ἀριθμόν.

[7] κατ' εἴδη διαιρεῖσθαι τὰ ὄντα (*Phaedrus* 273e); κατὰ γένη διαιρεῖσθαι (*Sophist* 253d).

[8] Its strong ties to χώρα, χῶρος, are evident in derivatives like χωρίτης, χωρικός for 'country-person, rustic'.

[9] He is strongly supported at this point by the logical grammar implicit in common usage: '*F* is "in" (ἔνεστι) or is "present" (πάρεστι) to *x*' would be a normal way of saying that *x has* the attribute denoted by *F*: 'temperance in you, is present in you' for 'you are temperate': *Ch.* 158e7, εἴ σοι πάρεστι σωφροσύνη . . . ἐνοῦσαν αὐτὴν εἴπερ ἔνεστιν.

on a point of fundamental importance in the debate: they would be left unaware of the fact that in part [a] of T2 forms are being *distinguished* from their participants, while nothing is said here to *separate* them from the latter. For this we have to go to part [b] of the text. And here another trap may be sprung for the unwary in a translation. This is how T2[b] comes through Allen's: 'And do you think that likeness itself is something separate from the likeness that we have' etc. The trouble here is of another sort. Strictly speaking there is no inaccuracy in rendering *einai ti chōris* 'is something separate': what is misrepresented is not the sense of the Greek words but the grammatical form of one of them; and this happens to be one of those cases where it is mandatory to preserve the grammatical form of Plato's Greek. For the precise Greek counterpart of 'is separate' would be *chōriston esti*: and Allen's translation would represent Plato as anticipating in the *Parmenides* the very word that was to figure so prominently in Aristotle's attack on him. In rejecting that translation of T2[b] (and parallel renderings of T4 and T5 below) we need not preclude the possibility that Plato might have wished to say that his forms are *chōrista*: at the end of this paper I shall be suggesting that this should be regarded as not only possible, but probable. But this will call for a separate argument which would be grievously at fault if it presumed that *chōriston* is the word Plato had put into the mouth of his Parmenides in our present passage. Since it is clear that he does not, it behoves us to stick to the least tendentious rendering of *einai ti chōris*: 'exists (or, still more literally, "is something") separately'.

I may now resume comment on T2[b]. When it is faithfully rendered it leaves no doubt that it is exactly [Q] to which Socrates is being asked to agree. When he does so he is presented with more examples of things he might believe exist 'themselves by themselves'.

T3 And of this sort of thing too—does a form of justice [exist][10] itself by itself and of beauty and goodness and of all such as these in turn?

(130b7–9)

Here we are back to [P]. But the next question returns to [Q]:

T4 And a form of man [exists] separately from us and our likes—a form of man itself—or of fire or of water?

(130c1–2)

---

[10] εἶναι is to be understood at 130b8 (as a carry-over from 130b4) and then again at 130c1. It is allowed a place of its own in the text at 130d1.

So does the one after that:

T5 And what about these, Socrates, which might be thought ridiculous, like hair or mud or dirt or anything else that is altogether worthless and trivial? Are you perplexed whether one should say that a form of each of these exists separately, as something other than the things we handle?

(130c5–d2)

So we have [P] in T1, then again in T3, and then repeatedly thereafter in the debate (133A, 133c, 135a–b), from which Parmenides feels free to shift at pleasure, with Socrates' concurrence, to [Q] at T2[b], T4, T5. There can be no reasonable doubt that [P] and [Q] are meant to enunciate the same metaphysical claim, sponsored by Socrates, attacked by Parmenides.

However, two objections could be raised to taking this equivalence to be Plato's firm, well-considered, doctrine:

First, it might be supposed that the relation of forms to their participants which is expressed in [Q] is symmetrical: And if this were true then, certainly [Q] could not be logically equivalent to [P], which Plato uses in dialogues of his middle period[11] and also in the *Timaeus*[12] to express the central affirmation of his theory of forms, for there can be no doubt that (P) is *not* meant to refer to a symmetrical relation between forms and their participants. Thus in the central books of the *Republic* the F is to its instances as is a model to its copies and as an object to its shadows; and this relation is strongly antisymmetric: the copies 'imitate' the model, but not the model the copy; the object is a causal condition of the existence of its shadows, but the converse is not true. But is there good reason for the supposition that the relation in [Q] *is* meant to be symmetrical? What evidence could be adduced on its behalf: Consider:

T6 Isn't death just this: on one hand, that the body, having got rid of the soul,

[11] That forms 'exist themselves by themselves' is built into the 'hypothesis' at *Phd.* 100b5–6 and into the description of the form's immutability at 78d5–6. Earlier on we were told that the forms are to be investigated 'themselves by themselves': 66a2, 83b1–2. In the description of the form of beauty perceived at the moment of climactic vision in the *Symposium* (211b) it reappears with redoubled emphasis, expanded into 'itself by itself with itself'. It is contracted to 'by itself' at *Cratylus* 386e3–4 and *R.* 476a11. It had first entered an epistemological context in Plato's corpus in the closing sentence of the *Meno*, portent of things to come in the *Cratylus* and the *Phaedo*.

[12] 1251c1 and d4–5, a passage of capital importance. Plato is raising afresh the question, 'Are there really such things as forms?' and he answers it from scratch. He puts the 'itself by itself' locution into the formulation of both the question and the resoundingly confident answer he gives to it.

has come to exist separately, itself by itself; and, on the other, that the soul, rid of the body, exists separately, itself by itself?

(*Phd.* 64c5–8)

(Cp. also 67a1: 'Then [at death] the soul will exist itself by itself, separately from the body.')

Here it is clear that the relation in 'X exists separately from Y' is not antisymmetric: it is reversible when X = the soul, Y = the body: the body *can* exist, albeit only for a short time, separately from the soul; the soul could exist for ever separately from a body. But what does that prove for the point at issue? Does it show that the relation in 'X exists separately from Y' is reversible for all values of X and Y? Clearly not: all it shows is that it is reversible for some values of the variables; it does not show that it is reversible when X = form, Y = its participants. That Plato thinks it irreversible in this latter case should be clear from the very analogies in the middle books of the *Republic* I cited above to show that the relation of forms to their participants is antisymmetric. Taking 'X exists separately from Y' to express the modal claim that X may exist when Y does not,[13] it should be obvious that while, say, trees may 'exist separately' from their shadows (they are there day and night, hence, regardless of whether or not they are casting shadows), their shadows cannot exist separately from them (no tree, no shadows); again, in Plato's creation story the existence of the eternal model only too obviously can and does exist separately from copies of it in the world of time. So the objection fails: there is no reason to believe that Plato would think that the relation in 'X exists separately from Y' is true for all values of X and Y, hence no reason here to doubt that [Q] at T2[b], T4, and T5 represents pukka Platonic doctrine. Only if one ignored the difference between [Q] and what is asserted in T2[a]— between asserting that forms *exist separately* from their participants at T2[b], T4, and T5, on one hand, and, on the other, *distinguishing separately* forms and participants from each other at T2[a][14]—would one be seriously tempted to think[15] that the position to which Socrates

---

[13] So (very reasonably, in my view) Allen (1980, 100–2 *et passim*) and Fine (1984, 58 *et passim*).

[14] In the latter assertion the relation is clearly symmetrical: if I distinguish X from Y I am *ipso dicto* distinguishing Y from X. It is not symmetrical *ipso dicto* in the former, and when one looks into the matter, one may find ample reason to believe that it is not symmetrical at all.

[15] So Allen: misled by his mistranslation of T2[a] he thinks that 'Parmenides' first question assumes that, if Ideas are separate, separation is a symmetrical relation' (1980, 100). Similarly Fine: "*chōris*" is . . . used to indicate a symmetrical relation (see, e.g.,

agrees in T2[b], T4, and T5 is out of whack with the ontology upheld by Plato throughout his middle period and even in the *Timaeus*.[16]

The other objection would be that the *Parmenides* is aporetic. Should this undoubted fact leave us in doubt that Socrates' concurrence with the equivalence of [P] and [Q] may be taken as firm, well-considered Platonic doctrine, rather than as a hasty, imprudent concession[17] wrested by a wily opponent form the immature, brash, unwary debater which Socrates is here made out to be for the nonce? So we might have cause to think, if that equivalence were something out of the blue, without strong antecedents in preceding dialogues of Plato's middle period. But it is nothing of the kind. If we look for antecedents we can find them as far back as the *Phaedo*. where the 'itself by itself' existence of the form is asserted repeatedly.[18] Here we are given the chance to understand what this phrase is supposed to *mean*. We get it when we see it used in the closely, though not entirely, parallel case of soul and body in their mutual relation. A second look at T6 above is in order here. There 'itself by itself' is brought in as a kind of tail to 'exists separately'. which could have easily sufficed without it to convey the message that death terminates the lifelong conjunction of soul and body, cutting them loose from one another to go their 'separate' ways. If Plato were striving for economy he would not have tacked on 'itself by itself' to 'exists separately' in each of its two occurrences. By bringing in that phrase the way he does here—as an appositional appendage to 'exists separately'—he gives his readers a perfect clue to what he means by that phrase, which is far from self-explanatory[19] and would have puzzled them if Plato had sprung it on

---

130b2–4)' (1984, 58), failing to notice that while distinguishing Forms from their participants is indeed symmetrical, the separate existence of Forms and participants is not (cf. the preceding note).

[16] Which is not to concede that it records the rejection of the ontology of Plato's middle period. As I argued years ago (1954, 231 ff), it is 'a record of honest perplexity'. Plato now recognizes the gravity of difficulties he had taken lightly heretofore, if he had even faced them at all. He is taking a second, very hard, look at his ontological theory—which is not to say that he is ditching it.

[17] Allen (98 ff) holds that it is, and Fine (58–9) allows that it might be, a 'wrong admission'. They seem unmindful of the question that should haunt anyone who has reached that conclusion Why should Plato make the great Parmenides direct his critique against a straw man?

[18] Cf. n 11 above.

[19] It is surprising how little curiosity this phrase has excited in students of Plato's technical vocabulary. That it enters his terminology for the forms in his middle period, having never been used in an epistemological or ontological context before the *Meno* (at its close, 100b) seems to have passed unnoticed by scholars who had been well aware of

them without supplying some such context as this. Here they should be able to see that to say of either body or soul that it 'exists itself by itself' is to reiterate, not to modify, the substantive claim that after death each exits 'separately' for a spell (a brief one for the body, an infinitely long one for the soul). And the context resolves completely the semantic incompleteness in 'separately', which would otherwise have left them wondering: separately from *what*? Thus what is said in the *Phaedo* shows that

for X = body, 'X exists *itself by itself*' = 'X exists *separately from soul*';
for X = soul, 'X exists *itself by itself*' = 'X exists *separately from body*'.

By the same token we may surmise that when it is form which is said to exist *itself by itself* what must be meant is that it too exists *separately*; and when we then ask 'separately from *what*?' we may surmise that the answer must be, 'from something which is to form as its body is to a soul'; and what could that be but the form's embodiments in the world of time—its participants? We do not need to rest content with just an educated guess that this would be the correct answer. Context makes it abundantly clear on all the occasions on which the 'itself by itself' phrase is brought in. Thus in the *Phaedo* the 'hypothesis' that beauty exists 'itself in itself' is precisely that it does so as something whose existence is completely separate from that of all those 'other things' (100c4), that is, other than *it*, which are beautiful 'for no reason other than their participation in *that* beauty' (100c5–6). So too in the *Symposium*, where the point made by insisting with redoubled emphasis that beauty 'exists itself by itself with itself' is that it is not '*in* some other thing' (*en heteròi tini*, 211a8), be it corporeal (some beautiful 'face or hands') or even incorporeal ('some discourse or knowledge'). Though the form is not *said* to 'exist *separately*' in either of these passages, nor any other before the *Parmenides*, it comes naturally to mind when one tries to explain their thought. So when we reach at long last in the debate in the *Parmenides* a passage where it blossoms out on the surface of the text, we can see it as the full

the fact that the leaner αὐτὸ τὸ Φ phrase had been fully anticipated in earlier dialogues (Riddell, 1857, 134; Lewis Campbell, 1894, 305–6; Burnet on *Phd.* 64c6, 65d5, 65e3; Ross (1951), 16–17; Allen (1970), 74–5). *A fortiori* enquiry into its special significance has never been put on their agenda. Most surprising is its neglect in the most laborious piece of research ever published on Plato's technical terminology, Constantin Ritter's *Neue Untersuchungen über Platon* (1910), containing a hundred-page-long chapter on '*Eidos, Idea* und verwändte Wörter': no allusion to the role of the 'itself by itself' phrase in the evolution of Plato's philosophical idiolect. The fault is not remedied in his massive two-volume work, *Platon* (1910, 1923).

articulation of what had been assumed all along, though never spelled out, in the earlier occurrences of the 'itself by itself' phrase. So there is good reason to accept the equivalence of [P] to [Q] as authentic Platonic doctrine. It makes explicit what Plato had been maintaining in other words throughout the great dialogues of his middle period and continued to maintain in the *Timaeus*.

II Aristotle on 'separation' in Plato

In explicit or implicit reference to the Platonic form Aristotle repeatedly uses appositional syntax to join 'is separate' to 'exists itself by itself' in exactly the same way as we saw Plato in the *Phaedo* (T6 above) join 'exists separately' to 'exists itself by itself' in speaking of the body and of the soul:

T7 And similarly with regard to [Plato's] Idea [of the Good], it is clear that even if there did exist some Good which is separate (*chōriston*), itself by itself (*auto kath hauto*), it would not be what human beings could do and possess.
(*Nicomachean Ethics* 1096b31–4)

T8 This is the question before us: to see if something exists which is separate (*chōriston*), itself by itself (*auto kath' hauto*), and not belonging to any sensible thing.   (*Metaphysics* (*Metaph.*) 1060a11–13)

In each of these texts Aristotle takes either of

'is separate',
'exists itself by itself'.

to make the same substantive ontological claim which he would know to have been made by Plato through either of

'exists separately'.
'exists itself by itself',

about the soul in the *Phaedo* and also, though not by the same syntactical device, about the forms in the *Parmenides*. Not surprisingly, Aristotle thinks of both statements as entailed by the same premiss, namely, that forms are substances:

For them the Ideas exist by themselves (*kath hautas*[20] *hyphistanai autois*), if they are substances.

---

[20] The contraction here of the 'itself by itself' phrase could be due to Alexander's paraphrase; but it *could* have been present in the original (Plato too occasionally clips off the first pronoun: cf. n 11 above).

(*peri Ideōn, apud* Alexander, *in Aristotelis Metaphysica commentaria* 83. 24–5)

They are right to separate the Ideas, if they are substances.

(*Metaph.* 1040b26–7)

In his illuminating study, '*Chōristos* in Aristotle' (1985), 89 ff at 92), Donald Morrison points out that the word is not known to occur anywhere before Aristotle and suggests that 'it is reasonable to suppose that Aristotle himself coined it'. The suggestion is certainly worth considering. But is it more likely or even as likely as is the alternative possibility that Plato had previously used the word himself in oral discussion in the Academy? Having asserted repeatedly in the *Parmenides* that the forms exist *chōris*[21], why should he have not found it natural to reach for the cognate verbal adjective when it could serve the needs of his discourse?[22] Anyhow there is independent evidence that reference to forms as *chōrista* was by no means confined to Plato's critic. For as Cherniss has pointed out,[23] Aristotle ascribes 'separately existing, non-sensible entities not only to Plato but to Speusippus and Xenocrates' as well and 'Aristotle's interpretation is here supported directly by Xenocrates, who defined the Platonic Idea as an *aita paradeigmatikē tōn kata physin synestōtōn*', asserting that it was '*chōristē kai theia*'. If *chōriston* had been invented by the bright young man from Macedonia to pillory as a colossal blunder a doctrine common to Plato and his closest adherents, it is hardly likely that the latter would have picked it up from him to put it at the centre of their own doctrinal self-description. In those circumstances it is more likely that Aristotle had found the term in current use inside the Academy and had voiced his dissidence in insider's language.

University of California, Berkeley

---

[21] With, or without, a dependent genitive (with at T2[b] and T4, without at T5). The latter usage comes closer to Aristotle's χωριστὸν εἶναι, which does not call for a dependent genitive, though it admits of one.

[22] If one starts off saying that something exists χωρίς one might well wish to say, in a back-reference to it, that it is χωριστόν, and would be able to say so if the word was within reach of one's effective vocabulary, as χωριστόν surely was in Plato's, for while (as Morrison points out (91)) χωριστόν never occurs in his corpus, ἀχώριστά does (*R.* 524c1); we may assume that anyone who controls the privative form of a verbal adjective, as well as the parent verb, would also have ready access to the word itself without the prefix.

[23] Cherniss (1942, 206 ff at 208–9), in the course of a powerful onslaught on the view, still influential at the time, that Aristotle's imputation of χωρισμός to Plato had been rank misinterpretation.

Bibliography

R. E. Allen, *Plato's Euthyphro and the Earlier Theory of Forms* (London, 1970).

——, *Plato's Parmenides*, translation and commentary (Minneapolis, 1980). John Burnet, *Plato's Phaedo*, text and commentary (Oxford, 1911).

Lewis Campbell, 'Platonic Diction', in *Plato's Republic*, ed L. Campbell and B. Jowett (Oxford, 1894), ii, 260 ff.

H. Cherniss, *Aristotle's Criticism of Plato and the Academy* (Baltimore, 1944).

F. M. Cornford, *Plato and Parmenides*, translation and commentary (London, 1939).

Auguste Diès, *Platon, Parménide*, the Guillaume Budé Plato, vol viii, Part I (Paris, 1922).

Gail Fine, 'Separation', in *Oxford Studies in Ancient Philosophy*, ii (1984), 31 ff.

Donald Morrison, '*Choristos* in Aristotle', *Harvard Studies in Classical Philology*, LXXXIX (1985), 89 ff.

J. Enoch Powell, *Lexicon to Herodotus* (Cambridge, 1938).

James Riddell, *Plato's Apology, with Digest of Platonic Idioms* (Oxford, 1867).

Gregory Vlastos, 'The Third Man Argument in the *Parmenides*', *Philos. Review*, LXIII (1954) 319 ff.

COULD ALEXANDER (FOLLOWER OF ARISTOTLE) HAVE DONE BETTER? A RESPONSE TO PROFESSOR FREDE AND OTHERS*

R. W. SHARPLES

IN HER article 'Could Paris (son of Priam)[1] Have Chosen Otherwise'[2] Professor Dorothea Frede, discussing my edition of Alexander of Aphrodisias' *de Fato*[3], raises issues which deserve further discussion. So too has Professor Nicholas White.[4] The points they make have a bearing on general questions of method in the study of ancient philosophy, and are worth discussing for that reason as well as for their own intrinsic interest.

I

Professor Frede and I agree that Alexander's discussion in Chapter IX of *de Fato*, in so far as it is concerned with (*A*) the distinction between cases where there are and those where there are not different possibilities *in general terms*, is not directly relevant as a criticism of the Stoic determinist position, while Chaper X, concerned with (*B*) the necessity or otherwise of *individual* events, *is* directly relevant (cf.

---

* © R. W. Sharples 1987
[1] Paris was also known as Alexander; so Alexander (of Aphrodisias), *de Fato* XVI. 187. 16 Bruns.
[2] *Oxford Studies in Ancient Philosophy*, II (Oxford 1984), 279–92; henceforth cited as 'Frede'. Cf. also her article 'The dramatisation of determinism', *Phronesis*, XXVII (1982), 276–98. I do not understand Frede's reference on 285 n 13 of her *Oxford Studies* article to my views on Ch XXXV of *de Fato*.
[3] London (Duckworth) 1983. Since the publication of this the Budé edition by Professor Pierre Thillet has also appeared (Paris, 1984; cf. my review of this at *Classical Review* 36 (1986) 33–35).
[4] *Philosophical Review* (PhRev), XCIV (1984), 31.

Frede, 283–5).[5] Where we differ is in our explanation of this aspect of Chapter IX. In my book and in an earlier article[6] I associated it with a tendency in Aristotelianism in general to emphasize (*A*) rather than (*B*). Frede explains Alexander's approach rather by the observation that 'it is always pedagogically and rhetorically effective if one pretends that the opponent stands in need of tutoring in basics'.

Even if Alexander's approach is a matter of conscious tactics, it is still significant that the basics are *Aristotelian* basics. There is, as Frede herself agrees (285), a 'preoccupation' in Aristotle with what is 'universal and eternally self-same or at least true "most of the time"'; and Chapter IX of *de Fato* would not, if Frede is right, be the only place where Alexander argues against the Stoics by interpreting their positions on the basis of Aristotelian assumptions and opinions which they would not necessarily accept.[7] He also tends to identify Aristotelian doctrine and natural conceptions.[8]

But can we be sure that Alexander *is* totally free from confusion on this issue? Frede is right to reject Hintikka's view that Aristotle's solution to the Sea-Battle paradox in *de Interpretatione* IX turns on (*A*) rather than (*B*).[9] But it is not clear that the distinction between the two issues was always realized in later ancient discussions of the issue.[10] And the treatment of necessary, assertoric, and contingent propositions in Alexander's own commentary on the *Prior Analytics*, if not also in Aristotle's work itself,[11] shows difficulties that may not be unrelated. A statement, be it particular or general, is either necessary or non-

---

[5] On my p 136 I referred to the issue as being whether something *can* be prevented (as is remarked by Frede, 284 n 11) precisely because I take it to be Aristotle's view that if an event is truly not predetermined then one cannot use the simple future tense '*will* be prevented' in connection with it; cf. *de Generatione et Corruptione* II. 11. 337b4, and below n 32.

[6] 'Aristotelian and Stoic Conceptions of Necessity in the *de Fato* of Alexander of Aphrodisias', *Phronesis*, XX (1975), 247–74.

[7] Cf. my commentary, above n 3, 20, and below n 51.

[8] Cf. *de Fato* VIII. 172. 17, and my commentary, 18 and nn 110–14.

[9] Frede, 284; Hintikka's view was expressed in 'The Once and Future Sea-Fight: Aristotle's discussion of future contingents in *De interpretatione* IX', *PhRev*, LXXIII (1964), 461–92, reprinted as Ch VIII of his *Time and Necessity* (Oxford, 1973).

[10] Cf. my article cited in n 6, 264–5, and especially Ammonius, *in Aristotelis de Interpretatione* (*in de Int.*) 137. I ff, discussed there at 265n 48. Chance, the contingent (again expressed in terms that emphasize the contrast between what is variable and what is not), and human agency appear as exceptions to fate in middle-Platonist writings, of which Alexander shows no direct knowledge (cf. my edition, 13–14), again without any very clear statement of the extent to which this has indeterministic implications.

[11] But cf. H. Tredennick in *Aristotle: The Categories* etc., ed H. P. Cook and H. Tredennick (Loeb, 1938), 192.

necessary (contingent); 'just being true' is not a third co-ordinate option, though Alexander tends to treat it as such.[12] But while from the general perspective (*A*) it is natural to confine 'possible' to the *non-necessary*, as Aristotle does in his treatment of the contingent as excluding both the necessary and the impossible, from the point of view of statements about individual events (*B*) it is natural to confine 'possible' to what is not *actual*; one does not naturally say 'it is possible that it is raining now' if one knows that it is. And a tendency to combine both general and particular perspectives may be partly responsible for the problems in Alexander's discussion.

My suggestion is not that Alexander could not have sorted out the difference between approaches (*A*) and (*B*) in de Fato IX if he had wished to, but rather that he tends to produce stock responses to certain issues, without perhaps always adequately considering the relevance of the points he was making.[13] And Chapter IX of *de Fato* comes (as I see it) at the end of a sequence of arguments concerned with the notion of exceptions to what is usual, a sequence which starts in chapter VI (see below, Section IV ad fin). As a non-determinist he may well have taken it for granted that some exceptions were indeed not predetermined; this would make the failure to distinguish explicitly between (*A*) and (*B*) easier to understand, if not to excuse.

I entirely agree with Professor Frede that Aristotle's preoccupation with what is true for all or most of the time has a physical and metaphysical basis in his system as a whole, rather than being just a 'foible for regularity' (ibid, 285); but I do not see that that in any way reduces the extent to which Aristotle and his followers *do* emphasize this perspective, or makes my explanation of Alexander's approach in chapter IX any less likely—if anything, the reverse. I also agree that accidental events can *sometimes* be subsumed under regularities and so explained (Aristotle, *Metaphysics E*. 2. 1027a25–6; Frede, loc cit); but what I insisted on in my 1975 article[14] was (i) that to the extent to which this happened the supposedly accidental *ceased to be* accidental, and (ii), *pace* Ross,[15] that the accidental could not be eliminated in this way altogether.

[12] Cf. R. W. Sharples, 'Alexander of Aphrodisias, Problems of Possibility—I', *Bulletin of the Institute of Classical Studies*, London (*BICS*), XXIX (1982), at 96–9.

[13] This judgement may be unduly influenced by the minor works attributed to Alexander, the *Quaestiones* and *Ethical Problems*; it may be questioned how far our assessment of Alexander should be influenced by works which are almost certainly not all by Alexander himself and are in any case only short school-discussions.

[14] Above n 6; at 263 f and n 44.

[15] W. D. Ross, *Aristotle: Metaphysics* (Oxford, 1924), I, 361.

The matter could be decisively settled if there was any indication from Alexander himself of a recognition of the difference between (A) and (B). But that is something I at least have failed to find in the text. (This was why I rejected Donini's suggestion that Chapter IX was not even intended to be directed against the same position as Chapter X;[16] but Donini was right to emphasize the extent to which Aristotelian texts and conceptions influence the course of Alexander's argument, here and elsewhere.) Frede observes (284 top) that 'the serious charge' (by Alexander against the determinists) 'in Chapter IX is that *even if* an event is in principle in the class of the contingent . . . *this* particular event cannot be considered as genuinely "open" . . . if it is ancestrally rigidly determined that it *will* or *will not* come about' (italics hers). What I miss in Chapter IX is an explicit statement of that 'even if'; Alexander writes as if contingency in principle is enough. It is true that in the second part of Chapter X he emphasizes the importance of whether an individual event is predetermined or not, but that is in arguing against the Stoic claim that 'there will be a sea-battle' (on a specified date) is not necessary because it will become false after the event; the question whether a statement about an individual event remains true for ever is a different issue from that of the distinction between (A) and (B), though not unconnected,[17] and it is not clear that Alexander connects the point he makes against the Stoic argument in Chapter X with the fact that a similar objection could be made against his own remarks in Chapter IX.

Frede remarks (284 n 10) that Alexander 'rather cleverly' starts with cases of random motion (i.e. what might plausibly be assumed to be non-predetermined, though the Stoics would not accept the point) and then moves on to what is in principle open (i.e. cases like that of water which can be either hot or cold, as opposed to fire which is always hot). The latter type of example proves nothing against the determinists unless it can be shown that the temperature of the water on any particular occasion is not predetermined. But since the random examples come *before* those of variation, Alexander does *not* in Chapter IX start by tutoring his opponents in basics and *then* go on to the real issue; rather, he introduces examples of contingency that are at least

---

[16] P. L. Donini, 'Stoici e Megarici nel *de Fato* di Alessandro di Afrodisia?', in *Scuole socratiche minori e filosofia ellenistica*, ed G. Giannantoni (Bologna, 1977), 190. Cf. my edition, 21, and J. Dillon's review, *Journal of Hellenic Studies* (*JHS*), CV (1985), 195–6 and n 1.

[17] Cf. my commentary, 137, second complete paragraph.

arguably relevant and then others that are less obviously so, without clearly indicating that the issues are distinct. (Or, if the *whole* of Ch IX is to be regarded as establishing basic distinctions before the more directly relevant arguments of Ch X, the tutorial is one that obscures the crucial distinction.)

It is true that the reference to water is introduced by 'at any rate' (*goun*); but 'at any rate' is not the same as 'I am now going on to make a general basic point which may be less directly relevant to the point at issue than what has preceded'. It *might* mean 'I know that the following point is weaker than the one I actually need to make', but in that case one would expect a clear subsequent indication of just how the weaker point is relevant—for example, 'It is true that *not all* these variations are necessarily exceptions to determinism, but can we really believe that *none* are?' Either, as I suggested, Alexander in Chapter IX neglects the difference between the two issues (*A*) and (*B*); or else he *deliberately* starts with examples that are at least plausible counter-examples to determinism, and then leads on to those that are less obviously so, with a view to misleading his readers into supposing that the determinist position cannot accommodate examples of the latter type either. I am not sure whether Frede would wish to attribute such a ploy to Alexander, though she *does* refer to 'much rather cunning manipulation and finagling' (284).

Frede speaks of the rhetorical effectiveness of pretending that one's opponent needs tutoring in basics. But doing this, rather than getting to grips with the real issue, is a tactic that may turn against its user. At any rate, it was precisely the apparent irrelevance of Chapter IX that led me, the first time that I myself read Alexander's *de Fato*, to suspect that what was interesting about Alexander's arguments was sometimes precisely the way in which they were beside the point.

II

Both Frede (291–2 and n 22) and White (129–30) have remarked on my relative neglect of the providential aspect of Stoic determinism. In a commentary, as opposed to a general discussion of Stoic doctrine, I was necessarily constrained by Alexander's own text;[18] and it seems

---

[18] It is an interesting question how far the lack of unity in Alexander's own discussion can be attributed to the fact that most of his writing was in the form of commentaries.

that the providential aspect of Stoic determinism is something to which he too fails to do justice.

When Frede says (291) that Alexander discusses the providential nature of Stoic determinism in Chapters XXII and following, I am not sure whether she has in mind Chapters XXII to XXV in particular, or the whole of the rest of the treatise. If the latter, it is true that the issue of divine providence is raised more than once.[19] But this is only in sections of a series of arguments whose unifying feature is not a concern with providence, but the fact that they are presented as defences of Alexander's own position against arguments put forward by the determinists for their own position (cf. *de Fato* XXII. 197. 26 ff, and p 17 of my edition); many of them make no reference to providence at all.

Chapters XXII–XXV are concerned with the Stoic argument that fate is needed as the unifying principle of the universe (Ch XXII); Alexander replies that a unifying principle, but one that admits of sublunary exceptions, is rather to be found in the movement of the heavens (Ch XXV). He does criticize the Stoics in Chapter XXIII by arguing that not everything produces an effect, and he argues in Chapter XXIV that for this reason explanation should start from final rather than efficient causes; but his own explanation of the unity of the universe in Chapter XXV hardly puts this suggestion into effect, and throughout it is the question of unity, rather than purpose, that is pre-eminent.

Frede can reply that this is what one would expect, since, she argues, for an Aristotelian unlike a Stoic teleology is a matter of the purposes of individual beings rather than of the universe as a whole (Frede, 291). But this only makes it the more natural that Alexander fails to do justice to the providential aspect of fate in the Stoic theory. Moreover, the reason why the providential nature of Stoic fate is

---

[19]   In Ch XXVIII Alexander raises the biggest single difficulty in the Stoic system, that of why, in a world ordered by providence, good men should be as rare as the phoenix (199. 7 ff). In Ch XXXI Alexander uses the Stoic belief in providence to criticize their attempts to exploit traditional mythological stories about oracles; and divine providence is implied in the argument set out and criticized in Ch XXXVII. Divine foreknowledge is discussed in Ch XXX, though it should be emphasized that this is a rather different issue. Foreknowledge is a necessary condition for providence in the sense of benevolent concern, but not a sufficient one; power and benevolence are also required. Cf. Plato, *Laws* X 901d–e, an influential passage in ancient discussions of the topic. Elsewhere in *de Fato*, too, Alexander complains that determinism is not compatible with divine providence; cf. my edition, 27. But this is a debating point against his opponents, not a serious attempt to consider their position.

important in a discussion of determinism is its relevance to the assessment of individual human action in the Stoic system. Alexander does tell us that for his determinist opponents living creatures are included among the things used by fate (XXXVI. 208. 3 ff, cf. XXII. 192. 27); but he sees this purely as a limitation of human autonomy.

These limitations reflect, naturally enough, aspects of Alexander's own approach to the questions of providence and of the place of human agency in the universe. As the late Professor Moraux observed, Alexander's own explanation of divine providence in terms of the influence of the heavenly bodies produces an idea of the operation of providence that tends towards the mechanistic.[20] Secondly, Alexander rejects determinism by the claim that nature, fate, or—as in Chapter XXV—the order created in the universe by the heavens admits of exceptions. But if human freedom is to be linked with such exceptions to a general order, the question arises of its value in the universe as a whole. Alexander does not consider this in the *de Fato* at all; as I have argued elsewhere, one of the short texts attributed to him does so, and runs into difficulties.[21]

For Alexander, the important question is whether human agents are capable of performing actions that are not entirely predetermined. For the Stoics, it was not just the autonomy of the individual human agent that was the important issue, but also his ability, if he so chose, to co-operate with the working of divine providence. Responsibility (in a soft-determinist sense) was something possessed by all human agents, but *freedom* belonged to the sage alone.[22] Moreover, while the Stoics did at times feel the need to defend their soft-determinist notion of responsibility against libertarian criticism,[23] there is perhaps a danger

---

[20] P. Moraux *Alexandre d'Aphrodise: Exégète de la noétique d'Aristote* (Paris and Liège, 1942), 200. Indeed, Alexander found it hard to rebut the charge that the 'providential' influence of the divine on the sublunary was a purely accidental by-product in his system as far as the divine was concerned; cf. R. W. Sharples, 'Alexander of Aphrodisias on divine providence: two problems', *Classical Quarterly* (*CQ*), n.s. XXXII (1982), at 204–8.

[21] *de Anima Mantissa* (*de An. Mant.*) 169–172 Bruns. Cf. R. W. Sharples, 'Responsibility, chance and not-being', *BICS*, XXII (1975), at 50–2. And for a similar problem in Aristotle himself cf. R. W. Sharples, 'Responsibility and the possibility of more than one course of action: a note on Aristotle *De caelo* 2. 12', *BICS*, XXIII (1976), 69–72. This is not the place to go into the question of whether man is a free agent for Aristotle himself; Frede rightly refers (279) to deterministic tendencies in his thought, but it nevertheless seems to me that his general assumptions are libertarian, and that he does not spell this out as clearly as we might like simply because, at the time when he wrote, the determinist position was not as familiar as it later became. Cf. my edition, 7.

[22] Cf. H. von Arnim, *Stoicorum Veterum Fragmenta* (*SVF*) (Leipzig, 1903–5), iii, 355 f, 362, 544.   [23] Cf. especially *SVF*, ii, 1000, at p 294. 30.

of a false perspective, especially in view of the hostile nature of most of our sources, Alexander included. From the point of view of the Stoic's own positive doctrine the concept of 'what depends on us', *to eph' hēmin*, may have been important in connection not so much with the debate about determinism as with the need to achieve a right understanding of the difference between those things that are up to us and those that are not.[24] The Stoic sage will realize that the one thing that matters—virtue—is in his own power (in a soft-determinist sense, of course) while the things that are not in his control, such as wealth, and health, are not goods. His attitude to them will then be, as Inwood has recently shown,[25] the correct one of an impulse which involves assent *with reservation*; for in addition to knowing that they are not goods, he will also realize that everything that happens is ordained by providence for the best, and that what is in the interest of the universe as a whole is in his own interest, even if it does not seem so. Of this aspect of the Stoic treatment of 'what depends on us' there is no hint in Alexander's *de Fato*. He may well, indeed, have regarded it as beside the point, if the Stoics could not first show—as they could not, if they were to be consistent with their own determinist doctrine—that human beings could be in control of their own actions and attitudes in a sense that would satisfy Alexander himself.

The notion of 'what depends on us' may not be the only case in which the nature of our sources may lead to a false emphasis in our assessment of the Stoic position. For while libertarian critics, ancient and modern, regularly link the Stoic doctrine of possibility to the question of responsibility, it is not clear that this was the perspective in which the Stoics themselves primarily saw it. Later accounts, at any rate, suggest that the Stoic doctrine of possibility originated in the context of discussions of possibility by Diodorus Cronus, Philo, and perhaps Aristotle himself;[26] and examples like the possibility of a log in the Atlantic burning or a stone at the bottom of the sea being seen do not suggest a primary concern with the ability of human agents to

---

[24] Cf. A. A. Long, 'Freedom and determinism in the Stoic theory of human action', in his (ed.) *Problems in Stoicism* (London, 1971), at 189–92; especially on Epictetus, but emphasizing the similarity with earlier Stoic thought.

[25] Brad Inwood, *Ethics and Human Action in Early Stoicism* (Oxford, 1985), 119–26.

[26] Cf. R. Sorabji, 'Five philosophical issues arising from *Metaphysics* Θ 1 and Θ 5', in *Notes on Eta and Theta of Aristotle's Metaphysics recorded by Myles Burnyeat and others* (Oxford, Sub-Faculty of Philosophy Study Aids Monograph no. 4, 1984), at 112–14.

influence events.[27] (If Simplicius, *in Aristotelis Categorias Commentarium* 196. 4 is to be connected with a Stoic position, I was wrong to suggest, on p 135 of my edition, that Alexander, *On Fate* X was the *only* text to suggest that the Stoics interpreted it epistemically; for Simplicius there refers to 'the absence of any *obvious* impediment'.[28] I am grateful to Dr David Sedley for pointing this out.)

III

There is a further way in which the providential nature of Stoic determinism may have a bearing on Alexander's argument. In my commentary I pointed out how Alexander often speaks as if Stoic determinism was fatalistic, in spite of the fact that Chrysippus himself rejected that interpretation by his doctrine of co-fated events. Sarah Waterlow has suggested[29] that this may be because Alexander operates with a notion of causation derived from human agency, where it is not the individual links in the causal chain needed to bring about an intended outcome that we have principally in mind, but the outcome itself. That is to say, Alexander may have assumed that fate must as it were have made up its mind *first* about the eventual outcome, so that that is fixed before the means are even taken into account. (This, after all, is the sequence of a standard Aristotelian deliberation.[30]) In Waterlow's view, then, Alexander's fatalistic interpretation of Stoic determinism results from certain assumptions of his own about causation in general. White (129–30) modifies this by linking it particularly to the Stoic conception of fate as providential and hence, in a sense, purposeful.

Alexander may however be influenced not so much by the general thought that fate has designs which it will definitely achieve, by whatever means, as by a particular point about deliberation. The very notion of deliberation seems to involve the possibility of alternative

[27] Cf. Sharples, above n 12, 91–6, and id, 'Alexander of Aphrodisias: Problems on Possibility, II', *BICS*, XXX (1983), at 99–100.

[28] Simplicius does not cite any authority for this position, unlike those of Diodorus and Philo; Alexander, *in Aristotelis Analytica Priora* 184. 10, in a similar context, attributes the view that what is possible is what is not prevented—here with no reference to *obvious* impediment—to Aristotle. But it seems clear that the Stoic view, too, was intermediate between those of Diodorus and Philo. Cf. Sharples, above n 12, 92 and n 33; M. Frede, *Die stoische Logik* (Göttingen, 1974), 107 ff.

[29] In her review of my edition, *Times Literary Supplement*, 17 February 1984, 173.

[30] Cf. *Nicomachean Ethics* III. 3. 1112b19 ff; Alexander, *de Fato* XII. 180. 17.

courses of action; so, if the outcome is predetermined—even through our deliberation as a stage in the causal sequence—deliberation may seem to be a link in the causal chain, indeed, but a *pointless* link.[31] And this thought might express itself, inaccurately to be sure, as the claim that in the Stoic system deliberation can make no difference to the outcome. After all, if the outcome is fixed, there is a sense in which *nothing* can make any *difference* to it, even though that does not mean that it does not *depend on* previous factors. It is true that if the agent had not deliberated at all, or had decided otherwise, the result might have been different, but in a system where everything is predetermined these are unreal hypotheses in any case.

The determinist might object to this that to talk about real, categorical possibilities of acting otherwise is unreasonable, and that we should be satisfied with the claim that an agent could have acted otherwise *if* the circumstances, or more importantly where moral responsibility is concerned the agent's character, had been different. Frede in effect argues in this way when she says (289–90) that determinism only implies that a given agent *will* act in a given way in a given situation, not that he cannot; for by refusing to say that the agent in a determinist system *cannot* act otherwise, she suggests that the possibility of doing otherwise *if* circumstances or one's character had been different, which a determinist system *does* allow, is a real possibility in the sense in which we usually use the term. But it may be doubted whether Alexander would have accepted this. It is true—even if Aristotle and Alexander would not have accepted the point[32]—that 'what will be will be' is a harmless platitude (cf. Frede, 289) if we are speaking of the logical relationship between events and their predictions; but it is not clear that that is still true when—like Alexander's opponents, and like Frede herself here, apparently—we are speaking of determinism in terms of physical causation.

Moreover, in explaining Alexander's interpretation of determinism as fatalism due weight needs to be given to his Aristotelian background. The implications of the Sea-Battle paradox *are* fatalistic; if the truth of a prediction of a sea-battle tomorrow did necessitate its

[31] Cf. Ammonius, *in de Int.* 148.24 ff., and my commentary, 142.

[32] Frede follows Carneades and Ryle in rejecting the paradox of truth about the future as a mere tautology (289–90). But as she recognizes it seems unlikely that Alexander took this route (cf. Frede, 286, where she perhaps overstates the degree of caution in my treatment—cf. my edition, 11–12 and 138), and later commentators on Aristotle certainly did not; cf. R. W. Sharples, 'Alexander of Aphrodisias *de Fato*: some parallels', *CQ*, n.s. XXVIII (1978), 263–4.

occurrence, it would do so in a way that would be completely unaffected by the admiral's deliberations between now and then, Aristotle explicitly mentions deliberation in *de Interpretatione* IX. 18b31 and 19a8; he also emphasizes, in a chapter of the *Nicomachean Ethics* which was influential for Alexander, the connection between deliberation and what is contingent as opposed to necessary.[33] Passages like these may have contributed to Alexander's expressing himself in a way which suggested, wrongly, that there was no place for deliberation in the Stoic system.

IV

The Stoics claimed that to deny determinism involved the assertion of uncaused or unexplained events or movements. This necessarily raises the question of what is to count as a cause or explanation. White is right to point out (130) that I could have discussed this matter more fully in my edition; but a comprehensive treatment would have involved bringing in many texts other than Alexander's and would have been a rather different enterprise.

We do not normally regard all the necessary conditions for the occurrence of an event as its 'causes', and we do not normally regard an event as insufficiently explained if we have not listed conditions which are jointly sufficient to explain why that outcome occurred rather than any other. What is acceptable as an explanation depends on the context in which an explanation is requested, as has often been pointed out.[34] The Stoics themselves did not regard all the factors involved in the production of an outcome as causes in the fullest sense.[35]

---

[33] Cf. *Nicomachean Ethics* III. 3. 1112b19 ff; Alexander *de Fato* XI. 178. 28 ff. *Ethical Problems* XXIX. 160. 5 ff. The taking over of arguments originally directed against astrology may have played a part; cf. my commentary, 150.

[34] Cf. e.g. R. Sorabji, *Necessity, Cause and Blame* (London, 1980), 29; J. L. Mackie, 'Causes and conditions', *American Philosophical Quarterly*, II (1965), 245–64, repr in E. Sosa (ed), *Causation and Conditionals* (Oxford, 1975), Sec II, 21–30 of repr.

[35] Cf. *SVF* II. 347; also II. 346a (Seneca, *Epistulae Morales* 65.4, which is indeed concerned with a special point, the role of god as the first cause; on this W. Theiler, 'Tacitus und die antike Schicksalslehre', in *Phyllobolia für P. von der Mühll* (Basel. 1946), at 44–8, and my commentary, 158. At Cicero, *de Fato* 34 ff it is questionable how much is Stoic doctrine being turned by Carneades against the Stoics themselves, and how much is Carneades' own contribution. Cf. M. Frede, 'The original notion of cause', in *Doubt and Dogmatism*, ed M. Schofield *et al* (Oxford, 1980), 220 and 228.

It might therefore be tempting to argue that, since a cause is normally something less than a sufficient condition for the occurrence of the outcome in question *and no other*, it is possible for an event to be undetermined and yet not uncaused even though there was no conjunction of conditions sufficient to necessitate one outcome rather than another. But, as a way out of the Stoic dilemma—either determinism or something without a cause—that is simply missing the point. A cause may be sufficient to explain why A_1 or A_2 occurs rather than B; but it is difficult to see how it can be open whether A_1 occurs, rather than A_2, without there being *something*—the occurrence of A_1 *rather than A_2*—which is unexplained and uncaused.[36] And, if there is no cause for the occurrence of A_1 rather than A_2, is not A_1 uncaused *qua A_1*, even if not *qua A* (rather than B)? Even the trajectory of a particular Epicurean atom after its non-predetermined swerve is presumably *to some extent* explicable, in that an atom can only swerve from the position it was in at a particular time, and its direction can only be changed to a very small extent (cf. Lucretius II. 244–50).[37]

It might be protested that only a committed determinist would ever think of putting the matter in this way and demanding that explanations should be so complete as to exclude all conceivable alternatives. But in that case the correct response is to say precisely this, that the determinists' whole approach to the question of causation is misguided; and this Alexander does not do as fully as one might wish. He does criticize the Stoic account of causation in Chapters XXIII–XXV, as already mentioned, and to some extent traces out an alternative approach—the unity of the universe can be preserved, not by the Stoic causal chain which leaves nothing uncaused, but by the movement of the heavens. But *this* unity, as he expressly points out, leaves room for exceptions; he says nothing in Chapter XXV about whether these are caused or not, and while Chapter XV argues that human actions *do* have causes, Alexander makes no attempt to spell out to us how the doctrine of Chapter XV and that of Chapter XXV are to be related to each other. It is all very well to argue that the world is not systematic in the way the Stoics suppose, and that the actions of human

---

[36] Cf. Sorabji, above n 34, 30–1, and my comments at *JHS*, CIII (1983), 177. Cf. also Chrysippus in *SVF* 2. 973.

[37] This is so unless something as strong as Heisenberg's uncertainty principle is implied by Lucretius II. 293, 'in no fixed region of space and at no fixed time', so that one could not even speak of an atom swerving *in* a place *at* a time at all; but this seems doubtful. Not being predetermined is not the same thing as being indeterminate. Cf. also A. A. Long, *Hellenistic Philosophy* (London, 1974), 59–60.

agents simply *are* exceptions to the general order;[38] but there is a difference between simply assuming that one's own way of looking at the world—or that of one's tradition—is the correct one, and arguing the point.

V

Alexander discusses the problem of allegedly uncaused events in two contexts, those of chance (Ch VIII and XXIV) and of human agency (Ch XV). Where chance is concerned, Frede argues that my comments place too much emphasis on the issue of regularity, and that the central issue is the absence of a final cause. She suggests (282) that, if a man dug with the conscious intention of looking for buried treasure, even in a place where there was only a small chance of finding some, Alexander would not describe the finding of treasure as due to chance. But is this really so? *Tuchē* also has the more particular meaning of 'luck', and even when the possibility of finding treasure was the primary motive for digging, we might still describe the finding of treasure in a particular place, or indeed in any one of the first hundred places, when the odds were a million to one against, as 'a lucky chance'.

Alexander argues that the cause of the finding of treasure is the digging (VIII. 174. 14–20); but he also refers in the same chapter to the 'absence of causation of', or by, 'the principal cause' (174. 28). Frede would I take it reconcile these remarks by saying that the chance event has an efficient cause, but no cause to which it is related as an end;[39] I would rather point to the fact that the digging does cause the finding of the treasure, but does not suffice on its own to explain it,

[38] Cf. Frede's remarks, in the context of teleology, at 291; above, Sec II.
[39] That is to say, finding buried treasure turns out *in fact* to be the result of the digging by accident, but was not the end or goal of the digging in the sense that the digging was directed towards this. It does not seem correct simply to say that a chance event itself has no final cause; firstly, it is the final cause of the digging rather than of the chance event itself, the finding, that is at issue; and secondly it is not always the case that, because the chance result occurs, the original intended result does not—the man who finds the treasure *may* indeed not bother to plant the tree, but the man who chanced to meet his debtor in the market-place may well have done whatever else he went there for in the first place. (It must be admitted, though, that Aristotle's and Alexander's explanation of *automaton* as 'itself in vain' does on the face of it imply the non-fulfilment of the original purpose; Aristotle, *Physics* II. 6. 197b22 ff, cf: Alexander, *de An.* Mant. 178. 26 ff).

since for this we need at least also the fact—obscure to human reasoning, until after the event—that someone in the past buried treasure in the place in question. I say 'at least', because explaining both why one man buried the treasure in the place in question, and why the other man dug in that place in order to plant, may not explain the coincidence as such. One may compare Sorabji's example; separate explanations of five different aircraft crashes on the same day do not explain why five aircraft crashed on the same day. That coincidence may have effects—the bankruptcy of the insurers, for instance—but it has no explanation as such.[40] The chance finding of buried treasure *would* be explained if one were to say, for example, that an all-knowing providence had arranged the 'coincidence' in order to reward the poor farmer for his honesty;[41] but then the finding would no longer be a coincidence, even if it seemed so to the finder.

It is natural to think of the cause of finding buried treasure as not just 'digging in order to plant' but 'digging in a particular place', and once the treasure has been buried the question of frequency does not arise—the first person to dig in that place will find treasure *whenever* he digs. But, in the case of another example used by both Aristotle and Alexander, going to the market place leads by chance to recovery of a debt when the debtor happens to be there at the same time; if he were *always* or *usually* there, it is not clear that the recovery of the debt would be described as due to chance. (If I go to the shops to buy bread, but suddenly realize I need some stamps, we don't say 'I *happened* to find the post office open' if it usually is, still less 'I was *lucky* to find it open'.)[42]

Examples like the finding of treasure are in no way incompatible with determinism; if it is predetermined that X will bury treasure in a

[40] Cf. Sorabji, above n 34, 10–11, and my edition, 13. Cf. also R. A. Heinaman, 'Aristotle on Accidents', *Journal of the History of Philosophy*, XXIII (1985), at 311–17. At 315 Heinaman seems to say in effect 'it would be indefensible to allow C [the man going to the well *at the same time* as the ruffians] as a cause of the man's death by violence, while disallowing as a cause the man's going to where the ruffians were [sc. without the time being specified]'. What does and does not count as a cause or explanation is a matter that admits of degrees, as argued above; but it seems to me to be precisely the coincidence in time that is here the crucial point.

[41] Cf. Boethius, *Consolation of Philosophy* V pr. 1 38 ff, especially 55; Sharples, *BICS*, XXII (1975), above n 21, at 58n 96.

[42] For the link between chance and the irregular cf. also *de An. Mant.* 178. 18–22 and contrast it with 177. 35–178. 5; Sharples, *BICS* XXII (1975), above n 21, at 56 n 74. This indeed only shows that infrequency is a necessary, not a sufficient condition for an event to occur by chance. [Plutarch], *de Fato* VII. 572b explicitly states that 'accidental' implies both 'rare' and 'unexpected'.

given place, and also that *Y* will later dig there in order to plant a tree, then it is predetermined that *Y* will find treasure when he digs. Alexander is closely following Aristotle's account of chance events in *Physics* II. 5–6, and that is not incompatible with determinism.[43] But Alexander clearly thinks that chance occurrences of this type are in some way relevant to his claim that fate admits of exceptions. Why so? If, as Frede argues, the point about chance events is that they do not come about in a purposeful way, it might be argued that they are exceptions to fate because fate is purposive (as Alexander points out at V. 168. 26–169. 3[44]). Chance events are incompatible with a *providential* determinism to the extent that, while they might still seem fortuitous to us, they would then be part of the plan of an all-embracing Providence, and not truly fortuitous. But Alexander does not make this point in Chapter VIII; his perspective is Aristotelian and particular, concerned with the purposes of individual agents, rather than universal and Stoic.[45] Moreover the *Aristotelian* argument for the purposiveness of nature rests largely on its regularity in any case.

If, on the other hand, the point about chance events is that they are not the *regular* outcomes of their accidental causes, it is at least possible to see why Alexander could have regarded them as exceptions to a fate identified with what is natural and hence usual. The discussion of chance events in Chapter VIII comes between the exposition of the view of fate as nature admitting of exceptions, in Chapter VI, and Chapter IX, discussed in section I above. Just as the chance events of Chapter VIII are not incompatible with determinism, and the variations of Chapter IX are not necessarily so either, so also with the exceptions to *individual* nature of Chapter VI; for it could perfectly well be predetermined, on every particular occasion, whether individual nature will be overruled or not. But an interpretation of Chapter VIII in terms of the *exceptional* nature of chance events does give Alexander a consistent train of thought throughout these chapters, even if not one that is proof against objections.

VI

The second context in which Alexander attempts to avoid the charge of introducing something without a cause is that of human agency. In

[43] As is noted, e.g., by W. D. Ross, *Aristotle's Physics* (Oxford, 1936), 41.
[44] Thillet, above n 3, xciv is wrong to say that fate is *itself* a *final* cause.
[45] Cf. Frede 291; above n 38.

Chapter XV he argues that human actions, though not predetermined, are not uncaused because their cause is the agent himself. As I remarked in my commentary (147–8), this is very similar to an argument attributed to Carneades in Cicero's *de Fato*. The key question in both cases seems to be: are these arguments simply failing to see that asserting that human actions are caused by their agents does nothing to escape the dilemma that *either* every outcome is the inevitable result of the circumstances obtaining before it, *or* there must at some point be a break in the causal chain? Or are they maintaining that discussion in these terms is simply inappropriate for human agency? Once again, it is not easy to decide. One might wish that, if Alexander and Carneades are taking the latter, anti-reductionist position, they had spelled it out more clearly; but it may be that they simply assume it to be self-evident, and indeed the similarity between their arguments may be due to an intuitive obviousness of such an approach rather than to any historical connection between the two.[46] (Sedley's recent interpretation of Epicurus as an anti-reductionist[47] may be relevant here, not in the sense that Alexander might have been influenced by Epicurus on this issue—he is silent about the Epicurean atomic swerve in the *de Fato*—but rather as a warning against excessively reductionist interpretations generally.)

Three positions which claim to retain human responsibility for actions can be distinguished, in addition to hard determinism which denies it. There is (1) the position of those soft determinists who argue that universal determinism does not rule out human responsibility, and wish to retain both. Then (2) there is the position which shares with hard determinism the belief that determinism and responsibility are incompatible, and denies the former in order to retain the latter—that is, asserts along with Epicurus that it is not the case that in every situation there is one and only one outcome that can result, and regards this as a necessary, even if not a sufficient condition for human responsibility. And there is also (3) the position of those who deny that responsibility is compatible with determinism, but also do not regard themselves as committed to indeterminism in the sense of (2). This may be (3*a*) because they hold that the question of whether

---

[46] Cf. my commentary, 13, 147–8, 150. Thillet (above n 3), cix argues that Alexander used no neo-Academic sources.

[47] D. Sedley, 'Epicurus' refutation of determinism', in *Syzetesis: studi sull' epicurismo greco e romano offerti a Marcello Gigante* (Naples, 1983), 11–51.

determinism applies on the physical or material level is simply irrelevant to questions concerning human action, this being something of an irreducibly different sort; or more generally (3*b*) because they regard the terms in which the determinist thesis, and hence also its denial, are stated as misconceived, on the grounds that even to ask whether in every set of circumstances there is one and only one possible outcome makes unwarranted assumptions about the possibility of specifying relevant sets of circumstances in the first place. (In fact, I do not myself believe that (3*a*) in coherent. Even if human decision and actions cannot be discussed entirely in the terms appropriate to the interactions of physical bodies, none the less human actions do affect the physical world, so the question whether or not unbroken physical determinism applies on that level is not irrelevant after all.[48] The supporter of (3*a*), if pressed for his view concerning determinism in the material world, will either have to accept it or to deny it. If he accepts it his position becomes indistinguishable from (1). If he denies it, then he agrees with (2) in rejecting determinism; he may emphasize that human actions are not uncaused, and play down indeterminism on the physical level, while the supporter of (2) may emphasize the randomness of some occurrences of the material level at least, in order to distance himself from the determinists, but both alike are agreed in rejecting determinism.)

The Stoic position against which Alexander argues is clearly compatibilist and soft-determinist—that is, of type (1)—as Frede recognizes (289). It seems likely that, in advancing his own theory of fate as admitting of exceptions, Alexander is attacking determinism as such, even if, as I have claimed, the presence of the issue of variation (*A*) as well as that of whether individual events are predetermined (*B*) does somewhat obscure the issue. This suggests that his view is not of type (1). On the other hand, he tries to escape the charge of asserting uncaused events, which Cicero rightly saw as implied in the Epicurean atomic swerve,[49] and he nowhere asserts radical indeterminism in the

---

[48] Cf. D. J. O'Connor, *Free Will* (Garden City, NY, 1971), 82–3 and 105–9. O'Connor discusses the issue from the point of view of the relation between mind and brain states, but the point can be generalized: if free human choice involves some break in determinism on the physical level, the relation between mind and brain is simply the most plausible place in which to look for it.

[49] Cicero, *de Fato* 46 ff. Cicero rightly sees that the Epicurean swerve is uncaused, but fails to see that that is the essential thing about it (on the level of individaul atoms, anyway;). His point does seem to be that there is no reason for each *individual* atom swerving when it does, and not just that, while there is a reason why human agents should exercise free choice, there is no reason why atoms *in general* should swerve.

physical world in the way in which Epicurus did. This suggests that his view is of type (3) rather than (2).

In my commentary I described Alexander's position as libertarian, intending by that to indicate that his view was of type (3) rather than type (1)—even if I had and still have doubts about how *clearly* he had formulated either of the theoretical bases (3a) and (3b) of such a position.[50] Frede, while emphasizing that terminological labels are relatively unimportant (289), prefers to see Alexander as advancing a type of compatibilism different from that which he attacks in the Stoics. The difficulty with this is that the forcefulness of his attack on Stoic compatibilism seems to fit ill with his holding any variant of such a position himself; it *may* be true that Alexander's version of position (3) is one that will *in the end* collapse into compatibilism, but that is a rather different point.

Where I saw Alexander as giving a distorted account of the Stoic position because it was so obviously unacceptable to him as a non-compatibilist, Free sees him as exaggerating the unacceptable features of Stoic compatibilism the better to distinguish it from his own version of compatibilism.[51] This may not be unconnected with the fact that Frede seems more favourable to compatibilism that I.[52] It is true that Alexander does represent his opponents' commitment to the preservation of responsibility as insincere and as designed only to deceive their hearers (XIII. 181. 7 ff, XIV. 182. 27 ff; though at VIII. 173. 23 he describes them as deceiving themselves *as well* as their hearers). But these are exaggerations for the sake of argument. It is characteristic of Alexander to represent his opponents as committed, not to things

[50] The matter is further obscured, I have argued, by the presence of the two issues of (*A*) invariance as opposed to variation and (*B*) the presence or absence of determinism; see Sec I above.

[51] Frede, 287. I agree, indeed, that Alexander's exaggeration of his opponents' position makes it easier for him to defend his own; but my point on p 140 of my commentary (Frede, 287 n 17) was *not* this, but rather that Alexander failed to give due weight to the Stoics' attempts to defend compatibilism because from his own *incompatibilist* point of view they necessarily came to nothing, which is a rather different point. How far Alexander is actually able to defend his own position, or even to make it coherent, is a different issue. Frede also overstates the issue in saying that Alexander presents the Stoics as *hard* determinists; he presents them rather as wanting to reconcile responsibility and determinism but failing to do so. It is true that at XIV. 183. 17 ff he criticizes their use of the expression 'what depends on us', but this is because responsibility is not preserved in their system according to his *own* conception of responsibility.

[52] Frede, 289; the libertarian way of formulating the problem is 'a (needless) dramatisation of the determinist's position'. Cf. her article cited in n 2 above, and also Sec III above, at n 32.

which they themselves maintain, but to what he himself sees as the implications of their position (cf. X. 177. 1–2 and 178. 6, and p 136 and 139 of my commentary); and by the amount of space Alexander devotes to his opponents' arguments for responsibility he makes it clear that they were not hard determinists who openly denied responsibility. So Frede's claim (289) that Alexander portrays his opponents as hard determinists seems overstated.

White, on the other hand, while happier than Frede with my description of Alexander as a libertarian, suggests that his position might better be classified as that of an action-theorist, comparing his position with that of Richard Taylor who, as White points out, drew a parallel between his own position and that of Carneades.[53] That is to say, White classifies Alexander's view as type (3*a*). 'Libertarian' White wishes to reserve as a description for those who *explicitly* adopt an indeterminist position—that is, for (2) rather than (3). But it is not clear that Alexander regards human agents as a unique special case where determinism is concerned, as action theory would seem to imply. So while I am happy enough to accept White's terminology. I am not sure that it captures all aspects of Alexander's position.

VII

Professor White questions my rendering of *to eph' hēmin* by 'responsibility', on the grounds that the connotations of that term are legal or moral, and that these aspects are not Alexander's primary concern (White, 128–9). It is certainly true that, while Alexander does mention the moral implications of determinism, his main concern is with other aspects of the issue—I suspect he would say with more fundamental ones, on the grounds that, in his view, the existence of truly autonomous human action has to be established before questions of moral responsibility can be raised.[54]

My choice of 'responsibility' to render *to eph' hēmin* was based on the apparent similarity between the way in which the two terms, ancient

[53] White, 127; cf. Richard Taylor, 'Determinism', in *Encyclopedia of Philosophy*, ed P. Edwards (New York, 1967), 369.

[54] Ethical questions do not in general seem to have been Alexander's primary concern; he left no commentary on the *Ethics*, and the *Ethical Problems* attributed to him are mainly concerned with a few specific issues (pleasure, voluntary action) and with *logical* issues of genus-species relations, contrariety, and the like. (I hope to discuss this more fully elsewhere.)

and modern, were each used both by soft-determinists and by libertarians. The English term used needs to be neutral if the Stoic attempts to argue for the existence of *to eph' hēmin* within their system are not to seem self-evidently false; and 'what is up to us' seemed to my (incompatibilist) ear to incline too far in the direction of libertarianism to the exclusion of a soft-determinist interpretation. And from the point of view of discussion, rather than of actual translation, both 'what is up to us' and 'what depends on us' suffer from the absence of a conveniently corresponding abstract noun like 'responsibility'.

VIII

Many of the issues here discussed turn on a central problem in the historical study of philosophy: how far should one endeavour to interpret a text in the way that makes it most philosophically interesting,[55] especially when the alternative is an interpretation that involves attributing confusion to an ancient thinker? The problem is all the more complex when both what one regards as philosophically interesting, and what one regards as confusion, are—as they sometimes are—influenced by one's own philosophical position.[56] The ways in which ancient authors approach particular questions may be of interest because their very limitations show the influence of a particular philosphical tradition; an interpretation which lays less emphasis on the limitations may risk obscuring the historical connections. Professor Frede suggests that I have unfairly attributed confusion to Alexander in my treatment of Chapter IX; Professor Dillon, on the other hand, thinks I have at times been over-kind to him.[57] These judgements may serve to indicate—as if that were necessary—the difficulties by which any attempt at interpretation must be beset.

University College, London

[55] Cf. e.g. a comment by Jonathan Barnes, 'I do not like to think that Plato was deeply troubled by something essential unpuzzling' (*Phronesis*, XXIX (1984), 102), and—on a different issue—R. A. Heinaman, 'I think that such an interpretation is too optimistic and that Plato's view is less sophisticated than scholars would like to admit' ('Communion of forms', *Proceedings of the Aristotelian Society*, n.s. LXXXIII (1982/3), 175).

[56] Cf., on one particular issue, R. W. Sharples, 'Necessity in the Stoic doctrine of fate', *Symbolae Osloenses*, LVI (1981), at 83.

[57] *JHS*, CV (1985), 195. Cf. Also J. Dillon, *The Middle Platonists* (London, 1977), 250, and my edition, 17 f.

Review Articles

KNOWLEDGE AND BELIEF*

A discussion of Julia Annas and Jonathan Barnes, *The Modes of Scepticism: Ancient Texts and Modern Interpretations*; and Harold Tarrant, *Scepticism or Platonism? The Philosophy of the Fourth Academy*[1]

CHARLOTTE STOUGH

AN increasing number of scholarly works on the history of scepticism of late has prepared the ground for lively debate on the issues and protagonists of the different sceptical philosophies. Now two books from the Cambridge University Press help to put much of that scholarship in philosophical and historical perspective. *The Modes of Scepticism* and *Scepticism or Platonism?* pick up different threads of the ancient tradition, examining in detail the philosophical views associated with Pyrrhonism and the Academy. They do much to deepen our appreciation of the complexities of philosophical enquiry in the Hellenistic period.

I

Harold Tarrant's *Scepticism or Platonism?* is a rich and fascinating study of the philosophy of the Fourth Academy from c 100BC to c AD150. The author gives scrupulous attention to the limited sources for the period and offers shrewd evaluations of their often conflicting testimonies. He reconstructs in painstaking detail the position of Philo of Larissa and his followers, who espoused a 'One–Academy thesis'

* © Charlotte Stough 1987
[1] Julia Annas and Jonathan Barnes, *The Modes of Scepticism: Ancient Texts and Modern Interpretations* (Cambridge University Press, 1985), vii + 203; hardback £22.50, paperback £7.50. Harold Tarrant, *Scepticism or Platonism? The Philosophy of the Fourth Academy* (Cambridge University Press, 1985), ix + 182; £22.50.

claiming allegiance to Plato as well as to the Academic sceptics Arcesilaus and Carneades. The author shows how the Carneadean criteria for the conduct of life might have been subtly but significantly transformed by Fourth Academics to yield a position more 'fallibilist' than 'sceptic' on the matter of knowledge. After carefully examining ancient uses of the terms 'sceptic' and 'dogmatic' he concludes that the Fourth Academic philosophy eludes the standard 'sceptic—dogmatic' categories of classification. Philonians were 'sceptical' in their examination of both sides of an issue, but they were not involved in a crusade against *dogma*. Philo himself was prepared to weaken the Stoic definition of apprehensibility to allow that things might be apprehended in a general sense, albeit not with the certainly required by the Stoic criterion. Tarrant is convincing when he claims that this was the 'heresy' of Philo's 'Roman Books' to which Antiochus of Ascalon vehemently objected. Antiochus defended the Stoic criterion (the Stoic definition of the apprehensive presentation) against Philo and finally broke away with his own followers to establish a 'Fifth' Academy. But Antiochus, Tarrant believes, had no discernible influence on Middle Platonist epistemology in which the apprehensive presentation as a guarantee of truth plays no part. Instead the author locates the origins of Middle Platonism in the Fourth Academy, which found a place in philosophy for evident concepts. He makes a strong case that the anonymous author of the *Commentary on the Theaetetus* was a Philonian of the late first century BC, possibly Eudorus of Alexandria, whom Tarrant believes to have been of Fourth, rather than Fifth, Academic persuasion and an important link to later Platonism. Tarrant supplements his historical thesis with an impressive argument that the Fourth Academic position on concept formation has stronger philosophical affinities with Platonism than does a radical empiricist epistemology of the Stoic variety. But the philosophical issues become clouded, and more complex, with Middle Platonism. As Platonic Ideas become thoughts in the mind of God, they assume a primarily epistemological role and appear to be accommodated as well by an Antiochean as by a Philonian position.

In *The Modes of Scepticism* Julia Annas and Jonathan Barnes (hereafter A–B) present a fine introduction to the sceptical thought of ancient Pyrrhonists. The authors provide a translation of, and commentary on, the Ten Modes, or argument forms, leading to suspension of judgement, preserved individually in the writings of Sextus Empiricus, Diogenes Laertius, and Philo of Alexandria. In separate chapters devoted to each Mode they translate the relevant passages from each text, identify and discuss the sources, set forth the arguments, elucidate their structure, and evaluate them in a broad context, citing passages from a wide range of philosophers, both ancient and modern, for clarification and criticism. The commentary is critical and philosophically sophisticated. It is, of necessity, selective but always informative. The authors' comparisons with other ancient and contemporary philosophers are extremely detailed in some cases, and for that reason alone they are valuable. The *Modes* is intended for the non-specialist, who must get along entirely without footnotes. The text itself contains an exhaustive discussion of sources alongside the rigorous treatment of arguments, but readers unfamiliar with the current debates will come across relevant articles only by looking through the selected bibliography. A–B follow Sextus' ordering of the Modes in their chapters, but preserve the original order of Diogenes' and Philo's texts in an Appendix. Other useful Appendices contain translations from Sextus Empiricus of The Eight Modes against Causal Explanation, The Five Modes of Agrippa, The Two Modes, and Textual Notes.

II

In the first two chapters of *The Modes* A–B subscribe to an important thesis about ancient scepticism.[2] A major difference between ancient and modern sceptics, they claim, lies in their different attitudes toward knowledge and belief. Modern sceptics doubt the possibility of knowledge, whereas the ancients 'did not attack knowledge: they attacked belief' (8). A consequence of the challenge to belief was that the ancient sceptic suspended all belief. Pyrrhonists viewed their scepticism as a way of life without belief, while Academic sceptics were professional critics of all dogmatic views taking no alternative position of their own. The implications of the thesis are striking. For, as the authors claim, we can get along very well without knowledge as long as our beliefs are left intact, and, for that matter, we can even doubt belief as long as our doubt is a philosophical doubt. Thus modern scepticism

---

[2] Put forth by M. F. Burnyeat, 'Can the Sceptic Live His Scepticism?', in *Doubt and Dogmatism* ed M. Schofield, M. F. Burnyeat, and J. Barnes (Oxford, 1980).

differs radically from ancient sceptical philosophies in having no effect on our everyday lives.

The picture is painted with a broad brush. Pyrrhonian scepticism was a way of life without belief in some sense of that term. But Pyrrhonists, unlike Hume and other moderns, thought that one *could* get along very well without beliefs. What they meant by a life without belief is no doubt a complicated question. But one thing, at least, is clear: they did not share with Hume a common conception of belief.[3] Hume's understanding of belief actually has closer affinities with what Sextus terms the 'broader' sense of '*dogma*', which requires no more than assent to affections necessitated in accordance with one's impressions (*Outlines of Pyrrhonism* (*PH*) I. 13). Sextus plainly disassociates himself from that use of the term '*dogma*' when he says that the sceptic does not dogmatize. The ancient Pyrrhonist does not try to keep from assenting to his affections. He can follow his impressions *without* holding any beliefs, because he takes no position about the reality of things.

Still there is much to be said for A–B's thesis as applied to ancient Pyrrhonism. The Ten Modes contain little explicit reference to belief, but the idea is implicit in the concept of assertion which figures prominently in Sextus' formulation of the arguments. As Sextus normally puts it, we are unable 'to say' how things really are because (1) we have no more reason to assert this than that (taken by A–B to be the standard argument schema based on equipollence of appearances, on which see III below), or (2) we have no reason to assert this or that (a variation noted by A–B (114, 134–6) in the Sixth and Eight Modes but also occurring in the Third Mode), or even (3) it is possible that things might be other than they appear (noted by A–B (150) as a rare argument form in the Ninth Mode but also occurring in the Third Mode). So even though not all the Modes depend exclusively on equipollence, with occasional exceptions noted by the authors they do call into question the grounds for belief.

We know also that Pyrrhonian sceptics claimed to be free of *dogma* in the sense in which, as Sextus defines the term, a *dogma* is 'assent to something non-evident' (*PH* I. 16). In fact that was how they distinguished themselves from other philosophers (*PH* I. 14–15). The Pyrrhonist neither claims to have discovered the truth nor denies that

---

[3] Hume defined 'belief' as 'a lively idea related to or associated with a present impression' (*Treatise of Human Nature*, I. iii. 7). Also '. . . belief is more properly an act of the sensitive, than of the cogitative part of our natures' (*Treatise*, I. iv. 1).

it can be discovered; he just goes on enquiring (*PH* I. 2–4). But Pyrrhonists were even more radical on the matter of *dogma* than might first appear from Sextus' definition. Their unwillingness to accept *dogmata* committed them to living without beliefs of any kind. As Sextus puts it, the sceptic follows appearances and lives *adoxastōs* (*PH* I. 23).[4] That of course does not mean that '*dogma*' and '*doxa*' have the same *meaning* for him, but merely that all beliefs, even the most ordinary everyday beliefs, *count* as *dogmata* for the Pyrrhonist. Sextus gives no parallel definition of *doxa*, but it is safe to assume that assent to 'it is day', and 'I am conversing', would have been accepted as standard cases of belief.[5] The Pyrrhonist's position is that even the most obvious things one assents to, propositions that both Stoics *and* their Academic critics would call 'evident', turn out on analysis to be non-evident, since they embody theoretical presuppositions to which one is committed in believing them (*M* VII. 365–9). When the Pyrrhonian sceptic says 'the sky is blue', his words are, or at least they are self-consciously intended to be, theoretically neutral. They make no ascription of properties to reality, however it may be constituted. They do not even commit him to common-sense assumptions about the heavens. That is why Sextus must continually remind us that he is using 'is' in the sense of 'appears' (*PH* I. 135). He is aware that his words *do* carry theoretical commitments which a Pyrrhonian sceptic disavows.

The above considerations give strong support to A–B's claim that ancient Pyrrhonists, at least, were concerned primarily with the challenge to belief. The thesis is more problematic, however, when we come to Academic scepticism. The positions of the Third and Fourth Academies are a matter of controversy as much today as they were in antiquity. We have already noted the testimony of Sextus Empiricus, who says that 'Clitomachus, Carneades, and other Academics' held the view that nothing is apprehensible, whereas Pyrrhonists just go on enquiring (*PH* I. 2–4). Sextus' testimony is

---

[4] On Sextus' use of *adoxastōs* cf. J. Barnes, 'The Beliefs of a Pyrrhonist', *Proceedings of the Cambridge Philological Society*, XXVIII (1982), 26 n 77. Barnes suggests three possible meanings (without attempting to decide among them) as follows: (*a*) 'having no mere opinions', (*b*) 'having no *dogmata*', (*c*) 'having no belief of any sort'. My reading of Sextus comes closest to (*c*), assuming that (*c*) is intended to pick up a generic, non-technical sense of 'belief'.

[5] The examples cited are classified as 'evident' by the Pyrrhonists' dogmatic opponents (*PH* II. 97, *adversus Mathematicos* (*M*) VIII. 144). Such obvious cases would fit the definition of *doxa* at *M* VII. 225, which may be Peripatetic.

plainly at odds with the thesis that Carneades and his followers were occupied with an attack on belief rather than knowledge.[6] In the first place, a denial of apprehensibility was a denial of knowledge not belief. To take a stand on apprehensibility meant that one became involved in the major controversy of the time over the Stoic 'apprehensive presentation' (Tarrant's translation). The Stoic criterion of truth *was* a criterion of certain knowledge. Secondly, in declaring that nothing is apprehensible one is taking a position on *akatalēpsia*. One is subscribing to an epistemological tenet, which is something the Pyrrhonian sceptic does not do. If the Academic took a stand on inapprehensibility, he would not likely have been occupied with a general attack on 'belief'.

Sextus' testimony to the contrary, however, one might still question whether Carneades took any firm position on inapprehensibility. The ancient evidence for Carneades' views is far from clear, and Sextus, himself a Pyrrhonist, could have had his own reasons for wanting to establish a distinction between Academic and Pyrrhonian positions. Tarrant's *Scepticism or Platonism?* makes an important contribution toward resolving some of these questions. Although the principal focus of his book is not the Third Academy, Tarrant's careful study of the Fourth Academic position identifies subtle but significant differences between Carneadean and Philonian views.

Tarrant argues that before the first century BC philosophers did not view themselves, or their objectives, in the light of the familiar 'sceptic-dogmatic' dichotomy, simply because the terms 'sceptic' and 'dogmatic' had not yet acquired the determinate senses we find in later writers such as Sextus Empiricus. Sextus uses the term 'sceptic' to refer uniquely to Pyrrhonists, implying by it the antithetic method of counterbalancing impressions and arguments to arrive at suspension of judgement. But the use of 'sceptic' to refer to a special group of philosophers is not typical of other ancient authors, who apply it descriptively to both Pyrrhonists and Academics. Tarrant calls attention to the original sense of 'sceptic', 'given to enquiring', a sense that does not pick out any particular philosophical school. He finds this use of the term in the texts of Philodemus and Philo of Alexandria. He notes that Gellius employed the term in the sense of 'examiner' when he suggested that Academics and Pyrrhonists alike could be called

---

[6] Sextus' testimony is supported by *Ac.* II. 28–9, which adds that Carneades did not claim to *apprehend* that nothing is apprehensible, which would be inconsistent. Cf. Tarrant (8–9).

both 'zetetic' and 'sceptic'. The Fourth Academic ideal of examining all sides of a question in search of the truth fits that meaning as well as the Pyrrhonist practice of counterbalancing arguments and suspending judgement. But Tarrant also discerns in Philo an occasional use of 'sceptic', in a 'newer' sense associated with 'destructive paradox' and 'sophistry', to refer exclusively to Pyrrhonians (23–4). He believes that

> it is natural to assume that because *scepsis* (*qua* 'enquiry') always led the Pyrrhonist to counter-balancing arguments, the word came to be applied to the practice of balancing arguments itself. Subsequently the adjective 'sceptic' would have developed a special usage, referring to those who employ the antithetic method as a road to suspension of judgment. (25)

Tarrant traces the use of 'sceptic' in the sense equivalent to 'ephetic' to Aenesidemus. He derives evidence for his thesis from Sextus Empiricus and two other important sources: the anonymous *Commentary on the Theaetetus* and the anonymous *Prolegomena to Plato's Philosophy*. The anonymous texts contain a certain 'extremist' interpretation of Plato, which Tarrant argues is not the view of their authors. These extremists try to demonstrate that Plato was 'ephetic', that is, he held no *dogmata* and favoured suspension of judgement. They use the term 'ephetic' as equivalent to 'sceptic' (modified later to 'purely sceptic' at *PH* I. 222), but they also call Plato 'Academic' to distinguish his type of scepticism from the Pyrrhonian variety. The arguments they deploy 'in general are directed towards showing that Plato sanctions the practice of treating things as non-apprehensible . . . Only the Academics positively treat things as non-apprehensible; the Pyrrhonist views even this question with neutrality' (74). Tarrant identifies the extremists as Pyrrhonists, in particular Aenesidemus, the found of revived Pyrrhonism. The Pyrrhonists tried to show that Plato held the doctrine of inapprehensibility in an effort to validate their own suspension of judgement.[7] Aenesidemus distinguished between two kinds of *scepsis* in the early sense that implies no more than the antithetic use of impressions. One could make initial use of *scepsis* for dogmatic ends, or

---

[7] They apparently found no difficulty in claiming both that Plato was anti-dogmatic and that he took a position on inapprehensibility. Sextus refrains from calling Third Academics 'dogmatists' at *PH* I. 2–4, even though he finds it important to distinguish them from Pyrrhonists. A 'dogmatist' is one who puts forth a positive theory about the nature of things. He 'assents to one of the non-evident objects of investigation in the sciences' (*PH* I. 13). Sextus apparently does not count the epistemological tenet that things are inapprehensible as a *dogma*, whereas to subscribe to the *pithanon* is dogmatic (230–231).

one could remain in *scepsis* without holding *dogmata* (*PH* I. 210–41). Those who did not abandon *scepsis* were 'purely sceptic' (*PH* I. 222), which was equivalent to 'non-dogmatic' and 'ephetic'. Thus, without using 'sceptic' as another name for Pyrrhonists, Aenesidemus was responsible for its coming to be used in the stronger descriptive sense of 'ephetic'.

Tarrant also believes that it was Aenesidemus who was largely responsible for generating the debates on the propriety of *dogma*, which became a common part of the repertory of later sceptics. Prior to Aenesidemus' defection from the Academy and the revival of Pyrrhonism, the question of whether or not one was a 'dogmatist' was very likely not the source of contention it became for later philosophers. Tarrant accepts that 'the principal sense of the term ["*dogma*"] for Sextus was undoubtedly something like "philosophico-scientific tenet"' (30).[8] But he doubts that in the first century BC '*dogma*' had yet acquired 'a number of clearly defined meanings rather than a semantic range' (30). The best translation for that period, he suggests, is 'doctrine' (29). There is no evidence that the Fourth Academy objected to *dogma* in a sense compatible with the open-minded examination of all points of view. Philo himself apparently had no problem in allowing that apprehensibility (in a non-Stoic sense) was a *dogma* (31–2, 53–5). Tarrant concludes that '. . . opposition to *dogma* in the old sense of the term was not a stated objective of the New Academy, and not an objective of the Fourth Academics in any way at all' (32). But for later philosophers, Pyrrhonists and Academics alike, for quite different reasons, it became a matter of considerable interest to determine whether Second, Third, and Fourth Academics subscribed to *dogmata*. Tarrant reasons that the author of the anonymous *Commentary on the Theaetetus* was thinking of Carneades and Clitomachus as the 'exceptions' to his claim that Academics had *dogmata* (62–3).[9] Aenesidemus complained that the Fourth Academy of Philo 'dogmatized' on many matters (63–4). And Sextus himself made it a basis for his classification of philosophers.

Tarrant's analysis provides a fresh context for considering the issue of *dogma* in the Third Academy. If Tarrant is right, the question of

[8] Established by Barnes (above n 4) as an important use of the term in Sextus Empiricus. Cf. also D. Sedley, 'The Motivation of Greek Scepticism', in *The Sceptical Tradition*, ed M. Burnyeat (Berkeley, Los Angeles, London, 1983), 9–29.

[9] It is not clear however whether the author intended to imply that Carneades took no stand on inapprehensibility. See above n 7.

whether or not inapprehensibility was a *dogma* could not have had the significance for Carneades himself that it came to have for later philosophers. It might not have been a live issue for him. If Carneades was confident that things were inapprehensible, it is not even clear that he would have thought of that as a '*dogma*'. The possible dogmatic implication of a position on inapprehensibility *could* have been an issue for Metrodorus, and it most certainly *was* an issue for Antiochus.[10] But one might reasonably suppose that Carneades, instead of being challenged on the issue of *dogma*, would more likely have been constrained to argue that his view on *akatalēpsia* did not logically commit him to *katalēpsis* (*Academica* (*Ac.*) II. 28, 109). One might also think that there would have been even *less* question about where he stood on *akatalēpsia* than on anything else, even though that, too, was one of the things about which he was unwilling, either directly or publicly, to commit himself (*Ac.* II. 60). Tarrant himself cautiously concludes that it is 'reasonable to argue that the traditional New Academy did have certain philosophical tenets in the realm of epistemology, notably the doctrine that nothing is apprehensible (at least in the Stoic sense)' (31, cf. 144 n 49).[11]

Carneades' position on ordinary beliefs is a rather different matter. Where he stood on that issue depends on the status of 'persuasive' presentations and his criteria for the regulation of life. Tarrant formulates the criteria as a principle of rational conduct (15):

(B2) One should follow a believable presentation p when, on investigation of all other presentations relevant to p, p is found to be consistent with them.

The key to (B2) as a guide to conduct lies in the consistency of the presentations and their consistent believability. Tarrant rightly stresses that for Carneades consistency is not confirmation of the truth of p. But Fourth Academics took the notion of consistency to imply positive agreement. They saw the 'absence of contrary testimony as some kind of limited confirmation in its own right' (15). Adding the notion of the 'evident' (introduced to the Academy by the former Epicurean Metrodorus) and employing it in a weaker sense not excluding the possibility of error, they applied the term 'evident' to concepts as well as presentations. Fourth Academics thus transformed (B2) into a

[10] Metrodorus is said to have denied that inapprehensibility was a *dogma* of the Academy (Augustine, *Academica* 2. 11), but the text is ambiguous and, in any event, does not establish Carneades' position. Antiochus claimed that inapprehensibility *was* an Academic *dogma* (*Ac.* II. 29, 109).

[11] Also propositions (B2) and (D4) below (14–21, 138 n 29); but cf. 41 and 146 n 1.

positive theory in which 'confirmation through consistency is closely
linked with the notion of the evident' (16). They ended with a 'fallible'
but seemingly reliable method for judging truth, which allowed for the
occasional fortuitous presentation which might pass the tests of
believability and consistency in spite of being false. Of course Fourth
Academic theory went far beyond Carneades' own practical principles.
But Tarrant believes that Carneades might have accepted, strictly as a
guide to conduct, an amended version of the Fourth Academic
position as follows:

(D4) If *Fx* consistently seems evident in all the many presentations which
purport to judge the *F*-ness of *x*, and if this impression is consistent with all
other relevant presentations, then *Fx* is evident.

(D4) defines a class of evident presentations (or propositions).
Construed as a regulative principle it makes evident presentations the
basis for acting. One should follow one's evident presentations. Where
does (D4) put Carneades on the matter of belief? Of course, we do not
know where Carneades *actually* stood on the issue, since he did not
directly reveal his views on anything. It is well known that in antiquity
there was a controversy over the question among his interpreters. And
even Carneades' own pupils could not agree about his views on the
permissibility of belief (*Ac.* II. 78). The problem of Carneades' real
views aside, however, one *can* ask whether, given his practical criteria
of conduct, it is likely that he would have abjured belief. Tarrant
interprets the criteria negatively. Referring to (B2) he writes, 'Strictly
speaking, consistency with other presentations is not a confirmation
that *p* is true, but rather the elimination of objections to believing *p*'
(15). Presumably, then, principle (D4), as Tarrant intends it, also
commits Carneades to having beliefs.

Tarrant has little more to say on the subject of belief, but for some
the issue will not be settled. This much at least is certain: if acting
commits one to beliefs, then (D4) would commit anyone who held it as
a regulative principle to whatever beliefs are necessary for following
evident presentations. Still it might be questioned whether belief is
necessary for action or whether Carneades thought that it was.[12]

One can surely follow a presentation without holding the corresponding belief, if there is some sort of countervailing evidence to keep

[12] M. Frede defends the negative general thesis in its application to ancient sceptics
in 'The Sceptic's Two Kinds of Assent and the Possibility of Knowledge' in *Philosophy
in History*, ed R. Rorty, J. B. Schneewind, and Q. Skinner (Cambridge, 1984), 255–78.

one from forming that belief. But that is not the issue with (D4), which would rule out all cases involving contrary evidence. (D4) requires that one's presentation be evident, which is to say, intrinsically persuasive and consistent with all other relevant presentations. The question is, then, whether one can follow an *evident* presentation that *Fx* without holding the belief that *Fx*. It would not be unreasonable to think that anything sufficient to keep one from forming a belief that *Fx* would be sufficient to render the presentation non-evident. The *pithanon* is what is psychologically persuasive and believable in itself. If a believable presentation is consistent, in relevant ways, with other such presentations, it becomes *so* persuasive as to be experienced as evident. One could still argue, I suppose, that it is at least *possible* that one might keep oneself from forming the belief that *Fx* even under such psychologically strenuous conditions. But we must ask whether Carneades is likely to have thought that one could follow a very believable presentation that *Fx* without actually believing that *Fx* with at least a minimum degree of confidence. To suppose that he did would mean he thought it appropriate to recommend following our most believable presentations, while yet making epistemological certainty a requirement for holding even the weakest and vaguest of ordinary beliefs, beliefs we tend to hold with a minimum degree of psychological conviction. The position would be: if one does not *know* that *Fx*, one ought not to, and will not, *believe* that *Fx*, no matter how persuasive one's presentations, but one will nevertheless *follow* one's persuasive presentations. That, I think, is a most unlikely position for Carneades to have held, given his choice of the *pithanon* as a basis for action.[13] A more plausible supposition would be that Carneades, differing from Arcesilaus on this score (*Ac.* II 67), was inclined more to the view that some presentations were so persuasive that one could scarcely keep from assenting to them. His practical guidelines took note of different degrees of persuasiveness that accrue to one's presentations, without mistaking psychological conviction for truth.

Carneades himself, I think, was very clear about the difference between psychological conviction and epistemological certainty when he drew a distinction between the apparently true and the true.

---

[13] It has been argued that Carneades himself did not subscribe to the *pithanon* but was merely arguing dialectically from Stoic premisses. Cf. P. Couissin, 'The Stoicism of the New Academy', trans Jennifer Barnes and M. F. Burnyeat, repr in *The Skeptical Tradition*, 31–57; G. Striker, 'Sceptical Strategies' in *Doubt and Dogmatism*, 54–83; M. Frede, above n 12; M. F. Burnyeat, 'Carneades Was No Probabilist' (unpublished).

Principle (D4) pertains only to what is apparently true, which means that no matter how great the difference in persuasiveness among presentations, there is no reason to think that one is more likely to be true than another. That would make Carneades' own view of the *pithanon* very different from what it became in the Fourth Academy under Philo, who allowed that things are apprehensible in themselves, even if not with the certainty required by the Stoic criterion (*PH* I. 235). The difference between the two views of the *pithanon* is the difference between psychological confidence and the likelihood of truth.

Nevertheless (D4), construed as a principle regulating conduct, does provide a different *order* of reason for believing and for following evident presentations. Tarrant takes Carneades' practical criteria to be something like principles of rational conduct, such that '. . . it is rational to follow a believable presentation . . . ' (15) But he does not explain why Carneades might have found a connection between rationality and persuasiveness, when he had found none between truth and persuasiveness. What sort of reasons for acting and believing does (D4) suggest? One might say that it contains, at the very least, a *rationale* for one's conduct and beliefs. The degree to which one's presentations are persuasive or believable will provide an intelligible basis for understanding and explaining one's actions and beliefs. That I have a very believable presentation that *Fx* makes my belief that *Fx* and my consequent action comprehensible and even predictable. But (D4) is a *practical* principle, so it must offer more than just a way of explaining why I do this rather than that. To function as regulative principles the criteria embodied in (D4) must only be workable. They do not need to provide a method for distinguishing true from false presentations. If Carneades thought that it was rational to follow believable presentations, that could only have been because he thought it rational, in deciding matters of conduct, to go by principles that work. His practical criteria actually do little more than record in canonical form the practices one normally observes, in both decision-making and justification, in ordinary life. And that could well have been all they were intended to do.

III

In *The Modes of Scepticism* A–B claim that the sceptic's arguments are *ad hominem*, based on propositions accepted by his non-sceptical opponents. The Pyrrhonist need not be committed to the premisses of his own arguments to accomplish his task of curing the rashness and conceit of the dogmatists. He 'only requires that *his opponents* believe the premisses' to be true (45). Typically these opponents are philosophers who put forth theories about how things really are. Sextus mentions Stoics, Epicureans,. Platonists, and Aristotelians, and he alludes to others indirectly through their doctrines. Thus one naturally expects the authors to point out significant instances of dogmatic theory incorporated into the sceptical arguments. In their elucidation of issues and problems they do provide valuable discussions of the Epicurean theory of perception, the Stoic conception of relatives, and the differences between scepticism and relativism. It is odd, then, to find no references to the Stoic theory of knowledge and perception. Although the force of the sceptical arguments is not dependent on the technical apparatus of any theory, Sextus' use of the term *phantasia*, which played a pivotal role in Stoic epistemology, can hardly be missed. A–B translate *phantasia* interchangeably with *to phainomenon* as 'appearance', on the ground that *phainesthai* is a 'common Greek term' for which *phantasia* is the cognate noun (23). But given that Stoics were prominent among the sceptics' dogmatic opponents, there is a presumption that Sextus (or his source) is incorporating the Stoic notion of impression into the statement of the arguments. An account of how Pyrrhonists came to use the term *phantasia* in a theoretically neutral manner, wholly uncontaminated by Stoic views, would be welcome.[14]

A–B's chapter on the Relativity Mode is of particular interest because of the highly complex interpretation offered, but also because (based on Sextus' remark at *PH* I. 39) it supplies the perspective from which the authors elegantly derive an argument schema for all the Modes. Each Mode, they claim, is grounded in oppositions of appearances, and appearances are always relative to something. Since, without exception, conflicting appearances turn out to be equipollent,

---

[14] The question is not answered by Sextus' remark, in the course of explaining the sceptic's practical criterion, that he is using *to phainomenon* virtually interchangeably with *phantasia* (*PH* I. 22).

the sceptic arrives at suspension of judgement. A–B find the following schema in each of the Modes:

(1) x appears F in situation S
(2) x appears F^* in situation S^*
(3) we cannot prefer S to S^* or vice versa;
(4) we can neither affirm nor deny that x is really F or really F^*.

'F' and 'F^*' in premisses (1) and (2) represent 'incompatible properties' or 'oppositions of appearances' in Sextus' language, predicates which in the Pyrrhonian view of things cannot jointly be true of a subject. Situations 'S' and 'S^*' are specified variously in the Modes, according to circumstances, positions, quantities, mixtures, and the many other relations noted by the sceptic. Premiss (3) claims *isotheneia* of appearances. Here A–B depart from the text in formulating the problem of equipollence as inability to prefer S over S^* rather than F and F^*, while Sextus consistently argues that we cannot judge the accuracy of our *phantasiai* (impressions, presentations) in different situations.[15] Does it make a difference to the argument? The conclusion is the same on either formulation, since we end by suspending judgement in both cases. But the problems are subtly altered by A–B's formulation.

Sextus commonly takes the line that we cannot prefer our own impressions in one situation to impressions that arise in another situation because we are a party to the dispute and not impartial judges (*PH* I. 59, 90, 98, 112–13). A–B note the legal tone of the reasoning in their commentary on the First Mode. 'The legal principle to which Sextus appeals is doubtless a good one in its legal context: we should not, in the law-courts, be judges of our own cases. But Sextus' application of it outside the legal context is dubious ... in the cases Sextus imagines we are not allocating rewards and punishments but attempting to discover the truth' (50). A–B argue that we can and sometimes do judge our own situations and on that basis defer to others' judgements about appearances. Commenting on the Fourth Mode they write, 'if I have a cold, and know that I do, then I prefer the judgement of other wine-tasters to my own; and in general we recognize the "conditions" we are in, admit that they affect the way things appear to us, and defer to the judgement of those in other "natural" conditions' (87).

---

[15] *PH* I. 59, 61, 78, 112, 113, 114, 117, 121, 123; at 114 he talks of judging both.

A–B's formulation of the argument schema translates the problem of choosing among impressions into a problem of assessing one's situation. Criticism of premiss (3) in some of the Modes then rests on the following claims: (*a*) we frequently modify our judgements about appearances on the basis of an assessment of our own situations; (*b*) we can be impartial judges of our situations when there is no question of reward and punishment. But that line of criticism, I think, will not do. When Sextus maintains that our judgements about appearances are biased, he is not alluding to the sort of impropriety we should find in the idea of a criminal defendant judging his own case. He is pointing to a problem more like that of two disinterested observers of the crime, who receive conflicting impressions from witnessing the same event and insist that their impressions are accurate. Each observer is a party to the dispute about what happened, but *not* in the way in which the defendant is a party to the dispute. Sextus is not suggesting that bias prevents us from disclosing a truth already known. He is alluding to the kind of bias that prevents us from knowing the truth to begin with, an epistemological rather than a moral or legal bias.

Sextus argues (*PH* I. 112–13) that we cannot make a judgement about appearance F or F^* without being in some condition C or C^* when we make the judgement. But by virtue of being in condition C or C^* we are a party to the dispute over F and F^*. Because we cannot be 'in no condition whatsoever' when we make a judgement our judgement cannot be impartial. But, he continues, neither are we in a position to compare F with F^* to arrive at a decision. Being in any one condition C or C^* when we compare F and F^* will affect our judgement, for we tend to 'assent to what affects us in the present'. To neutralize the kind of epistemological bias Sextus is thinking of would require being in neither C nor C^* or in both C and C^* at the time we make the judgement about F and F^*. The former would permit a judgement about F and F^* uncontaminated by C or C^*; the latter a comparison of F-in-C and F^*-in-C^*. Sextus is no doubt wrong when he says that we always assent to what is present: we *can* compare the present taste of the wine with our memory of how it tasted before we caught cold, perhaps giving the preference to the former. We can defer to the judgements of healthy wine-tasters. But Sextus' point is that even if we do defer to the judgement of others, we cannot conclude that their impressions are more accurate than our own. Whatever judgement we make about F or F^*—and Sextus' claim can easily be amended to include a judgement about the wine that might result from evaluating our situation—will be influenced by the condition we find ourselves in when we make that judgement. One *can* of course take issue with Sextus on the idea of bias and partiality in judgement. But to meet premiss (3) of the argument it will be necessary to attack his notion of epistemological bias. A–B do justice to premiss (3) only when they concede the epistemological problem of *justifying* one's judgement to defer to the impressions of others (96).

Proposition (4) of the argument schema records the sceptic's inability to make an assertion about appearances. His only recourse in the face of *isotheneia* is to suspend judgement about how things really are. A–B rightly note that (4) is not intended strictly as an inference from the premises of the argument. It is rather that 'once we recognise the premises, we shall in fact suspend judgement; suspension follow on, or is inferred from, the premises in the sense that it is the actual—perhaps even the inevitable—result of our recognising the force of the premises' (49). The Pyrrhonist likens his arguments to a drug applied to cure the disease of dogmatism. A good argument is one that is effective in bringing about the desired effect. Hence the authors claim that while others might be led to enquire about the logical properties of the arguments, '[the Pyrrhonists themselves] do not concern themselves with the *soundness* of their arguments but with their *efficacy*' (50). That is correct, as far as it goes, but A–B fail to mention that the disease itself is a rational one. And so must the cure be. One suspends judgement only if one is persuaded, and to be persuaded one must at least *believe* one is being persuaded by rational means. It is true, as the authors say, that for the sceptic a good argument is an argument that works. But the sceptic's dogmatic opponents were in some cases superb logicians, and of course the sceptics himself had to be persuaded of *isotheneia* before suspending belief. Not just any argument or set of arguments *will* work. What then is the force of the medical metaphor?

The conclusion of the argument schema is not a proposition inferred from the preceding premises. Instead proposition (4) records the sceptic's *epochē*, a '*pathos* that comes about in the enquirer after the investigation' (*PH* I. 7). The arguments we find in the Modes, though not always sound, are rational and, in some cases, surprisingly powerful. In that context, the medical metaphor likening the sceptical arguments to drugs, far from giving an irrational turn to the Pyrrhonian position, supports an interpretation of the Modes as a paradigm of reasoning to a practical end. That is consonant with the sceptic's stance against *dogma* as well as his adoption of appearances as a practical criterion for life.[16] But can *epochē* be defended as a *rational* conclusion of the sceptic's argument schema? A–B regard suspense of belief as 'something that *happens* to us, not a thing we are *obliged* or can *choose* rationally to adopt' (49). That view of *epochē*, however, is not altogether satisfactory. I *can* suspend judgement, of course, by just failing to believe something, by not being persuaded by the partisans on either side of an issue. I just find myself not believing, not coming around to either position. This is the passive kind of suspense of belief which the authors have in mind, I think. But it would be mistaken to equate it with an irrational attitude. We often judge a 'healthy scepticism' to be the *most* rational attitude to maintain, for example, in the face of exaggerated claims made by religious zealots, political ideologues, and automobile salesmen. In some cases Pyrrhonian unbelief will probably fit this model. But there are other ways of suspending judgement which also bear on the sceptic position. I can suspend belief as a consequence of weighing evidence for and against a proposition, which is something I must *do* and not something that just *happens*. When I am deciding whether or not the evidence supports the proposition, I am in fact deciding whether or not to assent to it. In this case it will not do to say that my withholding assent is no more than a failure to believe, something that just happens. Suspending belief can be thought of as a consequence of the activity of weighing evidence, but it is not an effect which is *caused* by that activity. The connection between the rational activity of evaluating competing claims and the outcome of that activity is such that (1) the outcome is just the *conclusion* of that activity, and (2) the process of evaluation itself determines what will count as a rational outcome. So the sceptic suspends judgement when the conflicting arguments appear to him to be equipollent. Suspending belief is not something he 'chooses', or is 'obliged', to do on each occasion after examining the arguments; *nor* is it something that just happens to him. It is the attitude he assumes as a consequence of *isotheneia*. The sceptic can be affected by the dogmatists' arguments in either of the two ways mentioned. Being altogether unimpressed, he might find that he just fails to be persuaded by the proponents of either side. Or, he might conclude a more or less lengthy assessment of arguments that turn out to be

---

[16] Cf. C. Stough, 'Sextus Empiricus on Non-Assertion', *Phronesis*, XXIX (1984), 137–64.

equally balanced by intentionally withholding assent. In both cases his suspense of judgement is a *pathos*, an attitude of mind. The sceptic either *finds* that he has it, or he consciously *assumes* it. But in neither case is his *epochē* a mental event which is the effect of being impinged upon by an external cause.

University of California,
Santa Barbara

HELLENISTIC ETHICS*

A discussion of Malcolm Schofield and Gisela Striker (eds), *The Norms of Nature, Studies in Hellenistic Ethics*[1]

C. C. W. TAYLOR

THIS volume contains the proceedings of the third of a series of international colloquia on Hellenistic philosophy, begun in Oxford in 1978, and is thus the successor to the two previous collections of proceedings, *Doubt and Dogmatism* (Oxford, 1980) and *Science and Speculation* (Cambridge, 1982). It maintains the high standard of those widely acclaimed volumes, and will, like them, prove indispensable for anyone interested in later Greek philosophy and its connections on the one hand with earlier work and on the other with modern issues.

The theme of the volume is ethics, which, in taking us to the central interest of the major Hellenistic schools and thereby to certain topics of common concern to them, such as the ends of life, allows the volume to achieve an admirably comprehensive coverage without sacrifice of thematic unity. The nine papers are printed in two series, the four in Part I dealing broadly with connections in various theories between reason on the one hand and moral belief and emotion on the other, the five in Part II devoted to various aspects of the discovery and pursuit of the supreme good. Cutting across that explicit division is a division according to schools. Two papers deal with Epicurean themes (Malte Hossenfelder on Epicurus' hedonism and David Furley on Epicurean attitudes to death) and three with Stoicism (Michael Frede on the passions of the soul, Gisela Striker on Antipater's doctrine of the supreme good and Troels Engberg-Pedersen on the discovery of the good), while Jacques Brunschwig's paper is directly comparative of the two schools, specifically in respect of their use of arguments from the alleged behaviour of infants to establish conclusions about what is natural and hence good. Two relate aspects of Hellenistic theory to

* © C. C. W. Taylor 1987
[1] Malcolm Schofield and Gisela Striker (eds), *The Norms of Nature, Studies in Hellenistic Ethics* (Cambridge University Press and Editions de la Maison de la Science de l'Homme, Cambridge and Paris, 1986), 287; £25.00.

that of Aristotle: Martha Nussbaum compares and contrasts Aristotelian and Epicurean conceptions of the relations between philosophy and the methodology of medicine, while T. H. Irwin constructs a dialectical confrontation between Aristotelian and Stoic conceptions of happiness and the good. The collection is completed by an illuminating comparison by Julia Annas of ancient and modern moral scepticism. There is a bibliography, index locorum, general index, and glossary of Greek and Latin technical terms. In the text of the papers all Greek is transliterated; in the footnotes the practice varies from author to author, some using the Greek alphabet, others transliterating. All the papers are in English; those by Brunschwig and Hossenfelder are translated by Jennifer Barnes, while Striker's paper, to judge from her opening acknowledgement, is a translation revised by the author of a German original.

The standard of the individual papers is high. Though Furley's is rather slight and those by Brunschwig and Engberg-Pedersen decidedly heavy going, all are worth reading, and I found the collection as a whole much more interesting than many similar volumes. The selective nature of the discussion which follows reflects the particular interests of the reviewer, without any implication that the other papers do not merit discussion.

One of the most intriguing topics dealt with is that of the Stoic conception of the good; its interest is reflected in the fact that it is the theme of the papers by Striker and Engberg-Pedersen, and is also treated at some length by Irwin. The early Stoic formulation of the good as a life in accordance with nature was elaborated by the second-century Stoics Diogenes and Antipater as 'rational behaviour in the selection of what is natural' or as 'doing everything in one's power to obtain the primary natural things' (see Striker, 187). These formulations were criticized by Carneades on the ground that, whereas the good is *ex hypothesi* the agent's goal, selection itself cannot be the goal, since all selection is made with a view to some further end, and therefore some further goal. Selection of natural things cannot, therefore, be the good. The Stoics' response to this objection was summed up in their example of the archer, reported by Cicero and Plutarch: the archer indeed aims at the target, but his having the target as his *aim* or *mark* is subordinate to his ultimate *end* or *goal*, which is shooting well. Provided that he shoots well he will have achieved his end, irrespective of whether external circumstances prevent him from actually hitting the target, as when a sudden gust of wind deflects his arrow. Hence the sage is immune to the vicissitudes of fortune, since what he seeks to attain is nothing external to himself, but merely a certain style of behaviour, or more strictly the exercise of practical rationality, which is wholly within his power. Both Striker and Irwin consider the adequacy of this response, in discussions of considerable subtlety. Striker points out first (191) that the Stoics are not open to a charge of formal circularity, as they would have been had they defined the goal of life as the selection of that which is of value for the attainment of the goal of life. They escape the circle by defining the goal of life as rational behaviour in the selection of what is of value for a natural life. But she further points out that this escape is only temporary; either a natural life has value as contributing to the attainment of the goal of life, in which case the circle is closed again, or it has value with a view to the attainment of some other goal, in which case, contrary to the Stoic hypothesis, there is not one goal of life but two (an outcome which generates familiar problems concerning the reconciliation of the two), or it has no value. Identifying the latter as the Stoics' actual choice, Striker then explores the viability of a concept of the ultimate value as consisting in rationality in the choice of things which have no independent value.

In general, as she observes (196–7) the practical arts do not provide such a model, since rationality in their performance is defined by reference to a goal, such as health in the case of medicine, which is of acknowledged value independently of its serving as the opportunity for the exercise of rationality. A more promising model is, however, available in games (to which one might add game-like activities such as various forms of puzzles), where the players' goal is to show skill in, or derive enjoyment from, the attempt to attain some *end*, such as driving a ball between posts, which is intrinsically valueless, and is valuable only as providing the occasion for the exercise of skill etc. (197–8). It seems, however, that this cannot provide an adequate model for the Stoic art of life, for two connected reasons. First, games are essentially parasitic activities; it is because we value, for independent reasons, such attributes as skill, strength, stamina, and competitiveness that we devise games as artificial milieux for their exercise. Given that, for example, rationality in the selection of means to ends already has a point in our lives, it makes sense to invent artificial contexts for the exercise of specialized forms of rationality, for example rationality in chess. But the whole point of living itself could not be to show rationality in the exercise of an intrinsically pointless activity. Secondly, the Stoic conception of rationality is rationality in the choice of natural things; but rationality in choice cannot be identified otherwise than as choice of such a nature as is likely to lead to the best result. Choice is not rational in virtue of its form alone, but in virtue of its content, as being the kind of choice which may be expected best to promote the agent's ends. In the restricted context of a game that end may be arbitrarily adopted to allow scope for the exercise of rationality; but by our first argument that cannot be the case for life as a whole. For the latter, practical rationality requires prior ends, which the agent must recognize as goods; rationality cannot then be the agent's sole good, as the Stoic conception requires.

While Striker's defence of the Stoic conception by appeal to the analogy of games is not, in the last analysis, persuasive, it strikes me as more plausible than the alternative suggested by Irwin. The core of this suggestion is a distinction between the *end* and the *objective* of an activity: the objective is the goal to the attainment of which the activity is directed, for example hitting the target, whereas the end is the conception of a state to be realized, which is 'conceived in the proximate cause' of action (229). The end, thus defined, is the final cause of action, which, *as it is conceived in the agent's decision*, is also part of the efficient cause of action in the Aristotelian-Stoic model of action. But what the agent decides to do, as Aristotle points out (*Nicomachean Ethics* 1111b26–30, 1112b11–16), is not to hit the target (since his success is not up to him), but to shoot in such a way as to maximize his chance of hitting the target. Hence the Stoics were right to say that the archer's end is not hitting the target but shooting well, and that the end of life is not achieving any external result, such as enjoyment of natural goods, but making the right choice of such goods.

Our previous arguments are, I think, sufficient to show that the distinction between end and objective could be at best a verbal manoeuvre, insufficient to defend the Stoic conception. For the conclusion of that argument, restated in terms of the distinction, is that the end can have value only if the objective has prior value, contrary to the Stoic hypothesis that only the end has value. But in any case the distinction itself is suspect.

The conception of the end of the action should appear in the efficient cause of the action; but Aristotle himself shows that it is the conception of the function, not the conception of the external result, that appears in the efficient cause of the craftsman's action. When we think about what to do now, we will guide our decision by what we think is required by competent practice of the craft; hence this competent practice will be our end. There is no point in thinking about the external result; for that depends on circumstances that cannot be controlled by our action.

(Irwin 230)

But all that Aristotle in fact shows is that we cannot be said to decide to be successful; that is far from showing, as Irwin's argument requires, that the conception of being successful does not figure in our decision on what to do. And plainly it does; when the archer thinks 'In a wind of this strength I'd better aim off five yards to the right' it is clear that the conception of hitting the target figures essentially in his practical thought. So far from its being the case that '[t]here is no point in thinking about the external result' the agent's practical thought cannot adequately be formulated *without* his thinking about the external result. Irwin might perhaps reply that the conception of the external result figures at an earlier stage than that of decision, which is the proximate cause of action. In our example the archer's decision is expressed as 'So I'll aim five yards to the right', which does not mention the hitting of the target. But on that view the agent's 'end' in any chain of means–end reasoning is not the goal, but the immediately available means. So when I reason that if I'm to go to London I must take the train, and if I'm to be at the station on time I must take a taxi, and if I'm to get a taxi I must phone for one, so I'll phone right away, my objective is getting to London, but my 'end' is phoning right away. It is clear that that conception of 'end' is now altogether remote from the Aristotelian–Stoic conception of *telos* which Irwin asumed at the outset of his argument in taking as his starting-point the uncontroversial Stoic assumption that happiness is the end of our actions (228).

The central point of this discussion has a more general application to ethical theory, indeed it is intriguing to observe that it applies both to Kant's theory of the good will and to Mill's utilitarianism, providing another point of contact between theories which are generally (though superficially) located at the opposite poles of deontology and consequentialism. The parallel with Kant is clear and, given the strongly Stoic overtones of his theory (for another instance see Irwin, 217 n14), not surprising. The Stoics hold that the only good is rationality, defined as rationality in choice of natural things, but rationality thus conceived requires that the natural things chosen are independently good, and are chosen because they are good. Kant holds that the only thing good without qualification is the good will, but the good will cannot be adequately conceived except as the will to do or achieve good, which likewise requires that the objects of the will have independent value. In fact the resemblance is closer than this parallelism suggests; first, Kant identifies the will with practical reason (*Grundlegung*, ch II, 36), thus assimilating his position even more clearly to that of the Stoics, and secondly both Kant and the Stoics support their position by the argument, originated by Plato (*Meno* 87e–88e, *Euthydemus* 280e–281e), that wisdom is the only good, since all other purported goods are liable to be misused and are therefore good only when directed by wisdom. (Irwin cites the Stoic use of this argument (220), but does not mention its use by Kant.) In Mill's theory the only ultimate good is happiness, anything else being good either as a means to or as a part of happiness. But happiness has to be construed as a state in which an agent is satisfied with his or her life as meeting or at least approximating to that agent's standards of value, which requires that the things that meet those standards have independent value. Just as in Stoic theory rational choice must be choice *of* independent goods, so in Mill's theory happiness is a second-order reaction, involving the belief that one has gained or will gain independent goods. The fundamental error of all these theories is the claim, not merely that there is a unique good, but that that good is located in the mind, whether the intellect as in Stoicism and Kant, or the affective side of the personality, as in Mill. The lesson to be drawn from the failure of all three projects is first that values are irreducibly pluralistic, and secondly that there is no favoured location for them.

Martha Nussbaum's comparison of Aristotelian and Epicurean treatment of medical methodology is characteristically inventive, wide-ranging, and well-documented. Her paper brings out, with a wealth of detail, some important similarities in aims and methods between Aristotelian and Epicurean ethics, and a crucial dissimilarity which has some disturbing implications. For both Aristotle and Epicurus the aim of ethics was practical, to help the student on the path to *eudaimonia*. Both regarded medical theory and practice as providing models for their ethical counterparts. This was partly because they inherited a tradition which stressed the role of various kinds of *logoi* in curing ills of the soul (to the evidence she cites (52), going as far back as Homer, one might add the story in pseudo-Plutarch *Lives of the Orators* about Antiphon's 'psychiatric clinic' at Corinth (833c, DK 87 A 6)), partly because both philosophers were impressed by the facts that in both areas there are no exceptionless generalizations and that the aim of theory is to enable the skilled practitioner to reach particular judgements based on informed perception of the facts of the particular case. But from this point the gulf begins to open. For Epicurus philosophy (not just ethics, but all philosophy) was literally a sort of therapy, a cure for the ills of life, above all the fear of death and the after-life, but also the disturbance caused by vain desires. Rational argument had value as the means of dispelling these fears and disturbances, but its value was purly instrumental, as is that of a drug. As Nussbaum, puts it (45), 'the Epicurean teacher has no *intrinsic respect for the standard values of rational discourse*, such as consistency, validity, clarity in definition'. Hence the well-known Epicurean contempt for logic and general culture, and the inculcation in the school of attitudes of uncritical adulation of authoritative figures, whose extreme expression was Colotes' act of prostration before Epicurus 'an act of obeisance appropriate to a divinity or a self-deifying monarch' (47). Indeed, the Epicurean school appears to have recommended and practised some of the more repellent features of the life of certain religious organizations and other coteries of ideological extremists, specifically the memorization of authoritative texts, confession of errors (known in some circles as 'self-criticism') and, most sinister of all, denunciation of backsliders to authority (the evidence, mostly from Philodemus, is chillingly set out on 48–50). In these respects Epicurus is at the opposite extreme from Aristotle, for whom rationality in all its aspects is valuable, not merely instrumentally, but also intrinsically, as an excellence of the soul in its own right and hence as a constituent of *eudaimonia*. No contrast could be greater than that between the Epicurean slogan 'We will obey the authority of Epicurus, according to whom we have chosen to live' (Philodemus, *peri Parrhesias* 15, quoted 47), and Aristotle's famous remark in introducing his critique of Plato on the Form of the Good that, while it is uncongenial to criticize one's friends, one must put the truth first, expecially when one is a philosopher (*EN* 1096a12–16, cited 64). Aristotle, that is to say, cared ultimately for the human intellect and the value of rationality as a good in itself, while Epicurus did not. The latter's philosophy is, indeed, benevolent in intention, but its lack of ultimate respect for rationality conceals a lack of respect for human autonomy, which is grounded in rationality. Subsequent ages, including our own, have provided only too many examples of benevolent theories which, fostered by quasi-coercive techniques such as those mentioned above, and lacking any intrinsic respect for the virtues of rationality, criticism, and tolerance, have pursued their admirable ideals to the point of tyranny and beyond. The divergence between Aristotelian and Epicurean theory has thus some practical relevance to contemporary issues, as Nussbaum points out in the closing sections of her paper. It is good that she raises these issues, but disappointing that her own commitment to Aristotelian values is expressed so tentatively and apologetically. What is missing from these final hesitant paragraphs is any sense of adherence to those values as a safeguard for freedom of thought and hence of political freedom.

In 'Doing without objective values' Julia Annas first of all sets out and criticizes the principal ancient arguments for moral scepticism; this part of the paper is admirably clear and careful, establishing beyond dispute just how weak those arguments are. She then turns to the rather more interesting task of comparing these arguments with modern versions of moral scepticism, in particular that of Mackie. Her main point here is that, while modern moral sceptics normally attack claims to moral knowledge by contrasting them unfavourably with the deliverances of some other domain of enquiry which is taken as paradigmatic of objectivity, typically the natural sciences, ancient moral scepticism was merely one campaign in a global war against dogmatism in *every* area. 'For the ultimate aim [sc. of the ancient sceptic] is a rejection of all beliefs, not a dogmatic retention of some after preliminary sifting' (17). Having reached this point, the reader might be pardoned for finding some difficulty in her claim in her opening paragraph (3) that '[a]ncient sceptical arguments about proof, say, or perception, are different from modern analogues, and in important respects *less* radical' (my italics). There is, of course, no *contradiction*; the overall ancient strategy is more radical, while particular arguments are less radical than their modern counterparts (e.g. as Burnyeat points out in the article referred to on 3 n 1, ancient scepticism did not, unlike the Cartesian version, call into question the existence of the perceiver's body and its location in the physical world). But it would have been helpful to the reader had that distinction been drawn explicitly in the paper. In her interesting final section Annas compares ancient and modern reactions to the acceptance of sceptical arguments. The ancient sceptic accepted that suspension of judgement on the objectivity of moral values required detachment from the ethical attitudes and beliefs which presupposed that objectivity; what was disputed was how far that detachment impeded the sceptic's capacity for action. What was not available to the ancient sceptic was the modern stance of 'quasi-realism', which combines rejection of objective values with acceptance of the truth of beliefs traditionally regarded as presupposing the existence of those values. Those who doubt the coherence of quasi-realism will conclude that here, at least, the ancient sceptic had the better of it.

In 'Epicurus—hedonist malgré lui' Malte Hossenfelder offers a revisionist account of Epicurus' hedonism. The thesis of this paper is that Epicurus' main aim, which he shared with the Stoics, was to establish the good for man as something attainable and invulnerable. (This theme is central to a number of the contributions, notably those by Frede, Striker, and Irwin.) This naturally leads to a conception of the good as consisting just in freedom from disturbance (*ataraxia*). But at the same time sensation gives us immediate awareness of pleasure as something intrinsically good and pain as something intrinsically bad. Epicurus attempts to do justice to both intuitions by defining pleasure as peace of mind or, equivalently, freedom from pain (252). The traditional view of Epicurus as having distinguished two qualitatively distinct kinds of pleasure, kinetic and katastematic, of which only the latter is identical with freedom from pain, whereas the former is the pleasure of the senses, is therefore mistaken. In all kinds of pleasure what is experienced is one and the same thing, namely freedom from pain. Katastematic pleasure is the experience of the healthy functioning of the organism, in which that state is experienced as painless. But that state can also be experienced in another way, as one moves towards it, for example when by eating one gets rid of the pangs of hunger. In this case what is felt is not, as on the traditional view, the special sensation of kinetic pleasure, caused by the process (*kinēsis*) of return to the natural, that is painless, state. Rather, it is that state itself, experienced (apparently) to a greater or less degree the more or less closely one approaches it. (That, at least, is the best sense I can make of the very obscure account on 254–8).

If I have understood Hossenfelder correctly, the view which he attributes to Epicurus is certainly incoherent, since it requires absence of pain to be a quality which both characterizes subjects, and is experienced as characterizing them, to greater or less degrees. (He actually makes things worse by calling pleasure (= painlessness, on his account) an '*emotion* that only varies occasionally in intensity' (255; my italics), but the reference to emotion can be ignored; what is crucial is that painlessness has to vary in intensity.) But there can no more be two states, one more painless than another, than there can be two buckets, one emptier than another. Painfulness, like many other qualities, can be present to a greater or less degree, but no quality can be absent to a greater or less degree. My main concern is not, however, with the merits of Hossenfelder's interpretation, but with the fact that he ignores the treatment of this topic by J. C. B. Gosling and myself in *The Greeks on Pleasure* (Oxford, 1982), Chs 18–19. In that work, while agreeing with Hossenfelder to some extent, notably in rejecting the traditional view of the kinetic-katastematic distinction, we give reasons for rejecting his positive thesis and defend, at some length, an alternative interpretation (the reader is referred to those chapters for details). Hossenfelder might indeed be able to show that we are wrong; but it is not undue partiality to claim that he ought to have tried to do so. While it is just possible that the original version of the paper, written for delivery in August 1983, was complete before *The Greeks on Pleasure* was available to Hossenfelder, that was obviously not the case for the published version, nor is the book cited in the bibliography. This is, I am glad to say, an isolated departure from the generally high standard of scholarship which characterizes the volume.

The quality of editing and production is also high; I have discovered (without assiduous checking) no more slips than are inevitable in such mechanical tasks as the compilation of indexes, most of them trivial. It is perhaps worth calling attention to one: on 84 n 19, Furley refers to a discussion of fear by 'Richard M. Gordon (1980)'. The work is not cited in the bibliography, and the author is misnamed; the correct reference is 'Robert M. Gordon, 'Fear', *The Philosophical Review*, LXXXIX (1980), 560–78'. A table of abbreviations would have been a useful aid to those following up citations, especially of less familiar works, in the index locorum. Finally, one or two of the renderings in the glossary are questionable. *Epigennēma* and its equivalent *epigignomenon* are rendered 'supervenient', but *epigennēma* is a noun, whereas 'supervenient' is an adjective; a more correct rendering would have been 'something supervenient'. (The participle could indeed be rendered by the English adjective, but not when the former replaces the Greek noun.) In view of the well-known inadequacy of 'happiness' as a translation of *eudaimonia* (touched on by Irwin, 228) it is surprising to find it given as the sole rendering, without any alternative such as 'well-being'. *Oikeiousthai* is rendered 'to appropriate', but that verb means 'to take possession of, make one's own', whereas the Greek verb stands for the process by which an agent comes to see (middle) or is made to see (passive) something as belonging to him- or herself (see

Engberg-Pedersen, 149 n 1). Here no single English verb answers to the Greek, which requires rather to be explicated as above.

The editors and contributors are thus to be congratulated on an excellent volume. The fine weather which blessed their deliberations (see Preface) has brought forth an equally fine crop.

Corpus Christi College, Oxford

INDEX LOCORUM

Simplicius
in Aristotelis Categorias Commentarium

Stobaeus
Eclogues

Strabo